Managing Risk in Organizations

J. Davidson Frame

Managing Risk in Organizations

A Guide for Managers

JOSSEY-BASS
A Wiley Imprint
www.josseybass.com

Published by Jossey-Bass
A Wiley Imprint
989 Market Street, San Francisco, CA 94103-1741   www.josseybass.com

Jossey-Bass books and products are available through most bookstores. To contact Jossey-Bass directly call our Customer Care Department within the U.S. at 800-956-7739, outside the U.S. at 317-572-3986 or fax 317-572-4002.

Jossey-Bass also publishes its books in a variety of electronic formats. Some content that appears in print may not be available in electronic books.

Library of Congress Cataloging-in-Publication Data

Frame, J. Davidson.
   Managing risk in organizations : a guide for managers / by J. Davidson Frame.—1st ed.
      p. cm.—(The Jossey-Bass business & management series)
   Includes bibliographical references and index.
   ISBN 0-7879-6518-9 (alk. paper)
   1. Risk management.   I. Title.   II. Series.
   HD61.F726 2003
   658.15'5—dc21

                                                            2003008144

Printed in the United States of America
FIRST EDITION
HB Printing   10 9 8 7 6 5 4 3 2

᠊᢯᠊ Contents

To Yanping and Koko

⟶ Preface

Toward the end of the 1990s, we approached the coming millennium with a foreboding that was similar to what our ancestors experienced a thousand years earlier. In 999, many of them envisioned the new millennium as ushering in Armageddon and the end of the world. Today, we are more sophisticated. Like our ancestors, we saw the new millennium as bringing chaos and uncertainty, but this time it assumed a peculiarly high-tech and secular cast in the form of what we called "the Y2K problem." We breathed a collective sigh of relief when January 1, 2000, came and went with no collapse of our economic infrastructure. But whatever security we felt did not last long.

For the proponents of doom and gloom, the new millennium has not been disappointing. Even as the economies of the industrialized world reached unprecedented peaks of affluence at the outset of 2000, they were caught in the grips of a free-fall decline within a year. Then on September 11, 2001, an event of terrorism shook the capitalist world to its roots. The attacks on the World Trade Center and Pentagon reinforced the view that despite all the appurtenances of wealth and stability that we have grown accustomed to, the world is a dangerous place. The subsequent anthrax attack on the U.S. postal system confirmed this perspective.

Fear of terrorism and uncertainty took a big toll on global stock markets. Stock prices plunged. Retirees who had jumped on the bull market bandwagon toward the end of the 1990s watched their savings being wiped out. The pounding of the stock market continued when the largest financial scandals of modern times were revealed. Major corporations such as Enron, WorldCom, and Global Crossing confessed that they had cooked their financial books, abetted by prestigious accounting firms such as Arthur Andersen LLP.

These events reminded us of something many of us had forgotten: the world is a risky place. Planet Earth itself is a bull's eye on a target; one day an asteroid will hit the mark, with devastating consequences.

Global warming is causing ice caps to melt and sea levels to rise. One portion of the planet experiences unprecedented floods, while another faces unparalleled drought. Meanwhile, malcontents around the globe justify unconscionable acts of murder and mayhem on religious, cultural, or political grounds. And financial markets regularly prove that Newton's views on gravity prevail: what goes up must come down.

Awareness of life's dangers has sparked an interest in risk and its consequences. Untoward events are occurring regularly throughout the world. We are loathe to stand by passively as they ruin our lives. The question many people raise is: What can we do to lessen the likelihood of their occurrence and to reduce their impacts when they do arise? That is, what can we do to manage risk?

This book is written to help you understand and cope with the risks you come across on the job. It examines the risks you routinely encounter and explains their origins. It offers prescriptions for assessing their impacts and developing strategies to cope with them. It suggests how you can organize your operations to deal with them. To help you manage risk more effectively, it offers an abundance of tools and techniques that risk practitioners regularly employ.

I have been teaching risk management in business schools and executive development programs since the mid-1980s. Although I have come across a fair number of risk management books over the years, I did not find any that addressed the risk management concerns of general managers in business and government enterprises. This created problems for me because there was little written work I could use to supplement my class presentations. The risk management books I encountered focused on narrow areas. There are a number of excellent texts on understanding and handling risk from the perspective of the insurance industry. I have come across other useful works that approach risk management from the purview of hazards and occupational safety. There are quite a few books written for investors in the stock market that show readers how to accommodate investment risks. Finally, there are substantial numbers of books that are heavily quantitative and approach risk management from the viewpoint of operations research. But there is very little that general managers would find useful.

I hope this book fills the information gap that I perceive. I have designed it to provide managers with all they need to know in the risk management arena. I have attempted to increase its relevance to general managers by offering a large number of practical examples and case studies that bring theoretical principles to life. I have even included a friendly primer on statistics: Chapter Seven will help managers appreciate better the quantitative aspects of risk management. Beyond this, I have worked to make the book as up-to-date as possible. For example, I show how real options concepts borrowed from the financial community can be employed to reduce project risk.

I encountered two major challenges in writing this book. The first was putting boundaries around the topic. Everyone who works in the risk area quickly recognizes that risk is ubiquitous. Insurance companies see it as the prospect of loss of or damage to assets. Financial investors see it in terms of returns on investments. Hazard and safety managers approach it from the perspective of loss of life and limb. Environmentalists worry about damage to the environment. Project managers are primarily concerned with the possibility of missing deadlines, or encountering cost overruns, or not achieving specifications. Operations managers view it as the prospect of the breakdown of basic processes. Scientists and engineers focus on their ability to work in uncharted terrain to achieve results that have never before been achieved. And the ordinary citizen encounters it in all of its manifestations: If I work in a room of smokers, will I get lung cancer? Where should I invest my retirement savings to maximize returns and minimize risk? Will I be able to handle a Christmas party with sixty guests? Are my smoke detectors working?

The book's title indicates the work's boundaries. *Managing Risk in Organizations* examines the daily risks we encounter as we carry out our jobs in a business setting. The title is not fortuitous. I have already written another book with the title *Managing Projects in Organizations* (2003). In that work, I stress that your success or failure in executing projects is more closely associated with organizational factors, such as your ability to handle project politics and to motivate team members, than with your skills in building a computerized schedule. Similarly, in the business world, managing risk occurs within an organizational context. If you ignore this context, your attempts at managing risk will surely fail.

The second major challenge I faced when writing this book was to establish a proper balance between the quantitative and qualitative dimensions of risk management. There are those who strongly believe that the quantitative perspective has little to offer, because real-world risks seldom lend themselves to ready and meaningful measurement. After the 2001 terrorist attacks, I had several students ask me whether I thought a quantitative approach to risk management could have predicted those catastrophic events. I answered no. But I added that a quantitative approach could be enormously helpful in assessing the economic, personal, and infrastructure damage resulting from a collapse of the twin towers. Thus, although it might not lead to accurate predictions of the occurrence of a risk event, it could provide valuable insights about its impact.

There are also those who believe that so long as risk management is based on anecdotes and qualitative assessments, it lacks sufficient rigor to make it truly useful. They are fond of quoting William Thomson, Lord Kelvin, who at the end of the nineteenth century stated that if you are trying to explain something without including measures, "your knowledge is of a meager and unsatisfactory kind" (Thomson, 1894). They point out that the tools of probability and statistics are enormously helpful in identifying risk events and predicting their impacts and that they provide important insights that you cannot gain from purely qualitative assessments.

The arguments of both sides have merit, which suggests that people interested in managing risk effectively must steer a course between the two extremes. We must acknowledge that there is much more to managing risk than plugging probability values into equations. And we must also recognize that tools such as expected monetary value analysis and Monte Carlo simulation have demonstrated their value over and over again and that to ignore them weakens our ability to handle risk.

In this book, I provide readers with the quantitative background they need to understand the basics of probability and statistics that can help them improve their risk assessment capabilities. Readers with good quantitative skills can breeze through the explanations. Those who have eschewed math courses since squeaking through high school algebra may have to work a little harder, but not that much. The quantitative skills the effective risk manager needs do not go much beyond what you learned in high school.

ORGANIZATION OF THE BOOK

Chapters One through Three establish the context for understanding risk management. Chapter One offers an overview. It defines the concept of risk and shows how it is closely tied to the amount of information that is available to make decisions: the less information is available, the more risk you face. It describes various types of risk you can encounter: pure risk, operational risk, project risk, technical risk, business risk, and political risk. Finally, it offers a framework for handling risk: risk planning, risk identification, qualitative and quantitative impact analysis, risk response planning, and risk monitoring and control.

Chapter Two looks at the practical limitations of risk management. It steps through the risk management process with a view to identifying things that it can and cannot do. The strengths and limitations of risk management are illustrated through two detailed case studies.

Chapter Three examines how enterprises can organize their risk management efforts. It emphasizes that effective risk management does not happen by accident; it requires sustained support from the most senior ranks of the enterprise and must be designed into the organization's processes. These processes should enable staff to conduct risk assessments, manage crises, and recover from disasters.

Chapters Four through Nine explore a systematic risk management process comprising risk management planning, risk identification, qualitative impact analysis, quantitative impact analysis, risk response planning, and monitoring and control. Chapter Four describes the importance of being able to identify risk events that you might encounter so that you are not surprised by untoward events. It presents a number of techniques to help you in this undertaking, including employment of weighted checklists, risk logs, brainstorming sessions, behavioral models, diagramming techniques, flowcharting, and the holding of productive meetings.

Chapter Five looks at qualitative approaches to determining the impacts of risk events. It explores different ways that scenario building can be carried out to assist in this effort. It also examines the applicability of additional qualitative techniques, such as the likelihood impact matrix, attribute analysis, and Delphi forecasting.

Chapter Six reviews quantitative approaches to determining the impacts of risk events. It begins by stressing the importance of developing quantitative risk models, which can be as simple as a budget captured on an electronic spreadsheet or as sophisticated as a fully developed Monte Carlo simulation that incorporates budget, schedule, and resource data. It introduces readers to one of the most important quantitative techniques in risk management, expected value analysis, and describes the utility of benefit-cost analyses to handle risks associated with decision making.

Chapter Seven is a probability and statistics primer. It explains the all-important concept of conditional probabilities and illustrates their use in a real-world example. It also shows why statistical distributions—in particular, the normal and PERT beta distributions—need to be understood and belong in the competent risk manager's toolbox. The chapter concludes with a discussion of what transpires behind the scenes when a Monte Carlo simulation is run.

Chapter Eight provides tips for developing strategies to handle the risk events that you have identified. It focuses on four standard treatments: risk avoidance, risk mitigation, risk acceptance, and risk transfer. In addition, it describes how contracts are, at their heart, risk management tools and shows readers how to calculate budget and schedule reserves on their projects.

Chapter Nine, which addresses risk monitoring and control, goes beyond assessment into the action phase of risk management. The fact is that it is not enough simply to prepare for risk. You also need to be able to deal with it once the risk events arise. Monitoring enables you to keep your fingers on the pulse of the organization and its environment. By continual review of pending issues, for example, you may be able to surface serious risk events while they are still small and manageable. Control requires you to get things back on track. If you are facing a very bad situation, it may even require you to be good at managing crises; consequently, current perspectives on crisis management are discussed in this chapter.

Chapters Ten through Twelve examine the special issues and features of business risk, operational risk, and project risk. In Chapter Ten, readers see that an interesting aspect of business risk is that it offers the opportunity for gain as well as the prospect of loss. (Up to this point of the book, the discussion has focused on pure risk, where concern is with loss.) It puts the spotlight on two special instances of business risk: risk associated with new product development and financial risk.

Chapter Eleven looks at operational risk, that is, the risk associated with carrying out operations. It examines sources of this type of risk, including poorly formulated procedures, incompetence, and poor maintenance of equipment and software. It also makes the case that quality management is a special case of risk management, because quality management is concerned with avoiding deviations from a norm. Consequently, the tools that have been developed in the quality management arena turn out to be excellent for managing all types of operational risks.

Chapter Twelve looks at project risk. It points out that Murphy's Law is hardwired into projects because of the way projects are carried out. It identifies four predictable sources of project problems that risk analyses should routinely monitor: organizational sources of problems, problems associated with poor management of needs and requirements, poor planning and control, and poor estimation. It describes how each of these sources of problems can be handled.

Finally, Chapter Thirteen concludes the book by summarizing the book's main themes.

ACKNOWLEDGMENTS

A book like this is the sum total of the education and work experiences an author accumulates over a lifetime. In my case, I began working on the periphery of risk management a long time ago, when I focused my attention on econometrics and statistics in graduate school in the 1960s and 1970s. My first serious job had me engaged in technology forecasting. The point of the forecasts was to anticipate technology needs in the short- and medium-term future so as to avoid technology-induced surprises—that is, to manage technological risk.

When I joined the management science faculty of the George Washington University (GWU) in 1979, I consciously included risk management as a study topic in my technology management and project management courses. When I left GWU and became academic dean of the University of Management and Technology (UMT) in 1998, I made risk management a core knowledge area of UMT management and education programs, since risk and uncertainty permeate all management decisions.

In the early years of teaching risk management in an academic setting, I pursued a fairly conventional approach. I preached the value of following a structured risk assessment methodology and exposed my students to a range of standard tools and techniques. My approach to teaching risk management underwent a dramatic metamorphosis in the early 1990s, when I began offering risk management courses to men and women in executive development courses. Suddenly I found myself surrounded by management practitioners who were dealing with risk issues urgently and on a day-to-day basis. One student who worked in the New Zealand park service indicated that a number of school children had recently died when the viewing platform they were standing on collapsed down a mountainside. Another group of five students informed me that they were sent to my class after they had mishandled a water quality crisis that caused widespread panic in a major metropolitan area. Still another student shared with the class stories of how corruption in the ranks of senior managers had forced his company into bankruptcy. There was nothing abstract about risk management in these classes.

Consequently, in acknowledging my debt to the people who made this book possible, I must highlight the contributions of my students over a twenty-five-year period. They challenged me to keep my courses relevant. They also provided me with a wealth of insights about the real world of risk in real organizations.

Thanks are directed to my colleagues at the Australian Graduate School of Management (AGSM), the business school for the University of Sydney and University of New South Wales. They have sponsored my risk management programs in Australia since the beginning of the 1990s. These programs have me working closely with risk managers from Australian business and government enterprises, and the input I have received from these folks has greatly influenced my views on risk. Special thanks go to Paul Dumble and Bruce Wallace at AGSM. Their steadfast support for the risk management program has ensured its success in Australia.

Thanks also go to Tom Tarnow of Morgan Stanley and Bill Jacobs at Credit Suisse First Boston. They enabled me to work with risk managers in their respective organizations, and this experience provided me with good insights into risk management practices on information technology projects on Wall Street. I must also thank Rich Humphrey of the Washington Group (formerly Westinghouse Government Service Group), a serious risk management professional in his own right, who got me up to speed on the employment of risk management perspectives on hazardous projects.

Finally, thanks go my family. My wife, Yanping, tolerated my mood swings over the past year and also served as a sounding board for some of my ideas. She has been managing high-risk ventures for years, and her feedback provided me with valuable insights. And my daughters, Katy and Lele, were a continuing source of inspiration owing to their talent, intelligence, and goodness.

Arlington, Virginia   J. DAVIDSON FRAME
May 2003

⏤ⱽ⟩⟩⟩⟩⟩ About the Author

J. Davidson Frame is academic dean at the University of Management and Technology, where he runs graduate programs in project management. Prior to joining the UMT faculty, he was on the faculty of the George Washington University, where he established the university's project management program and served as chair of the Management Science Department and director of the Program on Science, Technology, and Innovation.

Since 1990, Frame has also served as director of the Project Management Certification Program and director of education services at the Project Management Institute. Before entering academia in 1979, he was vice president of Computer Horizons and manager of its Washington office. While there, he managed more than two dozen information age projects. Since 1983, he has conducted project management and risk management seminars through the United States and abroad.

Frame received his B.A. degree from the College of Wooster and M.A. and Ph.D. degrees from American University, where he focused on econometrics and economic development. He has written seven books, including *Managing Projects in Organizations* (3rd edition, Jossey-Bass 2003), *The New Project Management* (2nd edition, Jossey-Bass, 2002), and *Project Management Competence* (Jossey-Bass, 1999).

Managing Risk in Organizations

CHAPTER ONE

The Big Picture

The best laid schemes o' mice an' men gang aft a-gley.

Robert Burns, To a Mouse

O n the night of July 17, 1999, John F. Kennedy Jr. took his personal six-seater aircraft on a one and a half hour trip from New Jersey to Martha's Vineyard. He had with him his wife and her sister. They were traveling to Martha's Vineyard to attend the wedding of a friend. Sixteen miles short of the airport at Martha's Vineyard, Kennedy's plane plunged into the sea, killing Kennedy, his wife, and her sister.

In 1982, seven people in the Chicago area died after taking cyanide-laced Tylenol tablets that had been doctored by a malicious prankster, who was never caught.

On December 2, 1984, a leak developed at a Union Carbide pesticide plant in Bhopal, India. Toxic gas spewed out into the community, killing six thousand people and injuring tens of thousands more.

In late 1999, the Mars Climate Orbiter crashed into Mars because an inexperienced engineer at the Jet Propulsion Laboratories failed to convert British measurement units to the metric system. Shortly after, a sister space vehicle, the Mars Polar Lander, also smashed into Mars because *a line of software code that triggered a vehicle braking process was missing.*

On September 11, 2001, hijackers slammed passenger jets into the World Trade Center and the Pentagon, killing thousands and causing billions of dollars of damage to the world economy.

Life is risky business. Newspapers are filled with accounts of mishaps people encounter—some dramatic, others minor. The dramatic incidents, like those just highlighted, are the ones that stick in our memory, but most risk situations people face are mundane. Not a day goes by without people encountering a myriad of risk-filled circumstances. These are so commonplace that we hardly give them a passing thought. Consider the following examples of mundane risk situations:

- On January 17, an electric power outage that occurred during the night disables Ronnie Petrowski's alarm clock, causing him to wake up late and miss his first-period calculus exam.

- Anita Singh promises a client that an enhancement to a software system will be fully operational by June 30. By the following September, the system still has not been delivered. The client is furious and threatening legal action.

- During a dinner party, Myron Baker's vegetarian lasagna dish is such a hit that there is not enough for everyone to have second helpings.

- As Sue Shaefer rushes out of her house to attend a meeting where she will brief her staff on the company's new marketing strategy, she forgets to grab her lunch from the refrigerator. This means that later in the day, she will need to order a sandwich from the deli.

- In February 2000, sixty-eight-year-old Iris Schmidt takes half of her life savings—about $50,000—and invests it in three high-technology Internet stocks. Soon after, the NASDAQ crashes and the value of high-tech stocks plunges, leaving Mrs. Schmidt with stocks worth $16,000.

As these examples make clear, risk is ubiquitous. You cannot get away from it. This reality poses a problem for authors who write books on risk. If they do not establish some boundaries on their inquiry, they find themselves writing about life in general, because all life is characterized by risk. A pensioner on a fixed income is worried about the effects of inflation on his lifestyle. A college freshman studying for a final exam in world history wonders whether she should focus on reviewing the text or going over class notes. A financial planner works closely with a client to put together an investment portfolio that balances the risks of individual investments. A commuter who has just learned on the radio that a car has broken down on her usual route to work wonders whether she should follow an alternate route.

To capture the ubiquity of risk, I recently asked a friend to create a diary describing a typical Tuesday morning in her life. I have annotated the diary entries to highlight the risk features of some of the key points.

RISK DIARY: TUESDAY MORNING

7:00 A.M.   I look out the window. The sky is overcast. I wonder if I should lug my umbrella to the office?

Risk is pervasive because the future is uncertain. One way to handle this uncertainty is to set aside contingency reserves. In this case, it entails taking an umbrella to work.

7:25 A.M.   While trying to prepare toast for breakfast, I discover that the new toaster is malfunctioning. Yesterday it was emitting a small buzzing sound. I guess I should have figured it was about to break. I must have my toast! So I bake two slices in the oven. Luckily, the toaster is still under warranty. I'll take it to the store tomorrow to have it replaced.

Risk events often are preceded by warning signs—in this case, an unexplained buzzing of the toaster. Good risk management requires that a systematic attempt be made to identify possible sources of problems. Two risk-handling strategies are highlighted here. One is employment of contingency reserves: the diarist's oven served as a backup to the toaster. Another is risk transfer, where through a warranty program, risk is shifted from the diarist to the vendor of the toaster.

7:55 A.M.   On my way to work, the news announcer announces that traffic is backed up on Thirty-Fourth Street owing to a disabled vehicle at the intersection of Thirty-Fourth and Olivet. I decide to travel the back route to the office and arrive at the office ten minutes late. My colleagues take note of my late arrival and smirk.

The radio announcement provides advanced warning of an impending problem. The diarist is able to implement a backup strategy to drive to work. Even so, the diarist arrives at the office late.

8:45 A.M.   I receive a disturbing e-mail from the printer. Because of a small fire in the print shop, she cannot get the corporate brochures delivered to us today, as promised. The best she can do is to deliver the brochures in two days. This creates a problem for us, because our direct mail contractor has scheduled time today to sort, label, and ship out the brochures through the postal system. If the contractor does not receive the brochures today, he will not be able to sort, label, and send them until next week. This means that our brochures may not reach our clients before the vendors' conference in two weeks.

A common phenomenon associated with risk events is concatenation. One problem leads to another, which may lead to another, and so on. Consequently, a small problem may grow into a major pain.

10:00 A.M.   Marvin was unable to attend the management briefing today because he had to go to an unscheduled client meeting. Consequently, we couldn't share with him the results of our market research findings. We will have to reschedule a meeting with him ASAP.

Risk events do not need to have catastrophic consequences, but the cumulative consequences add up and can eventually lead to dire results. One common consequence of coping with many small risk events is that it leads to inefficiency of operations. If risk events are not handled properly, we may find that we are continually redoing things that weren't handled properly the first time. Ultimately, this increases the cost of doing business, slows operations, and leads to customer disaffection.

10:40 A.M.   A paper jam in the photocopier has forced us to stop using the machine until it is repaired. The vendor says that a technician will be sent to us sometime between now and 4:00 P.M. It is possible that we won't be able to do any photocopying for the rest of the day. We need to get fifty training workbooks published somehow before the end of day. Our backup, the print shop, won't be helpful because of the problems it is having!

Even when backup procedures have been organized to handle risk events, it often happens that they are unable to serve our needs exactly. In this case, a delay in the availability of the repair technician will lead to interruption of business services. Also, the backup to the backup (the print shop) is unavailable owing to the fire they experienced at the shop.

11:20 A.M.   Accounts payable just telephoned me. They were contacted by the Paper Warehouse Co. and told that we are in arrears in paying last month's bill. This is nonsense. My records show that we paid these folks two weeks ago. I'll have to straighten this out quickly. This is the third time this year that Paper Warehouse has had problems with its accounts receivable. What a pain! Why don't they get their act together?

A common source of risk is the incompetence of others on whom you depend. Effective risk management requires a defensive outlook on partners, employees, and suppliers. The best risk management policy to guard against the incompetence of others is to avoid working with or hiring incompetents!

12:15 P.M.   Horrible news! The radio announced that our number one client, Globus Enterprises, has just filed for bankruptcy. There were rumors that it had some cash flow problems, but no one anticipated it was in this much trouble. Globus generates 30 percent of our revenues. Management has scheduled a 1:00 P.M. emergency meeting to discuss developments at Globus and its possible impact on our operations. I need to clear my afternoon calendar.

Bad things happen that can have serious consequences. With effective risk management procedures in place, you can reduce the number of unsavory surprises that you might encounter in the course of business. Still, surprises arise because you cannot anticipate every possible risk event that may affect you. Part of your risk management policy is to prepare for a broad category of bad things happening—the fabled unk-unks, or unknown-unknowns. While you may not be able to predict that Globus will fall into bankruptcy, you certainly can develop a risk-handling strategy that would reduce your excessive dependence on one client.

DEFINING RISK

If you ask someone randomly, "What does the term *risk* mean to you?" you are likely to hear the following response: "The prospect of getting hurt." Dictionary definitions assume this perspective. For example, the authoritative *Shorter Oxford Dictionary of the English Language* defines risk as "Danger; the possibility of loss or injury" (Stevenson, Bailey, and Siefring, 2002).

If you approach risk management as a discipline, you find that there is more to the definition of risk than the concept of danger, depending on your perspective. For example, with *business risk,* you are concerned with the opportunity for gain as well as loss. This may seem strange at first: How can gaining something be construed as risky?

However, a little reflection shows that this viewpoint has merit. Consider Figure 1.1. The figure portrays stock price data for two companies over a period of time. Although both stocks sell at an average price of $20 per share, the fluctuations in the price of Stock B are dramatic, while the fluctuations in the price of Stock A are small. (The peaks on the graph represent gains, the troughs losses.) Investment in Stock B is riskier than in Stock A because the future price of the stock is less predictable for B than A. Certainly, you can reap much larger benefits with B than A, but so can you lose more money if things do not work out.

Similarly, risk associated with making forecasts or estimates focuses more on the matter of predictability than loss. Some of the most significant risks facing project teams when carrying out projects are those associated with estimates. If the team estimates that pre-plumbing work that is being carried out on a house building project will take five days to carry out but it actually takes ten days, then this can contribute to schedule slippage in delivering a completed house. If the team estimates that pre-plumbing work will take five days to carry out but it is completed in only one day, this isn't good either because the

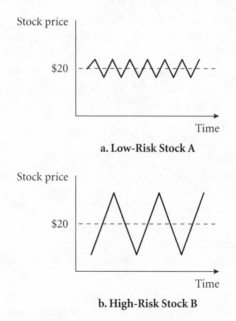

a. Low-Risk Stock A

b. High-Risk Stock B

Figure 1.1. Stock Price Data over Time.

plumbers won't show up until their scheduled time after Day 5. This means we waste four days of productive work time. Clearly, poor estimates, whether they undershoot or overshoot the target, can create problems for the project. They are risky.

Defining risk is complicated by the fact that it can be decomposed into two components: *likelihood* and *impact*. When a risk event is considered from the perspective of likelihood, this colors whether you think it is risky. For example, the likelihood that the earth will be hit by a comet in the next hundred years is near zero, so most people would view this prospect as a low-risk event, even though we realize that if the earth is actually hit by a comet, this event will have catastrophic consequences: all human life would likely cease. Consider a different example: the likelihood of encountering flies at a summer picnic in Maine is high. However, the presence of flies is low impact from a risk perspective. Although they are a nuisance, they do not pose a serious threat to the picnickers, so their presence would hardly be viewed as a significant risk.

In describing a risk event, it may be important to clarify whether the principal concern is with likelihood or impact.

This book approaches risk primarily from two points of view. First, it is principally concerned with bad things happening and takes the traditional view that risk is tied to the prospect of injury or loss. When an organization launches a risk assessment effort, the team conducting the assessment is looking for possible sources of trouble. It addresses questions such as: How might our operations fail? What weaknesses can we identify in our security system? Will we be able to deliver our goods by the contracted delivery date? The risk assessment team is not charged with identifying opportunities. (That task might be given to the marketing department.) This exclusive focus on bad things happening is called the *pure risk* perspective.

Second, this book sees risk as a reflection of information available to make good decisions. When decisions are made under conditions of ignorance, they are risky decisions and may lead to courses of action that create trouble. When decisions are informed, based on well-established fact, they are less risky. Viewed from another perspective, if a novice (someone who is inexperienced and uninformed about good practice) installs a new piece of equipment in a factory, there is a high likelihood that there will be problems with the installation. It may encounter delays. Once installed, the equipment may not work properly and may need to be reinstalled. However, if the installation is carried out by a seasoned professional—someone who has years of experience installing this type of equipment and is well informed about good installation practice—it is likely that the installation will go smoothly.

What these two perspectives have in common is that they both look toward the future, an occasion when outcomes are always uncertain. In his best-selling book about risk, *Against the Gods* (1996), Peter Bernstein makes this point when he notes that modern views about risk did not develop until the emergence of capitalism:

> But capitalism could not have flourished without two new activities that had been unnecessary so long as the future was a matter of chance or of God's will. The first was bookkeeping, a humble activity but one that encouraged the dissemination of the new techniques of numbering and counting. And the other was forecasting, a much less humble and far more challenging activity that links risk-taking with direct payoffs [p. 21].

Thus, risk management and forecasting are intertwined. We will look at forecasting and estimation in Chapter Twelve.

RISK VERSUS UNCERTAINTY

In management science, experts sometimes distinguish between the concept of *risk* and the concept of *uncertainty*. When making decisions under conditions of risk, you know the probability of the risk event you are examining. When making decisions under conditions of uncertainty, you do not. For example, if before leaving home to go to the office this morning I look out the window to check the weather and find that it appears as if it is going to rain, I am making a decision under conditions of uncertainty when I decide to bring my umbrella with me. However, if I telephone the weather bureau information number and learn that the probability of rain today is 80 percent and this leads me to bring my umbrella to work, I am engaging in decision making under conditions of risk.

If you know the probability of an event, you have more information available to you than if you do not. Thus, you make more informed judgments under conditions of risk than uncertainty. This distinction between risk and uncertainty may appear to be academic hair-splitting, but it is not. It is important, because it provides guidance on what tools are available for making decisions. With decision making under conditions of risk, you have access to distribution-based statistics to support your decisions. These statistical tools are potent and can add great power to your decisions. More will be said about using them in Chapter Seven. With uncertainty, the tools you can access are much cruder. Decision making under conditions of uncertainty has a strong element of guesswork built into it.

The link between information, risk, and uncertainty is pictured in Figure 1.2.

This distinction between risk and uncertainty was first made by the economist Frank Knight of the University of Chicago (Knight, 1921).

CLASSIFYING RISK

There is an old saying that fits here: "Where you stand depends on where you sit." The point is that your perspective on life is heavily colored by what you do for a living. This fact certainly holds true in the arena of risk, where risk can be sliced and diced in a number of different ways. The following list portrays various approaches to classifying risks:

- Pure (or insurable) risk
- Business risk
- Project risk
- Operational risk
- Technical risk
- Political risk

These risk categories are not mutually exclusive. Thus, technical risks can also be pure risks as well, and operational risk may contribute substantially to project risk.

Figure 1.2. Risk, Uncertainty, and Levels of Information.

Pure (or Insurable) Risk

Pure risk addresses the possibility of injury or loss. It focuses exclusively on the occurrence of bad things. The reason it is often referred to as *insurable* risk is that when you take out an insurance policy, you are protecting yourself from the consequences of damage or loss. You don't purchase insurance to cover beneficial events.

Business Risk

With business risk, there is the opportunity for gain as well as loss. This chance for gain, offset against the prospect of loss, energizes and excites many entrepreneurs. A defining characteristic of entrepreneurs is that they are risk takers. They recognize that nobody makes it big in life by being cautious, that is, by being risk averse. The bigger the risk is, the greater is the prospect for gain—and for loss.

Project Risk

Murphy's Law is the governing law of project management: if something can go wrong, it will. Projects are filled with risk because they are unique efforts, so the past is an imperfect guide to the future. There are major variations in the levels of risk that projects face. State-of-the-art projects are enormously risky, while risk levels for routine projects that have been carried out many times are low. A substantial portion of risk management on projects addresses risks associated with estimation. If task durations are not estimated accurately, or cost estimates are off-target, or resource needs are not correctly identified, the target project will face trouble.

Operational Risk

Operational risk addresses the risks associated with carrying out operations. Included here are such matters as running an assembly line, managing an office, and operating a computer facility. Risk arises when events occur that threaten operations in some way. For example, if a tourist bus runs out of fuel, it cannot continue on its mission of serving clients, and they will be greatly inconvenienced. Or if order takers in a mail order firm frequently make errors when taking orders, their inattention will ruin the company's reputation and lead to a loss of business. Or if a factory experiences a power failure, its assembly lines will stop, and it will be unable to produce its manufactured products on schedule.

Technical Risk

When a task is being done for the first time, the risk of not achieving budget, schedule, or specification targets is substantial. This is a situation frequently experienced by men and women who work with advanced technologies. The nature of new technology is that its development faces more than the usual levels of uncertainty. For example, a technical team may believe that a given job will take three days to carry out. However, during the effort, unanticipated problems arise, and dealing with glitches causes the effort to extend to ten days.

Political Risk

Political risk refers to situations that exist when decision making is heavily colored by political factors. For example, when investing in the construction of a manufacturing plant in a developing country, investors may have to contend with the possibility that an unfriendly government may move against them, possibly expropriating their assets. Within organizations, political risk refers to problems that can be triggered by office politics, as when a new product idea initiated by the marketing department is derailed by key players in the information technology department owing to territorial disputes.

EXTERNAL VERSUS INTERNAL SOURCES OF RISK

Risk has its origins both within and outside a given organizational environment. For example, many of the risks you face lie outside your control because they arise outside your realm of operations. Government regulations fall into this category. Companies that produce hazardous substances, for instance, chemical companies, are always concerned that government will change environmental laws in such a way that it becomes difficult to produce their products cost-effectively. Other examples of external sources of risk include the actions of competitors (for example, they have just introduced a new product that makes one of your product lines obsolete), demographic trends (for example, the aging of the population reduces demand for your youth-oriented products), or acts of nature (for example, a sustained drought causes a dramatic drop in the output of agricultural products).

Because external risks lie outside your control, you are limited in the direct actions you can take to handle them. Nonetheless, you can still manage these risks by developing strategies to deal with them effectively once the untoward risk events arise. In the 1980s, DuPont, one of the largest chemical companies in the world, selected a chief executive officer who was a lawyer, rather than a scientist or an M.B.A. graduate, in order to prepare DuPont to deal with the possibilities of antitrust actions directed at it by the government and growing regulations of hazardous substances. Through this action, DuPont was attempting to handle the serious regulatory risks it faced. Or consider how you can obtain insurance to contend with natural disasters, such as floods, winds, earthquakes, and fire.

Other risks lie more directly in your realm of control because they occur within your particular organizational environment. These are internal risks. Examples include risks associated with using aging equipment, risks posed by employing an incompetent workforce, and risks associated with organizational politics. Many of these risks, particularly those associated with carrying out operations, can be mitigated by fixing the source of problems. Old equipment can be replaced, employees can be trained, and competent workers can be hired. Even within a defined organizational environment, however, there are internal risks that are difficult to handle directly. Office politics is an example. Still, there are defensive steps you can take to deal with them indirectly. For example, you can nurture good relations with two parties who are at political loggerheads, thereby avoiding some of the flack that might arise when they join each other in battle.

THE PRINCIPLE OF CONCATENATION

A common experience encountered in risk situations is concatenation. What this means is that one incident contributes to another, which in turn contributes to another, and so on down the line. Back in the mid-twentieth century, a cartoonist named Rube Goldberg drew pictures of fantastic contraptions; for example, a man in bed might pull on a cat's tail, causing the cat to leap and land on a teeter-totter, which would hurl a stone into the air that would land on a switch and turn on the coffee maker. These Rube Goldberg machines illustrate the principle of concatenation humorously. The principle was captured nicely in an entry by Benjamin Franklin in his *Poor Richard's Almanack* in 1758: "For want of a nail, the shoe was lost; for want of a shoe the horse was lost; and for want of a horse the rider was lost."

A feature of concatenation is that the individual incidents in the chain of events may not be fatal in themselves. However, the cumulative impact of the incidents can lead to disaster. The investigation of the Valujet crash in Florida on May 11, 1996, shows that there were several safeguards in place to keep hazardous materials from being stowed in the cargo hold of a jetliner. However, in the case of the canisters of chemical oxygen generators that were loaded onto Flight 592, the fatal cargo passed through a series of checkpoints and owing to incompetence and sloppy procedures was ultimately loaded onto the aircraft (National Transportation Safety Board, 1997).

When concatenation is prevalent, the results often seem fantastic. In retrospect, people lament: "If only X had happened, or Y had been checked, or Z had occurred five minutes later, this tragedy would never have occurred." The strange character of incidents involving concatenation is illustrated in the following story published in the *Washington Post* on September 8, 2001:

A Loudoun County woman who was horseback riding near Middleburg was killed yesterday after she was stung by a bee, fell off her horse and was run over by a neighbor who was driving to her aid, Loudoun authorities said.

Janice L. Ruetz, 52, of Edgewood Farm Lane in Purcellville, who was highly allergic to bee stings, was riding with a group near Leith Lane shortly before noon when she was stung, sheriff's officials said.

Disoriented, she fell from her horse onto a private road and used a mobile phone to call emergency workers and a neighbor for help as her riding partners also sought assistance.

Sheriff Stephen O. Simpson said Ruetz was obscured by an overgrowth of grass and brush along the road, and the neighbor, whose name was not released, could not see her as he approached in his Ford pickup truck.

"A friend ended up driving out there to try to assist her, and she was laying in a private road not visible because of tall grass and weeds," Simpson said. "He's coming to help her, doesn't see her and runs her over. It's just a real strange thing" [White, 2001, p. B4].

A RISK MANAGEMENT FRAMEWORK

Because life is filled with risk, smart people and well-run organizations set out to manage it as effectively as possible. Otherwise, they find that they are controlled by events. Good management is concerned with operating proactively, initiating action that takes the organization where it needs to go rather than responding to a steady stream of mini and major crises that lead the organization to wherever the prevailing currents carry it.

Risk management is a process of handling risk in a conscious fashion. In this book, I loosely adopt the risk management framework promoted by the Project Management Institute (PMI) in its *A Guide to the Project Management Body of Knowledge,* known by its abbreviation, *PMBOK* (2000). There are a number of risk management frameworks that can be pursued beyond the PMI perspective. For example, a thoughtful framework has emerged in Australia and is known as the Australia/New Zealand Standard 4360:1999 (1999). This framework, developed by the Standards Association of Australia, serves as the leading guide to risk management in Australia and New Zealand. The good news is that different frameworks that exist pursue the same basic message. They all are predicated on the view that effective risk management requires organizations to plan and deal with risk proactively, identifying risk events, developing strategies to deal with them, then handling them when they arise.

The risk management framework followed here has five steps, as adapted from the *PMBOK*:

Step 1. Plan for risk. Prepare to manage risks consciously. Effective risk management does not occur by accident. It is the result of careful forethought and planning.

Step 2. Identify risk. Routinely scan the organization's internal and external environment to surface risk events that might affect its operations and well-being. Through this process, you develop a good sense of the bad things you might encounter in your projects and operations.

Step 3. Examine risk impacts, both qualitative and quantitative. After you develop a sense of the risk events you might encounter in Step 2, systematically determine the consequences associated with their occurrence. Think through hard-to-measure consequences by means of a qualitative analysis. Model measurable consequences with a quantitative analysis.

Step 4. Develop risk-handling strategies: Now that you know what risk events you might encounter (Step 2) and the consequences associated with them (Step 3), develop strategies to deal with them. For example, would it be helpful to take out insurance on a shipment of goods to Thailand? Should you purchase new equipment to replace the old machines that are on the verge of breaking down?

Step 5. Monitor and control risks. As projects and operations are underway, you need to monitor the organization's risk space to see if untoward events have arisen that need to be handled. If the monitoring effort identifies problems in process, then steps should be taken to control them.

Steps 2 through 4 constitute risk assessment. Together, they comprise an intellectual exercise that allows you to explore your risk space in order to prepare yourself to handle the occurrence of untoward events. Step 5 takes you into the realm of action by having you deal with problems that are unfolding. You are now out of the domain of brainwork built on hypothetical scenarios and focused on solving a real problem. Risk management is the combination of risk assessment and action.

As you will see later in this book, there is often a tremendous chasm separating what you have prepared yourself to deal with through your risk assessment and the reality of what has actually transpired. Even when you engage in serious risk management efforts, you are seldom able to predict untoward events accurately and may encounter a series of unhappy surprises as a risk event unfolds. One of the great challenges people face in managing risk is to bridge the gap between the anticipated events surfaced through risk assessment and reality.

CONCLUSION

The big picture perspective offered in this chapter captures the basic features of risk that individuals and organizations face today. It demonstrates that risk is ubiquitous: you encounter it in all aspects of your life. It arises from both internal and external sources. To a large degree, risk is tied to information: the more information you have about something, the better you are able to deal with it. This is most evident when you find yourself trying to make decisions with little or no information. Under such circumstances, your decisions are not likely to be very good.

Although I focus primarily on the harmful aspects of risk in this book, you should recognize that when viewed broadly, risk presents opportunities for gain as well as loss. A well-known characteristic of entrepreneurs is that they are risk takers. What drives them to take risk is the opportunity for gain. The bigger the risk, the bigger the gain.

CHAPTER TWO

Practical Limitations of Risk Management

~~~

In the fall of 2001, I conducted a five-day project management program in the United Kingdom, soon after the September 11 terrorist attacks on the World Trade Center and Pentagon. On the second day of class, we discussed the role of risk management in project environments. In view of the recent events in New York and Washington, the students were quite engaged in the discussion. After we examined a number of commonly employed risk management tools, one student asked: "Do you think that if people had employed best-practice risk management tools, they would have been able to predict that on September 11, 2001, nineteen terrorists would hijack four aircraft and crash two of them into the World Trade Center and one into the Pentagon?" Some of the students chuckled when they recognized the wry thrust of this question, while others sagely nodded their heads, saying, "Good point, good point."

It was a good question, because it got to the crux of the matter. After all is said and done, do risk management and its affiliated tools and techniques make a difference? If not, then let's quit wasting time with this topic and move on with our lives. If so, then let's make sure we understand how they help.

My answer to the question was: "No, the employment of best-practice risk management techniques would not have predicted the September 11 disasters with the level of detail you specify."

I paused for effect, and waited for the inevitable follow-up question. After a few seconds, it finally came: "Then why bother studying risk management?"

Why indeed study it? Why bother learning its tools and techniques?

This chapter examines the practical limitations of risk management. It demonstrates that the value and versatility of risk management are dependent on a number of factors. How much experience do we have in conducting our operations? Do we operate in a stable or volatile field? Do we operate in a stable or volatile business environment? Has our organization made an attempt to archive its work experiences, providing us with metrics we can employ to conduct meaningful risk analyses? To what extent are our senior managers committed to dealing with risk?

Ultimately, risk management will not work miracles. However, it can prepare us to reduce the number of surprises we encounter in our work efforts and prepare us to handle untoward events when they arise.

WHAT RISK MANAGEMENT CAN AND CANNOT DO

To understand what risk management can and cannot do, you need to review the basic risk management process described in Chapter One. The process has five steps:

Step 1. Plan for risk.

Step 2. Identify risk.

Step 3. Examine risk impacts, both qualitative and quantitative.

Step 4. Develop risk-handling strategies.

Step 5. Monitor and control risk.

The first step, *plan for risk*, forces people to deal with risk at a conscious level. No accidental risk management here! The planning effort addresses a range of important questions: Who has ultimate risk management responsibilities? How should you organize your efforts to handle risk? What tools and methodologies should you prepare to use?

The second step, *identify risk,* has people systematically trying to identify the risk events that they may have to contend with. They do this by going through checklists of risk events, brainstorming in groups, and using various analytical tools that focus on risk vulnerabilities. At the end of this step, you have a good idea of what bad (and good) things can happen. The chance of being blindsided by and unprepared to deal with unexpected events is dramatically reduced.

Nevertheless, there are limits as to how specific you can be in identifying risks. In the case of the World Trade Center, a range of risks to the physical integrity of its buildings could be identified at a general level, though not in specific detail. In fact, in 1995, a group of engineers and risk specialists conducted a risk identification exercise with respect to the World Trade Center. It was triggered by the 1994 attempt to blow up one of the twin towers with a powerful bomb. They concluded that the single greatest threat to the World Trade Center was that *the towers could be struck by an aircraft, with catastrophic consequences.* Such an act could be deliberate (for example, as a consequence of a terrorist attack) or accidental (as when an aircraft struck the Empire State Building in the 1940s). Beyond this, they could not be more specific.

The third step, *examine risk impacts, both qualitative and quantitative,* requires people to examine the consequences of bad things happening. If risk event X occurs, what will be the physical consequences? The financial consequences? The impact on the well-being of the public? The impact on the reputation of the organization? And so on. The more thorough you are in conducting this step, the more aware you are of the likelihood and impacts of different risk events. The information garnered at this point is valuable in developing strategies for dealing with specific risk events. For example, highly likely high-impact risk events (the *red zone* events) should receive top-priority attention, because there is a good chance they will actually happen, and when they do, they will cause substantial damage. Risk events of low likelihood and low impact (the *green zone* events) do not warrant much attention. Don't waste time and resources preparing to deal with them.

The fourth step, *develop risk-handling strategies,* focuses on preparing to deal with the risk events that you have identified. As you will see in Chapter Eight, there are some standard strategies that you can employ. For example, with risk transfer, you may attempt to shift the burden of dealing with a risk event to a third party (for example, an insurance company). Or with risk acceptance, you recognize that bad things happen and are prepared to move forward nonetheless; however, you set aside contingency reserves to deal with the possible consequences of untoward events. Or with risk mitigation, you try to fix the problems so that they will not arise. Or finally, with risk avoidance, you stay away from doing things that get you in trouble.

In the case of the World Trade Center, the people charged with dealing with threats to its physical integrity recognized that there were limits to what they could do to prepare for untoward risk events. As we have seen, they determined that the single most serious threat to the World Trade Center was having an aircraft crash into one of the twin towers (they never reckoned on two towers being struck). But what could they do to deal with this possibility? They did not control air traffic or the air defense system in the northeastern sector of the United States. Clearly, there was nothing they could do to avoid the risk event directly. They were, however, able to take steps to see that the towers could be evacuated quickly in the event of a disaster. Consequently, they made sure that the stairwells were usable (when the World Trade Center was built, the stairwells were made extra wide to deal with the potential need for quick evacuation of the structures) and developed effective evacuation plans. Thus, although they could not prevent an aircraft collision with a tower, they could minimize casualties if such an event occurred.

The fifth step, *monitor and control risk,* is the action step. At this point, you have determined that a risk event is no longer a theoretical possibility but is actually transpiring. If you have anticipated the risk event correctly and are prepared, you deal with it.

In practice, the problem with the fifth step is that when a risk event plays out, it is often quite different from what you are prepared to deal with. The gap between reality and the plan can be substantial. For example, in New York City, the plan for dealing with a major catastrophe was to have it handled out of the mayor's command center (a bunker). However, the bunker was located at the World Trade Center itself. Because the terrorist attack focused on the World Trade Center, the $13 million bunker was unusable. In fact, it was completely destroyed along with the rest of the World Trade Center complex.

A review of the five-step risk management process highlights what risk management and its tools can and cannot do:

• They encourage people to take a conscious, systematic approach to dealing with risks. Thus, they help move risk management from the realm of the accidental to the realm of the proactive.

- They surface risk events that otherwise would not be recognized. Consequently, they reduce the number of surprises that managers encounter in their work efforts.

- They enable managers to calculate the consequences of untoward events. With this information on the impact of risk events, managers can make informed judgments on what directions they want to travel in.

- They provide managers with guidance on what steps they can take to reduce the likelihood of untoward events arising, and when they do arise, what steps they can take to minimize their negative impacts.

- They do not provide managers with sufficient insights to predict untoward events with high levels of specificity.

- Their usefulness is limited by the quality and quantity of information available to managers for making informed judgments.

HOW ELABORATE SHOULD RISK MANAGEMENT EFFORTS BE?

How sophisticated do you need to be in managing risk? Should you be conducting Monte Carlo simulations? Should you be building decision trees? Should you employ concepts of mathematical expectation into your decision processes? Most significant, if you were using sophisticated techniques, would it make any difference?

There is no best way to carry out risk management efforts that apply to all circumstances. The amount of risk management one can engage in and the degree of sophistication of these efforts are conditioned by at least three factors:

- *How much good-quality information is available to guide you in the risk management undertaking?* The data processing adage holds true here: garbage in, garbage out. Your risk analysis is no better than the quality of the information on which it is based.

- *How many resources can you afford to expend on preparing for risk events?* Conducting risk assessments is not cost free. It requires the allocation of qualified resources to study current processes within the organization and the environment external to the enterprise, identify possible risk events, examine their possible impacts, and suggest strategies to handle them. If resources are not available to conduct effective risk analyses, then their value will be limited.

• *What difference would it make whether you are prepared thoroughly to handle risk events?* In some cases—for example, red zone events that are highly likely and that can have major consequences—it may make sense to conduct careful risk analyses. The hassles and costs of such analyses will be worth it if they can help avert a catastrophe. In other cases—the green zone events—the benefits of a careful risk assessment are outweighed by their costs.

HOW MUCH GOOD-QUALITY INFORMATION IS AVAILABLE?

At its heart, risk management is a process of harnessing information to help people make informed decisions. If information is lacking, this restricts the amount of effective risk management that can be carried out. If information is bountiful, then risk managers may be able to employ a full range of risk management tools. The irony is that the need for risk management is often greatest in situations where information is lacking or faulty. If you know exactly what the consequences are of doing something, you don't need to expend much effort conducting formal risk management exercises.

An Information-Poor Scenario: Web-Based Advertising Campaign

Katy is trying to determine what kind of advertising campaign to launch in order to promote a new product her company has developed. She has recently read that Web-based advertising can help her reach a huge audience—literally, an audience of millions of people. With traditional targeted direct mail advertising, her audience has been restricted to the 80,000 to 100,000 prospective clients on her standard mailing list.

Intrigued by the possibilities of Web-based advertising, Katy reads a dozen articles about it. These articles offer contradictory conclusions. Proponents support it eagerly, emphasizing that vendors can reach very large audiences of potential customers with modest financial outlays. They argue that if even a minuscule percentage of the audience responds to an advertisement, this may translate into a large number of responses. Skeptics see it as a waste of time and money, pointing out that untargeted promotion campaigns seldom work. Furthermore, they maintain, Internet users are so bombarded with unsolicited advertising that they ignore it entirely.

The fact is that Katy has little information that she can use to guide her on the risks of launching a Web-based advertising campaign. Such campaigns are so new that even advertising experts have little consensus on their efficacy. Yet before committing hundreds of thousands of dollars to pursuing Web-based advertising, she feels compelled to conduct an analysis of the risks of such an undertaking. What kind of a risk analysis makes sense here?

The principal constraint Katy faces is lack of information. Not only does she personally have no experience with this new form of advertising, the industry itself has almost no track record that she can draw on. The level of sophistication of her risk assessment will necessarily be low.

Let's examine what Katy can do as she steps through the standard risk management process.

STEP 1. PLAN FOR RISK. Katy needs to lay out what her objectives are in examining the risks associated with the Web-based advertising venture. Is she simply trying to get a rough sense of the risk issues? Does she want to engage in a serious analysis? In our example, Katy decides she wants to conduct a reasonably serious analysis, since more than $100,000 in advertising outlays is at stake. Furthermore, if the advertising campaign does not work, her company has lost the initiative in introducing the new product. In planning for the risk assessment, she decides to do further reading on the subject and to interview experienced salespeople who are familiar with Web-based advertising. She will also do a spreadsheet analysis to identify the financial impacts of a highly successful advertising campaign, a likely campaign, and a failed campaign.

STEP 2. IDENTIFY RISK. In going through this step, Katy decides to divide risk events into two broad categories: (1) standard risks associated with advertising a new product and (2) risks specifically tied to Web-based advertising. Katy has plenty of information for the first category of risk events, since she has been engaged in new product rollouts for fifteen years. She goes through her standard checklist to identify what these are. They include such items as customers are unfamiliar with the product, the best advertising vehicle is unknown, and the market for the new product is minuscule.

In order to gain information on the second category of risk events, she carries out a literature search. She buys three books on Internet marketing and peruses a year's worth of marketing and sales magazines. As a consequence of her readings, she begins to develop a good idea of what the key issues are. She also contacts a number of highly experienced salespeople whom she has worked with over the years to determine what they see as the risks and benefits. The principal risk event she identifies is that the Web-based ads will not generate sufficient sales.

STEP 3. EXAMINE RISK IMPACTS, BOTH QUALITATIVE AND QUANTITATIVE. If the Web-based advertising campaign does not work, this will lead to a number of qualitative consequences. For one thing, her company's new product will not have gained the exposure it needs. Without such exposure, competitors' products may achieve the upper hand in the marketplace. For another thing, because reactions to Web page ads are hard to assess, Katy suspects that she will be unable to diagnose why the campaign failed and whether there are any bright spots that can be addressed in future advertising campaigns. That is, she will not get the kind of feedback she needs to evaluate what worked and did not work.

Katy's assessment of the quantitative impacts of a failed campaign is carried out on a spreadsheet, where she models three scenarios: (1) the campaign leads to large sales, (2) it leads to modest sales, and (3) it leads to no appreciable volume of sales. The model investigates such things as anticipated profit levels for each scenario (scenario 2 leads to break-even, scenario 3 to substantial losses) and anticipated market share.

STEP 4. DEVELOP RISK-HANDLING STRATEGIES. After reviewing the results of her impact analysis, Katy decides to go ahead with a Web-based advertising campaign. However, she hedges her bet by sending direct mail brochures to twenty thousand targeted clients. She knows from experience what the likely response rate will be from the brochures.

STEP 5. MONITOR AND CONTROL RISK. Two months after initiating the Web-based advertising campaign, it becomes obvious that the campaign is not generating sales. A quick look at the results of the direct mail campaign shows great customer response. Katy decides to kill the Web-based campaign and send out brochures to sixty thousand targeted clients on her standard mailing list.

An Information-Rich Scenario: Public Seminars

This second scenario contrasts dramatically with the first because it deals with a situation where historical data exist and can be used to offer guidance on what strategies a manager should pursue.

Shivraj is the director of operations for Events Plus, a management training company that offers public seminars on a range of management topics of interest to the private and public sectors. Events Plus holds an average of 120 seminars a year. The company has developed a database of enrollments for its past seminars. The information contained in the database enables Shivraj to determine which programs will have sufficient enrollments to make money and which will not.

Events Plus's marketing department has great hopes for a new seminar the company recently developed that shows managers how to conduct 360-degree reviews. They created a brochure advertising the course and sent it to fifty thousand managers on their mailing list. Shivraj's job is to monitor enrollments in order to determine whether a particular course will have sufficient sign-ups to warrant offering it. If enrollments are below a predetermined threshold, the seminar may be cancelled. The risk event Shivraj is concerned with is that a seminar will not have enough enrollments to cover costs.

Events Plus is so experienced in offering public seminars that it can offer them in automatic pilot mode. It has a standard checklist of eighteen items that helps in identifying risk events when preparing to offer seminars. The database allows the company to compute the probability that a seminar will generate good revenue streams. It even has developed standard risk-handling strategies to deal with different events that might arise.

Based on experience, Shivraj knows that a key indicator of enrollments is the number of course registrations six weeks before the seminar is to be offered. The data show that if at the six-week marker the course has already broken even financially, then there is a 91 percent chance that it will be held. If more than 70 percent of expenses have been covered at the six-week marker, there is a 70 percent chance that it will be held. Finally, if less than 70 percent of expenses have been covered at the six-week marker, there is a 60 percent chance that it will be held.

Six weeks before the seminar on conducting 360-degree reviews is scheduled to be held, Shivraj learns that only 55 percent of seminar costs have been covered. These results are not encouraging and warrant investigation. Random telephone calls to some of Events Plus's loyal customers suggest that the market for seminars on 360-degree reviews is glutted. Based on data garnered from the calls, Shivraj conducts a Monte Carlo simulation where he factors in data for best-case, most likely, and worst-case scenarios. The results suggest there is only a 35 percent chance that the seminar will break even. Shivraj pulls the plug on the seminar.

Review of the Scenarios

The big difference between the situations facing Katy and Shivraj is the amount of information they have available to conduct risk assessments. Because Katy operates in an information-poor environment, her attempt at risk assessment is largely qualitative and informal. Nevertheless, even with limited information, she is able to step through a standard risk management process.

In contrast, Shivraj operates in an information-rich environment and is able to conduct a formal, quantitative risk assessment. He even has data that enable him to compute conditional probabilities: if X percent of seminar costs are covered by early enrollments six weeks before holding a seminar, then the probability of the seminar's actually being held is Y.

The point is that the lack of good information should not keep anyone from conducting a systematic risk analysis. Clearly, information-starved Katy can make better-informed decisions going through the five-step risk management process than if she operated according to no process at all. However, lack of information severely limits the type of analysis she can conduct. For her, risk management boils down to structured common sense. Shivraj, in contrast, has sufficient data to enable him carry out fairly sophisticated analyses. If he wants, he can build decision trees, compute conditional probabilities, and conduct Monte Carlo simulations. Who is likely to make better-informed decisions: Katy or Shivraj? The answer is clear: Shivraj, because his decisions are rooted in analyses based on historical fact.

ARE QUANTITATIVE ANALYSES BETTER THAN QUALITATIVE ANALYSES?

There is a strong consensus among risk management specialists that risk managers should try to employ quantitative data in their work to the extent possible. The rationale for this bias is caught in a famous quotation of William Thomson, Lord Kelvin:

> When you can measure what you are speaking about, and express it in numbers, you know something about it; but when you cannot measure it, when you cannot express it in numbers, your knowledge is of a meager and unsatisfactory kind: it may be the beginning of knowledge, but you have scarcely, in your thoughts, advanced to the stage of science [Bartlett, 1992, p. 504].

Lord Kelvin makes a good point. When you can demonstrate that a particular risk event has a 75 percent chance of occurring, you are making a more meaningful statement than when you declare: "I think that the risk event is likely to occur." Narrative statements are inherently fuzzy and subject to multiple interpretations. Often they are not testable, so it is difficult to determine whether they are correct. Quantitative statements are usually quite clear and testable. When a quantitative statement is wrong, you can readily demonstrate its degree of wrongness.

Beyond this, if you can create a quantitative model of a scenario, then you can subject it to what-if analyses. For example, in project management it is common practice to model projects with PERT/CPM networks. (The term PERT was created by the U.S. Navy in the late 1950s and stands for Program Evaluation Review Technique. The term CPM was coined by DuPont Corporation and stands for Critical Path Method.) These networks show how tasks are interconnected and also capture data on budgets and resource allocations. They lend themselves to quantitative risk impact analyses. You can raise and answer questions such as: What is the impact on delivery date if task Z is delayed by one week? What are the budget implications of hiring outside contractors to carry out task M? What happens to the project schedule if we are able to carry out tasks F, G, and H in parallel?

There are two significant problems with quantification in risk analysis. First, as we have seen, there may not be adequate data to support efforts for quantification. And second, many people in the work world suffer from innumeracy: owing to their inadequate knowledge of mathematics and measurement, they are incapable of conducting quantitative analyses or interpreting the results of such analyses. Each problem will be discussed briefly in turn.

The Absence of Data

To quantify something, you must have data, which need to be collected in some fashion. If you are dealing with events that you seldom encounter (such as terrorist bombings of buildings), you do not have the basis for collecting enough valid and reliable data to create a usable database. But if you are engaged in repeatable processes, such as the installation of automatic teller machines (ATMs) in banks, you have the opportunity to develop a rich database that enables you to predict the amount of time an ATM installation takes under different conditions, the number of people needed for the installation, and the cost of such an installation. You can, in fact, build a checklist that enumerates all the problems you encounter in ATM installation projects, and this checklist can serve as a tool to help you carry out the risk identification step. Furthermore, you can create a mathematical model of a typical ATM installation and employ this model to simulate different risk scenarios.

In the 1990s, many businesses launched serious efforts to develop what they called business metrics. They began collecting data on all aspects of a business, from the number of complaints received by call centers, to the costs of carrying out certain processes, to sources of project failure. The measures can be employed in many ways, including providing fodder for risk analyses. The concept of using process data in risk management is not new. For many years, engineers have used measures such as mean-time-between-failure (MTBF) metrics for risk management purposes, enabling them to predict malfunctions in mechanical and electronic systems.

To a large extent, businesses do not have data that can be used for risk management purposes because they never have bothered to collect this information. Recent attempts to develop business metrics can help remedy this situation. Still, there are many situations where the data do not exist because the conditions they reflect seldom occur. Consumer response to adjustments in advertising campaigns, project delays tied to changes in the ranks of senior managers, and the collapse of a company's stock price because of accounting irregularities do not lend themselves to data-rooted statistical analyses. Nonetheless, you should not give up. One common practice is to see if you can get a group of experts to generate measures based on their collective gut feeling (this approach lies at the heart of a respected technique called Delphi forecasting). Obviously, these made-up numbers do not have the force of hard data. Still, they may provide risk analysts with insights that they would not otherwise have.

The Problem of Innumeracy

The problem of innumeracy reflects declines in the quantitative skills of men and women in industrialized countries. Until the 1960s, children were required to undergo fairly rigorous education in mathematics, from primary school through secondary school. Universities and colleges made education in mathematics part of the core curriculum of liberal arts programs. Then in the late 1960s and throughout the 1970s, students throughout the industrialized countries began demanding that course work be "relevant" to social issues and their personal lives. Requirements for math literacy were tossed out of the curricula of many institutions of higher education, replaced with courses dealing with issues of current interest, such as the problem of social injustice and the role of popular culture in the arts. Innumeracy flourished.

The phenomenon of innumeracy has been explored in detail by Temple University statistician John Allen Paulos. In his highly readable and entertaining books, he describes the quantitative illiteracy of large portions of the American population, including people with advanced degrees (Paulos 1989, 1995). In one book, *A Mathematician Reads the Newspapers,* he shows how even thought leaders and knowledge formers, such as editors and reporters, regularly misrepresent and misinterpret what is happening in the world (Paulos, 1995). By transferring their incorrect interpretation of events to the public, they contribute to an environment of ignorance. Paulos's books are amusing until you realize that he is describing a society whose citizens are largely unable to make informed judgments. Then they no longer seem so droll.

What does innumeracy have to do with risk management? The answer is simple. Many of the people charged with monitoring and handling risk lack the quantitative skills to engage in quantitative analyses.

In fact, they may be unable to interpret correctly the implications of the quantitative analyses offered to them. You may find that even if your organization has quantitative data that can be employed in risk analyses, it may lack analysts who can make sense of the numbers. The best way to deal with this problem is to establish a risk management training curriculum where people charged with conducting risk assessments are educated about the rudiments of probability, statistics, model building, data collection, and the use of heuristics. Chapters Six and Seven of this book provide a primer that highlights some of the key quantitative insights that the basic risk analyst should possess.

BEING PREPARED TO DEAL WITH UNTOWARD EVENTS

New York City has been fully committed to preparing for disasters for decades. It has developed the most sophisticated antiterrorism strategies of any police force in a major American city. Its police department spent heavily on purchasing emergency equipment, trained regularly in mock disaster situations, and maintained a high-tech command center to deal with disasters. It also helped design a $13 million emergency command center bunker built for the mayor. But the bunker was located in the World Trade Center and was lost with the collapse of the buildings (Rashbaum, 2001).

The preparations paid off handsomely. Within moments of the terrorist attacks, police erected barriers to keep people out of harm's way. They also began emergency evacuation of the two towers. Two dozen of their leaders died in the collapse of the towers. But thanks to the effectiveness of police and firefighters, thousands of lives were saved in the World Trade Center. Over the weeks that followed the disaster, the police continued to operate effectively owing to their training and preparations.

CONCLUSION

Risk management has its limitations. When dealing with stable, well-defined environments, it almost assumes the aspect of science. Such environments are information rich, and this information can be employed to estimate the likelihood of such untoward events as schedule slippages, cost overruns, and resource bottlenecks. However, today's business environment is characterized by chaos and uncertainty. Product life cycles are impossibly short, customer loyalty has vanished, boom cycles are followed by busts, today's business leaders are tomorrow's phantoms.

Ironically, today's risk-filled world demands that organizations develop good capabilities to handle risk, even as chaos and complexity make it difficult to implement effective risk management policies. At a minimum, they need to implement a structured approach to managing risk. Efforts to identify risk, assess its impacts, prepare to handle it, and control it must be carried out explicitly. While the employment of formal risk management processes may not allow you to estimate the likelihood of specific risk events accurately, it will increase the risk sensitivity of managers and employees and reduce the number and impact of the surprises the organization is likely to encounter.

CHAPTER THREE

Organizing to Deal with Risk

E ffective risk management does not happen automatically. Managers who aspire to enable their organizations to be good at managing risk must recognize that the road to effective risk management is long, twisting, and occasionally hazardous. Beginning the journey is not difficult. It may be triggered by a one-page directive issued by the chief operating officer following a small disaster, exhorting the organization to implement good risk management practices. But after the initial hoopla, when the confetti has settled and the noisemakers have been thrown away, the journey toward effective risk management grows difficult.

In some measure, what happens at this point is typical of many high-sounding corporate initiatives. When light shines on the initiative, everyone scrambles to support it. Once senior managers turn their attention to other issues, the initiative loses momentum, and without active support from the top, it flounders. It may hang on for a while before it dies and is buried. Employees are aware of this pattern and often grow cynical about management initiatives, referring to them as the *fad du jour*. They feel: "Yesterday, Total Quality Management was hot. Today it is self-managed teams, and tomorrow it will be 360-degree reviews. I wonder what's in store for us next week?"

To the extent that initiatives to establish risk management capabilities take on the flavor of a fad, then you should expect the initiatives to fail. But beyond faddism, risk management initiatives face another challenge: a large number of stakeholders in the organization may feel threatened by them and may work to water them down. To understand why these initiatives may be threatening to some people, consider what risk management processes do: they force people in organizations to approach their efforts in a deliberative fashion and to be aware of the dangers that lurk in the shadows. Overall, they encourage a measure of caution in decision making. A salesperson who is about to sell a large data management system to a client does not want to hear that a risk review shows that the three-month delivery date she promised the client cannot be achieved. She will certainly see risk management efforts as a deal killer. Or a project team charged with installing a power generator at a large laboratory may view some of the safety procedures imposed on them as a childish waste of time. Consequently, they bypass these procedures to the extent possible.

Of course, effective risk management is not alien to a wide range of organizations. For example, risk assessment has been a cornerstone of the insurance industry since its crudest incarnation, as reflected in the Code of Hammurabi (circa eighteenth century B.C.). The industry began adopting actuarial tables in the eighteenth century, enabling it to compute insurance premiums and payouts based on statistical data on life expectancies. (Interestingly, life expectancy tables were first published in 1693 by the British astronomer Edmund Halley, of Halley's comet fame. For a readable and fascinating history of risk, see Peter Bernstein's *Against the Gods*, 1996.)

Other financial institutions have also had a long association with risk management. Banks, for example, take risk issues into account when making loans. With risky loans, they charge higher interest rates to accommodate a risk premium. Investors in stocks and bonds routinely conduct risk analyses on investment possibilities before committing resources. In fact, finance majors in business school spend enormous amounts of time dealing with financial risk concepts, such as the beta value of a stock, estimating the cost of capital with the capital asset pricing model, and adjusting stock portfolios to reflect different risk levels.

Companies that produce or handle hazardous substances, as well as those that have danger-filled worksites, are required by law to have safety-oriented risk management policies in place. For example, in the United States, the Department of Energy requires companies in the nuclear power industry to establish and implement integrated safety management plans for each of their sites.

What is interesting is that even organizations that have incorporated risk management processes into defined areas of their operations, owing to the nature of the work they engage in, do not see how risk management can be applied to all of their operations. For example, if you were to visit the information technology shops of well-known investment banks, you would find that none of the concerns for risk management issues has migrated there from the investment floor. Or if you visit major engineering players in the chemical manufacturing industry, you would find that for all their expertise in employing risk management tools to deal with safety concerns, their business offices are clueless about what risk management is and how it can help them function more effectively.

Certainly managers are more sensitive about risk issues today than even a few years ago. This increased sensitivity was spurred by a number of serious concerns that unfolded with the onset of the new millennium. In a sense, it began on January 1, 2000, with the possibility that computer systems throughout the world would experiences failures tied to the Y2K problem. Worries about the consequences of Y2K computer failures did more to highlight the need for good risk management practice than any other event in modern history. In the United States and Europe, technicians, engineers and scientists spent about five years and billions of dollars rewriting software code and developing disaster recovery plans to contend with the Y2K challenge.

After surviving Y2K with no serious incidents, corporate executives breathed a collective sigh of relief, only to face a new threat soon into the year 2000 with the rapid collapse of dot-com companies and the weakening of the whole telecommunications industry. At this time, many investors saw the value of their stock portfolios plummet 70 to 80 percent overnight. Then the suicide attacks on the World Trade Center and Pentagon on September 11, 2001, forced people to realize that ours can be a dangerous world physically, where the unthinkable suddenly becomes plausible. Not only can a handful of fanatics kill thousands of people through their efforts, their actions can cause whole economies to reel. As with the looming threat of Y2K, the September 11 attacks put risk management under the spotlight.

The World Trade Center attack was followed immediately by the collapse of Enron, the seventh largest company in the United States, and the parallel tainting of the reputation of the Arthur Andersen accounting firm, at that time one of the most prestigious professional service operations in the world. This event contributed to a continuing sense of vulnerability among men and women in industrialized countries. If organizations at the top of the pyramid can come tumbling down in a matter of weeks, who can feel secure? An irony of the Enron case is that a government-promoted risk-handling strategy to ensure that workers save enough money for their retirements, 401(k) pension plans, contributed to wiping out the life savings of thousands of Enron employees.

The point is that at the outset of the new millennium, managers within organizations became highly receptive to learning more about managing risk and incorporating basic risk management procedures into their operations. What remains to be seen is whether this new concern has staying power. There are lessons to learn from our experiences with implementing quality management precepts into organizations throughout the 1980s and 1990s.

LEARNING FROM THE TOTAL QUALITY MANAGEMENT EXPERIENCE

Prior to the 1980s, quality management, like risk management up until today, was seen to lie in the domain of specialists. Specifically, it was pursued by men and women who worked in the quality assurance departments of manufacturing divisions. The work itself was not viewed as prestigious, and jobs in the quality arena were not jobs snapped up by people on the fast track to senior management slots. This is not to say that quality management was a total backwater. Tremendous improvements were made in the quality of goods produced by manufacturing enterprises owing to the application of quality management principles espoused by quality gurus such as W. Edwards Deming, J. M. Juran, Phil Crosby, and Kaoru Ishikawa. However, quality improvement activities occurred exclusively in manufacturing; little thought was given to extending these principles to other areas of the organization.

By the 1980s, the word *quality* became the mantra of all forward-thinking organizations. A new term was coined to reflect an all-encompassing, comprehensive view of quality: Total Quality Management (TQM). TQM taught that all areas of an organization can benefit by adopting quality management principles, from the customer complaints department to the accounts receivable department to the manufacturing division. Ultimately, implementing TQM became the rage in high-performing and low-performing organizations alike.

Without question, there was a large element of faddism associated with the spread of TQM. Many organizations jumped on the bandwagon because they did not want to be left behind. Nonetheless, in many organizations, TQM lessons stuck and transformed how business was transacted. Every now and then, someone asks me: "Whatever happened to TQM? Was it another one of those here today, gone tomorrow phenomena?" My response is: "TQM was implemented so successfully that we don't need to beat the TQM drums any more." It was TQM, after all, that put customers at the center of business activity and introduced concepts such as Six Sigma and zero defects to the service components of enterprises. Without the TQM movement and all the ancillary training, education, self-assessments, and process improvements associated with it, it is likely that the level of the quality of goods and services produced by organizations would be far lower than it is today.

Why did TQM succeed? Are there lessons from the TQM experience that can be applied to implementing risk management processes in organizations?

TQM was able to take root and transform business and government organizations for at least three reasons. First, there was a compelling reason for organizations to adopt good quality management practices: quality-based competition from Japan and the Four Tigers of Asia was harming Western manufacturing enterprises seriously. Prior to 1980, the hegemony of Western industry, particularly American companies, was unquestioned. American and European companies dominated global manufacturing. Then at the outset of the 1980s, they saw their lead disappear with breathtaking speed. The most visible cases were in the automobile and consumer electronics areas. Almost overnight, Toyotas, Datsuns, and Hondas became the cars of choice for middle-class drivers. U.S. and European manufacturers of televisions disappeared, and Sony, Hitachi, and Panasonic conquered the television market. When investigations were carried out to determine why consumers preferred Japanese products, the answer was clear: Japanese products were of superior quality to goods manufactured in Western enterprises. If American and European companies wanted to regain their competitive position, they would need to improve the quality of the goods they produced.

Second, an international quality standard emerged in the 1980s and 1990s under the rubric of ISO 9000, which enabled enterprises to focus their quality improvement efforts in a targeted way. The standard, which required manufacturing enterprises to demonstrate that they have processes in place that lead to the production of high-quality goods, began as a European initiative. Then members of the European Community announced that if you want to do business in Europe, your work units had better achieve ISO 9000 certification, where they are audited to demonstrate that they implement the processes that support the production of high-quality goods. Otherwise, you could not gain access to European markets. Any reluctance that old-line companies had to adopting the ISO 9000 perspective evaporated when they witnessed companies in Singapore, Korea, and Taiwan quickly become ISO 9000 compliant. It soon became obvious that adoption of ISO 9000 standards was an entry ticket that companies needed to acquire if they wanted to enter into world markets.

Third, owing to the compelling rationale to improve the quality performance of business and government enterprises, the senior management of these enterprises provided sustained support for quality initiatives. In fact, one of the preconditions for obtaining ISO 9000 certification is evidence of top management's knowledge of good-quality practice and commitment to supporting such practice in their organizations. During visits by teams of ISO 9000 auditors, top managers are queried: "What does Six Sigma mean? How can you employ the PDCA cycle to improve quality practices in your organization?" The top managers better do their homework, or else they may be fingered as the reason their organizations did not achieve quality certification.

CAN RISK MANAGEMENT REPLICATE TQM'S SUCCESS?

Can the success of TQM be replicated in the realm of risk management? Do the three conditions that contributed to the success of TQM exist in the risk management arena?

A review of the three conditions that led to the successful implementation of TQM processes in business organizations suggests that
only one of them is found in the realm of risk management today: the
existence of an external threat. In the case of TQM, the threat came
from the Far East in the form of companies that produced goods
faster, better, and cheaper than old-line Western companies. In the
area of risk management, the threat is more amorphous, tied to a
mélange of concerns, ranging from fears of terrorism to worries of
economic and political instability that appear to accompany the move
toward more globalization.

The fact that there are perceived external threats, as ill defined as
they are, provides a major impetus to establish risk management programs in organizations. The Y2K threat forced virtually all modern
enterprises to take stock of their computer operations to identify possible weak points. Later, stories coming out of the World Trade Center disaster caused managers in many organizations to ask a number
of questions about their own operations: Do we need to limit public
access to our facilities? Is it smart to have all of our people located in
a single facility? Do we have backup files of our databases situated at a
site far from headquarters? Do we have building evacuation plans in
place? Should we be more diligent in monitoring the risk management
plans of our vendors? With the bankruptcy of Enron and the loss of
billions of dollars of employee pension funds, the U.S. government
stepped in to review the relationship of companies with their auditors
and to establish new rules governing the management of pension
plans.

The second source of TQM's success, the emergence of a global
standards certification process that enabled companies to direct their
quality improvement efforts in a targeted fashion, is lacking in the
risk management arena. Risk management has no ISO 9000–style
standards-setting process. The most sophisticated attempt at creating
risk standards comes from the Australian Standards Association with
its publication of *Risk Management* (1999). This rather short document, containing some fifty pages, provides a general framework for
viewing risk. It is more a taxonomy than prescription. Organizations
that have attempted to apply it to their operations in order to establish risk management processes complain that it offers no guidance
on how to implement good risk management processes.

Without the existence of universally accepted risk standards and
an agreed-on process for implementing risk management procedures

in organizations, it is difficult for leaders to know how their organizations should set about establishing solid risk management capabilities. Certainly, they would be reluctant to push their organizations down a road that leads into a wilderness. In the days of TQM, there was no shortage of world-class companies (such as GE, Toyota, and Motorola) that became models for others to follow. ISO 9000 gave industry a road map that provided all the detailed information that companies needed to take them on their journey. What's more, everyone followed the ISO 9000 prescription. In fact, the European Community mandated compliance.

The upshot is that a key component of TQM's success is missing in the risk management arena. While the time has come where managers throughout the world see a need to improve the risk management capabilities of their organizations, they have encountered no vehicle for implementing this vision. The absence of an ISO 9000–type institutionalized process does not bode well for the universal adoption of good risk management principles in organizations in the near future.

The presence of the third component of TQM's success, sustained management support for improving the quality of the goods and services produced in their organizations, is questionable in the risk arena. Certainly, if queried about the importance of risk management to their organizations, senior managers will give an assuring response. They will say: "It is enormously important. We live in a risky world. An organization that is not prepared to deal with risk is not serving its customers, employees, or stockholders." Yet as a Wendy's television advertisement so aptly asked back in the 1980s, "Where's the beef?" It is not enough to mumble the right response. Are these same senior managers who are preaching the virtues of risk management supporting their words with funding? Have they adjusted the corporate mission statement to include the sentiment: "In this risk-filled world, we feel that our enterprise must be prepared to deal with all manner of untoward events to protect our clients, employees, and stockholders from their deleterious consequences"? The answer is a clear no.

When comparing developments in the risk management arena with those associated with the TQM movement, there are some major shortcomings. Three factors that contributed heavily to TQM's success are only partially present in the risk management arena. Does this mean that an enterprise cannot establish effective risk management processes? Of course not. An enterprise whose senior managers are obsessed with establishing the capacity to deal with risk issues in the organization and are willing to support establishing this capacity over the long term will develop solid risk management capabilities. However, it will not be an easy undertaking. They will not be supported by a groundswell consensus on what they should do. Still, by employing good sense and maintaining a long-term view of what needs to be done, they can build excellent risk management capabilities in their organization.

ORGANIZING FOR THE EFFECTIVE MANAGEMENT OF RISK

Organizing for effective risk management has two dimensions to it: one entails implicit organization for risk and the other explicit organization. With implicit organization, an enterprise has arranged its operations in such a way that if it carries them out in a prescribed way, it will lessen the chance that it will encounter troublesome events. Simply stated, good organization yields good management, and good management means fewer problems. You can argue that all well-managed enterprises practice implicit risk management.

With explicit organization for risk, an enterprise consciously sets out to establish a risk management process. This entails identifying who owns risk within the organization, establishing and documenting risk management methods and procedures, training personnel on risk management principles, building risk reviews into status reports, and possibly developing and staffing a structure to serve the organization's risk management needs.

Implicit Organization for Risk

Anything that enables an organization to function effectively contributes to risk reduction. In this section, three specific items are examined: the establishment of good operating procedures, organizational structure, and the use of contracts. Although these items are not specifically geared for the purpose of risk reduction, when they are implemented properly, they contribute to an operating environment where troubles are reduced and things run smoothly.

THE EMPLOYMENT OF GOOD PROCEDURES. Well-run enterprises are designed to function effectively, where effectiveness is defined as the capacity of the enterprise to achieve its fundamental goals. If one goal is customer satisfaction, then processes are established to increase the likelihood that the enterprise serves its customers well. For example, it may establish a sunset rule that states that all customer inquiries received before 3:00 P.M. must be answered before the close of the business day. It certainly will implement processes to achieve the highest level of quality in its goods and services. And it may create a customer hot line, where customer inquiries and complaints can be handled quickly and thoroughly.

If another goal is to carry out operations in the most cost-effective manner possible, then purchasing processes might be established to avoid overspending on supplies and services. Cost control points might be embedded in all operations, enabling financial managers to track cost performance. A reward system might be implemented: people and teams that realize major cost savings in their operations are given bonuses.

If yet another goal is to maintain the safety of clients and employees (for example, in the airline industry), then safety-oriented procedures will be practiced. Anyone who travels routinely by air can attest to the central role that safety considerations play in airline operations. For example, if even one passenger is standing in the aisle, an aircraft is not permitted to leave the gate.

What does all this have to do with managing risk? A lot. Well-managed enterprises establish procedures in order to have some assurance that their operations will be carried out smoothly. Most procedures emerge from experience. When something doesn't work well, adjustments are made to procedures to fix the problem.

If procedures are poorly conceived or poorly implemented, then problems arise. Customers complain that the enterprise does not care about them. Costs go through the ceiling, and profits plunge as rework becomes the order of the day. Accidents happen, and people get hurt.

When organizations lack effective processes or do not properly implement the processes they have, they are elevating the level of risk they must contend with. They are poorly managed. The establishment of effective business processes, then, is a good risk management strategy. We call this *implicit* risk management, however, because the principal purpose of having good processes is to operate effectively as an enterprise. The risk management aspect of good processes is only a secondary consideration.

STRUCTURAL FACTORS. The most famous precept of architecture in the United States was formulated by the Chicago school of architecture in the nineteenth century: form follows function. What this means is that in designing a structure for a defined space, an architect should first determine how the space will be used (function). Only after developing a thorough understanding of this can the architect design a structure that will serve the users' needs and also be attractive.

When considering organizational architecture, it is useful to take a reversed look at the Chicago school precept and consider a modification of it: function follows form. That is, show me the structure (form) of a work unit (a team, a department, or the entire enterprise), and I will be able to anticipate with a high degree of accuracy the risk implications emerging from the structure.

Risk can be designed into or designed out of organizational structures. To see this, consider two common structures encountered in business enterprises: a centralized decision structure and a decentralized one. The centralized structure is pictured in Figure 3.1a and the decentralized one in Figure 3.lb.

In the centralized decision-making structure, all decisions are made by a single decision maker, portrayed by the black circle in Figure 3.1. Three strengths of this decision-making structure are that (1) it can lead to consistent decisions, since all decisions come out of the head of a single player; (2) decision making can be quick, since the decision maker will not be spending time establishing consensus among the other players; and (3) the single decision maker can exercise strong control over the whole decision-making process.

The risks associated with this structure are obvious. One common phenomenon experienced by project teams structured this way is that

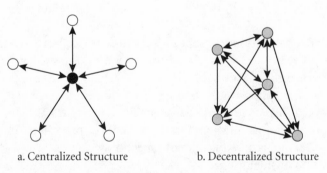

a. Centralized Structure   b. Decentralized Structure

Figure 3.1. Decision-Making Structures in Business.

the single decision maker (the team leader or project manager) soon grows overwhelmed with the volume of decisions that need to be made. Progress on the project then grinds to a halt as the decision maker becomes the principal bottleneck to achieving on-time delivery of goods and services to the customers. Another predictable risk is that decisions are not subjected to any checks and balances, so if the sole decision maker is making some bad decisions, this may not be detected until the project is over. Yet another risk emerging from this structure is that the decision maker is out of touch with what is happening in the field. This is a common complaint of team members out in the field whose actions are controlled by headquarters: How can the folks back home presume to call all the shots? What do they know about what is really happening out here in the field?

In the decentralized decision-making structure in Figure 3.1, decision making is distributed among all the players who are pictured. The strengths of this approach are clear: individual team members who are close to the client can make better client-focused decisions. Because there are multiple decision makers, you don't have all of decision-making eggs in one basket: if one decision maker is off-target, there are four others who can straighten him or her out.

The risks inherent in this structure are equally evident. If decision making is distributed this way, there is a good chance that the team may encounter a measure of decision chaos: when everyone is in charge, no one is in charge. One manifestation of the chaos is inconsistency: if each player is making decisions independently, it is likely that decisions made by Player A will be out of sync with decisions made by Players B and C, and so forth.

Figure 3.2 pictures a commonly encountered organizational structure employed on construction projects. In this structure, the owner has direct authority over both the contractor and architect-engineering firm. The owner can issue directions, and the contractor and architect-engineering firm are obliged to do his or her bidding. This degree of control over these two key players is what makes this structure appealing to owners.

Figure 3.2 also shows that the contractor has a measure of control over subcontractors. Where risk is introduced into this structure is the split authority of the contractor and architect-engineering firm. The architect-engineers have authority over design issues, and the contractor has authority over the physical building effort. A common problem that arises is when architect-engineers design structures that

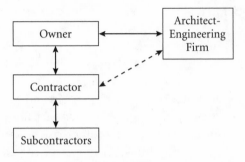

Figure 3.2. Typical Configuration of Players in a Construction Project.

contractors view as unbuildable. Since neither party is in charge of the overall construction effort, hostile feelings can develop between them. Progress can halt on the project as they try to work out their differences. In theory, the owner should be able to resolve the conflict, but owners seldom have the technical knowledge to know what to do, so poor relations may fester.

The point is that the way you structure your teams, departments, or overall enterprises has inherent risk implications. There is no single best design that an organization can pursue. What is best must be determined by the circumstances the organization faces. Thus, in one case, a centralized structure may be appropriate for a team, and in another, a decentralized structure makes more sense.

CONTRACTS. Contracts may be the oldest risk management tool employed by humans. They have been used by businesses since the time of the Sumerians and Babylonians more than four thousand years ago. Not many people recognize the risk management character of contracts, because they perceive them to be not much more than a formal agreement by one party to provide a good or a service to another in return for financial consideration. A little reflection shows that contracts are more than a simple exchange agreement. An important function they carry out is to apportion risk among the parties who have entered into the agreement. "If you deliver the goods late, you must pay a penalty of ten shekels a day for each day of delay." "If I do not supply you with the equipment you need to do your job, I will not hold you accountable for any delays you encounter in delivering the goods." "You will not be held accountable for meeting the terms of this contract if during its duration, flood, fire, or political mayhem interferes with the performance of your duties" (making provisions for uncontrollables like this is called *force majeure*). In formal risk management terminology, we say that contracts are a *risk transfer* (or *risk deflection*) vehicle, allowing risk to be shifted from one party to another.

How contracts are formulated has substantial risk management implications. The best-known example is the different risk consequences associated with fixed-price contracts (also called lump-sum contracts) versus cost-plus contracts (also called cost-reimbursable contracts). With fixed-price contracts, contractors agree to deliver goods or services by a particular date and at a specific price. If the costs to the contractors are greater than the contract price, then they must eat the loss. If they can produce the good or service for less than the contract price, the difference between the two is profit. Thus, contractors assume the risk burden on fixed-price contracts.

With cost-plus contracts, the contractor's expenses are reimbursed by buyers. If the expenses get out of hand, it is the buyers who suffer the consequences, since the reimbursement funds come out of their pockets. Thus, buyers assume the risk burden on cost-plus contracts.

Explicit Organization for Risk: Adopting Good Risk Practices

In the discussion of implicit organization for risk, we saw that well-managed enterprises carry out a range of activities that strengthen their risk position, even without people being aware that they are managing risk through these activities. Thus, by defining their business processes carefully, structuring their teams appropriately, and taking great care in formulating contracts, they are implicitly managing risk. Now we examine how the managers of enterprises can *explicitly* organize and employ the enterprise's resources in order to strengthen their risk management capabilities.

The most obvious thing that can be done is to adopt good risk management practices into the enterprise's business activities. The details of some of these good practices will be described fully later in this book. Here I will simply provide a listing of key good practices for purposes of illustration:

• *Conduct risk assessments on any ventures above a threshold size before launching them.* In conducting the risk assessments, the risk assessment team should follow an explicit methodology. The approach offered in this book has three steps: identify risks events, analyze the qualitative and quantitative impacts associated with the risk events, and develop strategies to lessen or avoid untoward risk events. If risk assessments are carried out before resources have been committed to funding the new venture, weaknesses might be identified and remedied before money has been expended. In the worst case, a decision might be made to kill the initiative.

• *Have issues logs incorporated into monthly project status reports.* Issues logs identify issues of concern to the project team at the time of the status report. An issue may be relatively benign, as in: "The head of software testing says she will be taking a two-week vacation beginning August 4. We are scheduled to have three software components tested during this two-week time period." Or an issue may be more serious, as in: "All of the staff we have been working with in the client organization have been fired. The status of our contract is uncertain." By surfacing and addressing issues systematically, you are less likely to be caught off guard by sudden, unanticipated shocks.

• *Have disaster recovery plans developed for critical business operations (for example, database maintenance operations, software development efforts).* Disaster recovery planning prepares an organization to deal with worst-case events, where owing to a catastrophe, it is unable to carry out its basic operations. A common type of catastrophic event is loss of important data. The loss might be caused by a computer failure, a fire, water damage, a power outage, or even theft. The best way to prepare for this type of event is to back up the important data. The backup protocol might be something as basic as making backup tapes of all data files at the close of business day or something as elaborate as running a parallel data processing facility in another city (standard practice when dealing with large amounts of financial data).

• *Develop a crisis management plan.* A passenger jet crashes . . . A tire manufacturer's top-selling tire is found to be defective . . . A psychopath is putting cyanide tablets into bottles of Tylenol . . . A chemical facility experiences a major leak of cyanide gas in a heavily populated community . . . The senior managers of a dot-com company have been accused of fraudulent behavior in preparing financial reports . . . When events like these occur, organizations need to be prepared to handle a bevy of issues. For example, experience shows that they must be able to make a public statement that demonstrates their integrity and their intent to deal with unfortunate circumstances quickly and honestly.

• *Use risk checklists.* Before an airplane can take off, the cockpit crew must go through a detailed checklist review of the status of the aircraft. When they are sloppy in this respect, as occurred in 1982 with Air Florida flight 90, disaster may ensue. What checklists do is capture experiences and insights in a listing that individuals cannot keep straight in their minds. Risk checklists reflect things that might be encountered on projects or in processes that can lead to problems. In building a software routine, how many interfaces do we need to work with? (The larger the number is, the higher is the likelihood of systems disconnects.) Are our test plans well developed? (If not, the project is risky.) Have we been given an adequate budget to do the job? (If not, the project is risky.) After you have systematically worked your way through the checklist, you should have a good sense of the overall level of risk facing your project.

• *Institutionalize risk management processes in the organization by creating a risk assessment group.* Every now and then, I get involved in discussions that address the question: Does it make sense for organizations to create risk management departments that are similar in purpose to quality management departments or possibly even marketing and finance departments? I believe that creating a risk department is unnecessary. To me, it makes more sense to embed risk management processes in existing departments rather than to create a new department that handles risk in a centralized fashion. Certainly, a standard-setting risk office can be established, much as project support offices proliferated in the 1990s and into the 2000s. But to create a whole department of risk management is overkill. One approach some major companies have experimented with is to create risk assessment groups (RAGs), which are resident experts on risk issues. They can serve a risk audit function where they review project proposals and plans before they are funded in order to make sure that what they promise is achievable. They can take on short-term assignments to help different players in the organization embed risk management processes into their operations. They can mentor senior managers on risk management principles. And so on. What is attractive about RAGs is their flexibility and cost-effectiveness. They enable organizations to institutionalize risk management procedures without indulging in excessive bureaucracy (Block and Frame, 1998).

CONCLUSION

The implementation of effective risk management processes in organizations will not happen by chance. Risk management must be consciously embedded in organizations. To function properly, it must be adapted to address the organization's special circumstances. This means that resources need to be made available to implement risk management processes, which implies that risk management must receive attention from top management.

CHAPTER FOUR

Identifying Risk

An important rationale behind risk analysis is to avoid surprises. You may not be able to stop the hurricane that is rushing toward your home, but if you know that it is on its way and will reach your area in six hours, you can prepare to deal with it. If you are unaware of its impending arrival, you will be caught unprepared, and this may have serious consequences for your home and personal safety.

Risk identification is the first step in the risk assessment process. Its purpose is to surface risk events as early as possible, thereby reducing or eliminating surprises. As a consequence of risk identification, risk analysts can develop a good sense of possible sources of problems (or opportunities) that will affect their organization's projects and operations. They then examine the quantitative and qualitative impacts of the identified risk events, which constitutes the second step of the risk assessment process and is covered in the next two chapters. Once the impacts of the identified risk events have been reviewed, the risk analysts, working with managers and employees in the enterprise, engage in risk response planning to develop strategies to handle the risk events. This is the third and last step of the risk assessment process and is covered in Chapter Eight.

This description of risk assessment pictures the process as linear, moving from one step to the next. In practice, the process is more dynamic. Its dynamic nature is pictured in Figure 4.1, which captures the process in a conventional flowchart. The figure shows that the risk assessment function is ongoing. During each management review cycle, an effort is made to identify risks. For example, during the monthly status review meeting, time may be set aside to deal with issues that have arisen since the previous meeting. If no significant risk events are identified, then no further action is needed until the next management review meeting. If significant risk events have surfaced, their impacts are assessed, strategies are developed for handling them, and the strategies are incorporated into the organization's business processes. This does not end the risk assessment effort, however. At the next management review meeting, the cycle resumes.

In this chapter, we examine different ways that risk identification exercises can be carried out:

- Checklists

- Brainstorming sessions

- Issues logs

- Behavioral models

- Diagramming techniques

- Flowcharting project and process models

- Regular meetings

CHECKLISTS

Airline pilots are not permitted to take off until they have worked their way through the preflight checklist. As they are going through the list, they make sure that the aircraft is in a condition to fly safely. The checklist forces them to be conscious of all the things that need to be dealt with before the aircraft is ready to take off. If the checklist shows that something is not working properly, they have warning of a malfunction that might jeopardize the aircraft's capacity to fly. The problem must be fixed before they are allowed to take off.

You can develop checklists for just about everything. Your fifteen-year-old daughter is about to take her first solo train trip to her grandma's, so you prepare a checklist of things she needs to be aware of during the trip. To be sure that the mechanics at the motor pool conduct their routine car maintenance chores properly, you require them to step through a checklist of maintenance activities that must be carried out. To make sure they have not overlooked anything, the people who pack computers into cartons before shipping them go through a checklist of items that must be packed before sealing the carton.

A little reflection suggests that what checklists do is capture the experiences of experts. Working with a checklist is like having an expert standing alongside you, reminding you of things you should know and do. In today's parlance, checklists are a form of artificial intelligence.

Checklists can be quite useful in risk management, particularly when trying to identify risks before a work effort is initiated. Exhibit 4.1 shows a generic risk identification checklist that can be used before launching a project. It addresses factors that reflect the types and amount of risk a project might encounter. By asking, "Have we estimated project costs accurately?" the checklist reminds us that a leading

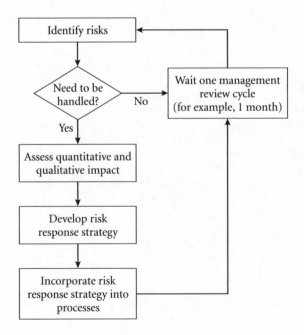

Figure 4.1. The Ongoing Nature of Risk Assessment.

1. Have we estimated project costs accurately?
   a. Costs are overestimated. (weight = 1)
   b. Costs are on target. (weight = 1)
   c. Costs are underestimated. (weight = 4)

2. Have we estimated project benefits accurately?
   a. Benefits are underestimated. (weight = 1)
   b. Benefits are on target. (weight = 1)
   c. Benefits are overestimated. (weight = 4)

3. Will benefits exceed costs?
   a. Benefits exceed costs. (weight = 1)
   b. Benefits equal costs. (weight = 1)
   c. Costs exceed benefits. (weight = 4)

4. Is our project addressing real market needs?
   a. It is right on target. (weight = 1)
   b. It is partially addressing market needs. (weight = 2)
   c. It is not addressing market needs. (weight = 4)

5. What positions are our competitors taking in the market?
   a. They have no presence. (weight = 1)
   b. They have some presence. (weight = 2)
   c. They are actively pursuing this market. (weight = 4)

6. Is the project focused on the right customers?
   a. It is right on target. (weight = 1)
   b. It is focused on some of the customers. (weight = 2)
   c. It is focused on the wrong customers. (weight = 4)

7. Will customer needs be captured correctly?
   a. Yes. (weight = 1)
   b. Some needs will be captured. (weight = 2)
   c. Most needs are not addressed. (weight = 4)

8. Have customer expectations been properly set?
   a. Expectations are right on target. (weight = 1)
   b. Some expectations are realistic. (weight = 2)
   c. Expectations are set too high. (weight = 4)

9. Are communications channels between the project team and customers open?
   a. There are excellent communications. (weight = 1)
   b. Communications are marginally good. (weight = 2)
   c. Communications are weak. (weight = 4)

10. Will the team be able to acquire needed resources?
    a. All resources are ensured. (weight = 1)
    b. Some resources are ensured. (weight = 2)
    c. Few or no resources are ensured. (weight = 4)

11. Is the project work likely to be completed on time?
    a. It will be completed early. (weight = 1)
    b. It will be completed on time. (weight = 2)
    c. It will be completed late. (weight = 4)

Exhibit 4.1. Weighted Checklist for Risk Identification on Projects.

12. Can the team operate as a well-integrated unit?
    a. Yes. (weight = 1)
    b. No. (weight = 4)

13. Is the team likely to follow a disciplined project management process?
    a. It has a highly disciplined process. (weight = 1)
    b. It has a moderately disciplined process. (weight = 2)
    c. It has an undisciplined process. (weight = 4)

14. Have customer needs been translated effectively into customer requirements?
    a. They are right on target. (weight = 1)
    b. Some needs have been translated. (weight = 2)
    c. There is a poor match between the two. (weight = 4)

15. Are the requirements clearly articulated?
    a. They are right on target. (weight = 1)
    b. They are partially on target. (weight = 2)
    c. They are ambiguous. (weight = 4)

16. Are the requirements formulated at the right level of detail?
    a. They are right on target. (weight = 1)
    b. There is too much detail. (weight = 2)
    c. There is insufficient detail. (weight = 4)

17. How experienced or familiar is the team with the work that needs to be done?
    a. They are very familiar with it. (weight = 1)
    b. They are partially familiar with it. (weight = 2)
    c. They are unfamiliar with it. (weight = 4)

18. How complex is the deliverable being developed?
    a. Not complex—a routine effort. (weight = 1)
    b. Somewhat complex. (weight = 2)
    c. Highly complex. (weight = 4)

19. What is the scale of the effort being undertaken?
    a. Small. (weight = 1)
    b. Middle scale. (weight = 2)
    c. Very large. (weight = 4)

Scoring
19–30: The issue is not likely to present a problem for the organization.
31–39: It is possible that the issue will cause a problem for the organization.
40–76: The issue will create a problem for the organization.

Exhibit 4.1. Weighted Checklist for Risk Identification on Projects, Cont'd.

contributor to project failure is poor estimation, so let's make sure that our cost estimates are on target. Similarly, by asking "Is the project focused on the right customers?" we are reminded that too often, in developing requirements and implementing the project work, we are talking to the wrong set of people.

The checklist in Exhibit 4.1 provides weights for each of the responses. The greater the weight is for an item, the riskier is that item. Consider, for example, the following question from the checklist:

• Will the team be able to acquire needed resources?

All resources are ensured. (weight = 1)

Some resources are ensured. (weight = 2)

Few or no resources are ensured. (weight = 4)

If all resources are ensured, then lack of resources will not be a problem contributing to project risk. Therefore, it is given the lowest weight of 1. If some resources are ensured yet others are lacking, this becomes problematic. The absence of some of the needed resources may be a source of trouble on the project, so it is given a weight of 2. If you know at the outset that there are not enough resources to do the job, then you have a real problem. Their absence is certain to create difficulties. Give it a weight of 4.

When weights are tallied for all items, you develop an overall sense of the total risk facing the project. On the weighted risk checklist provided here, the lowest total score a project can receive is 19 (low risk) and the highest 76 (very high risk). A score in the mid-thirties represents moderate risk. Projects with high scores should be handled as red zone efforts: projects that are sure to encounter problems. Projects with midrange scores should be handled as yellow zone efforts: there is enough uncertainty about their risk status that they should be approached with caution. Projects with low scores should be handled as green zone undertakings: they do not require special consideration from the perspective of risk.

Organizations that employ risk checklists use them principally at the earliest stages of the project life cycle. Certainly, employment of risk checklists is appropriate when selecting projects. If a project scores in the red zone, then perhaps it is not worth pursuing. Use of risk checklists is also apposite during the early portion of the project planning effort. By highlighting areas that are likely to encounter problems, the plan can accommodate them.

BRAINSTORMING SESSIONS

Checklists enable risk analysts to identify risks through systematic means. They focus on risk sources that experience suggests may affect their operations. By going through the checklist item by item, established sources of risk will not be overlooked.

In contrast, brainstorming focuses on novel risk sources. With brainstorming, a group of people get together and ask: "What can we *imagine* happening in our operations?" The participants are asked to come up with crazy possibilities—the wilder the ideas, the better. During the session, no one is permitted to criticize the contributions of others. Participants are encouraged to build off each other's inputs. As ideas are generated, they are written down. At the end of the session, the group goes over the list of ideas that have been generated, and at this time they deal with them critically.

Recently, people have had success conducting structured brainstorming sessions that are built around SWOT analyses. SWOT is an acronym for strengths, weaknesses, opportunities, and threats. With SWOT analyses, participants in the brainstorming session are first asked to identify strengths associated with an initiative they plan to undertake. Strengths refers to internal factors. For example, Alpha Enterprises is about to develop a new product called Product X. One strength associated with this product is that it builds on the technological capabilities Alpha already possesses.

After strengths have been identified, attention focuses on weaknesses. As with strengths, weaknesses refers to internal factors. For example, a problem with launching Product X today is that it may burden Alpha's already strained cash flow situation.

The discussion of strengths and weaknesses highlights internal issues that need to be addressed. Now it is time to look at opportunities—external possibilities that may work to the organization's advantage. For example, Alpha's market research department may identify strong market demand for Product X.

Finally, threats focus on external factors that may create problems for Alpha Enterprises as a consequence of launching Product X. For example, Alpha's operations director may have learned that Beta Enterprises and Gamma Enterprises are also working on developing products that are similar to Product X. If they are successful in their development efforts, the market for Product X will be crowded.

ISSUES LOGS

In recent years, risk-sensitive enterprises have begun using issues logs as part of the process of reviewing the status of their projects and operations each month. The issues log is a simple listing of issues— things that warrant consideration—that have surfaced since the previous status meeting. Issues need not be bad. For example, an issue placed on the issues log might be: "Next month will have three holidays. Will this have any effect on our operations?" Or they can reflect something serious: "Delta Enterprises, our number one client, has just filed for Chapter 11 bankruptcy."

When identifying issues, it is a good idea to tie them to an action item to make sure that they are not treated as interesting curiosities but entail some concrete investigation—for example:

Issue: Next month will have three holidays. Will this have any effect on our operations?

Action item: Report on this by March 25.

Item: Delta Enterprises, our number one client, has just filed for Chapter 11 bankruptcy.

Action item: Write a memo on possible consequences and submit this to the Executive Committee by March 25.

Exhibit 4.2 presents a typical issues log. The document is divided into two parts: *pending issues*, which reflect issues that need to be addressed, and *closed issues*, which have been handled and resolved. Ideally, the pending issues part should remain short, and the closed issues should grow long. If the pending issues portion gets longer and longer month by month, this means that the number of issues that needs to be handled is growing faster than the capacity of the organization to deal with them.

An important element of the issues log is the assessment of the anticipated impact of each issue in the list. Routine no-impact issues are color-coded green. They are not likely to present problems to the organization. Issues that might have untoward consequences are color-coded

Issue		Action	Owner	Date Opened	Date Closed	R, Y, G	Status
			Pending Issues				
1							
2							
3							
4							
5							
6							
			Closed Issues				
1							
2							
3							
4							
5							
6							
7							
8							

Key: R = red zone; Y = yellow zone; G = green zone.
Exhibit 4.2. Issues Log.

yellow. It is possible that they will cause problems and should be explored a little more fully. Those that will certainly create problems are color-coded red. These red issues might be put through a formal risk assessment process. The issues log exercise has identified them as items that warrant further investigation. Their possible qualitative and quantitative impacts should now be determined; then strategies for dealing with them should be developed.

BEHAVIORAL MODELS

There are certain human behaviors that are reasonably predictable, and effective risk analysts should be good at predicting their occurrence and consequences. This gets us into the area of "reading" people and involves more art than science. Still, understanding crude models of behavior allows us to anticipate both good and harmful behaviors in a reasonably objective fashion. The models can be valuable in the risk identification effort.

In his book *The Critical Chain,* Eliyahu Goldratt (1997) emphasizes the importance of being aware of human psychology when scheduling work efforts. If you have good psychological insights, you may be able to predict whether your team will be able to achieve the task deadlines they face. He puts two behavioral models at the center of his theory. One is what he calls the *student syndrome.* This is the tendency of people to put off doing a job until the last minute. The student syndrome is often a consequence of multitasking, the situation where people are required to engage in a variety of independent tasks simultaneously. When people try to do several things at the same time, they focus on dealing with the most pressing items first and put off addressing lower-priority items until later. They become "firefighters," struggling to put out fires as they arise. Regrettably, today's low-priority item becomes tomorrow's crisis, as the student syndrome leads to hurried solutions and missed deadlines.

So here is a risk-relevant behavioral principle that arises from the student syndrome phenomenon: if you give busy people work to do, don't be surprised if they put off doing the work until the last minute and consequently miss their deadlines.

A second behavioral model Goldratt poses is Parkinson's Law. The original statement of the law was articulated by C. Northcote Parkinson in *Parkinson's Law: And Other Studies of Administration* (1993) Parkinson's Law postulates that "work expands so as to fill the time for its completion." Goldratt adapts Parkinson's principle to the context of scheduling project and process efforts. He states that no matter how much safety you put into an estimate for a task's duration, your team members will eat up that safety and will probably spend more time doing the job than allotted. (In risk management, *safety* is known as *contingency reserve.*)

Let's say you know from experience that it takes three days to carry out Task A. In order to make sure that the team gets the job done on time, you schedule four days to do it. That is, you add an extra day of safety. Backed by an abundance of data, Goldratt maintains that there is a good chance that the team will spend at least four days on this task. Furthermore, had the team been asked to carry out the task in three days (a reasonable time), they probably would have done the job in three days or a little more—but in less than four days.

There are several reasons that Parkinson's Law holds true. For example, truly busy people may use the extra time you give them to work on other chores they have. Or if people are given more time to do a job than they need, they tend to approach their work with a relaxed attitude. Whatever the explanation, experience and research confirm that Parkinson's insights into human behavior are on target.

The risk-relevant behavioral principle associated with Parkinson's Law is: recognize that your team members will spend all of whatever time you give them to carry out a chore. If you establish contingency reserves for tasks, they will likely consume them, no matter how generous the reserves are. If you give them two days to do a two-day job, they probably will do it in two or more days. If you give them three days to do the same job, they will probably do it in three or more days.

The point is that by having a grasp of basic models of human behavior, you are able to identify risk issues that may arise in the ventures you are undertaking. Goldratt's *Theory of Constraints* describes a number of useful models. Clearly, many other models exist, including such well-known examples as Maslow's hierarchy of needs (1954), Herzberg's two-factor theory of motivation, and Argyris's concepts of espoused theories of action and theories of use (1990). The important thing is to select a handful of behavioral models that you find helpful in predicting risk issues rooted in human behavior and use them.

DIAGRAMMING TECHNIQUES

Various diagramming techniques can help risk analysts surface risk issues. Normally, when dealing with risk issues, people address them verbally. They talk them through. What is attractive about diagrams is that they force you to take a different approach—a visual perspective. This likely will give you a fresh point of view.

We look at two diagramming techniques in this section as representative of a much larger range of techniques that you can employ. One is a leading tool used in quality management to surface quality problems: the fishbone diagram. Another is a tool that is used when trying to identify customer requirements: the process/environment (P/E) diagram. In the next section, we examine a third diagramming technique that is valuable for surfacing risks: the flowchart.

Fishbone Diagrams

Fishbone diagrams (also called cause-and-effect diagrams) were originally developed by Kaoru Ishikawa, probably the most famous quality expert coming out of Japan. They are one of the most important tools used in quality management. What they do is to identify components of a process that feed into the core process, which, in turn, leads to a final "effect" (for example, a product).

The fishbone diagram in Figure 4.2 shows a portion of a process whose ultimate deliverable is "friendly data entry screens." Two factors that lead to the production of friendly screens are identified: "manpower" and "design." That is, an organization needs competent manpower in order to be able to create friendly screens. In particular, it needs "qualified designers." For their part, the designers need adequate "training" to make sure they have the skills necessary to do their jobs.

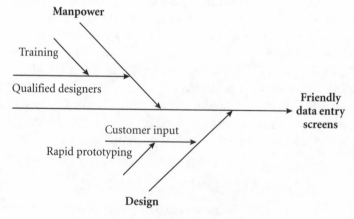

Figure 4.2. Fishbone Diagram.

As the diagram shows, friendly screens must be well designed. An important component of good design is that the screens are easily navigated by customers. Thus, the design must reflect customer needs and wants. These can be elicited through "rapid prototyping," a technique that enables customers and developers to work together to design a good product.

Once the fishbone diagram has been created, it enables you to focus on key areas that contribute to an operation's success. If these areas are not well developed or supported, then troubles are likely to ensure. In the example in Figure 4.2, the fishbone diagram leads us to ask a number of important risk-related questions:

Manpower Issues

- Do we have enough people to do the job?
- Are they qualified to do the job?
- Do we have training programs in place to help them to be qualified?
- Are the training programs any good?

Design Issues

- Do we have adequate customer input?
- Are we dealing with the right customers?
- Are we using the right mechanism to capture customer needs and wants (for example, rapid prototyping)?

If the answer to any of these questions is no, then we have a potential risk source. In this case, Steps 2 and 3 of the risk assessment process need to be carried out; that is, the qualitative and quantitative impacts of the identified risk events should be investigated, and then response strategies should be developed to deal with them.

Process/Environment Diagrams

Process/environment (P/E) diagrams focus on how core processes needed for doing a job interact with their environment. Clearly, core processes are not carried out in a vacuum. When you build a house, you need to deal with regulators, suppliers, neighbors, and a host of other players in the environment; when you are running a customer hot line, your operations must be sensitive to the roles and actions of business law, the telephone company, and your vendors. By explicitly examining the interactions of your processes with environmental factors, you are likely to develop a better sense of hidden risk issues that can emerge, thereby avoiding surprises.

Figure 4.3 presents a P/E diagram developed for a project to hold a picnic for a social club. The diagram is developed by the picnic-organizing committee members. The principal elements of the core process for holding the picnic are intentionally kept sparse. In this case, they are reduced to five basic tasks: make arrangements with caterers, have discussions with park officials, issue final instructions to the picnic attendees, check the weather the night before the picnic, then hold the picnic. Even with large complex undertakings, it is important to portray the core process simply in just a handful of steps.

Once the core process has been identified, the members of the picnic-organizing committee attempt to identify environmental factors that need to be taken into account. First, they need to identify pertinent environmental players and rules, and then they need to discover what risk issues, if any, these players and rules present to the picnic-organizing effort. In this case, the picnic-organizing committee uses a brainstorming process to identify eight players and rules. Following is a listing of these players and rules and a brief description of possible risk issues associated with them:

Picnic attendees: Are they aware of the arrangements? Do they have any interest in attending the picnic?

Park officials: What concerns might they have hosting a group of two hundred to three hundred people? Are they aware of the impending picnic, and do we have their support to hold it?

Weather bureau: Have we made preparations to deal with holding the picnic in the event of rain?

Entertainment committee: Has the entertainment committee done its job? Are activities well planned? Has the entertainment committee taken into account gathering equipment that may be needed for games?

Park regulations: What rules do we need to be aware of (for example, the park closes at sundown; no alcoholic beverages are permitted on park grounds)?

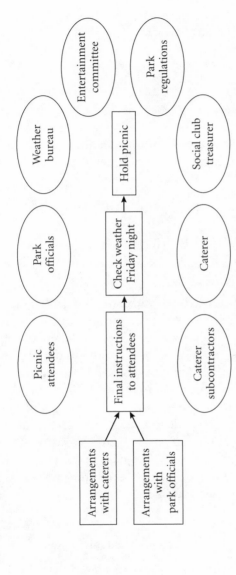

Figure 4.3. Process/Environment Diagram.

Social club treasurer: Is there enough money in the treasury to cover the costs of holding the picnic? Will attendance fees cover the costs of the picnic? Has the treasurer established a process to collect all the attendance fees?

Caterer: Does the caterer understand her role? Does she understand the food requirements for the picnic? Is she aware of the agenda for the picnic (in particular, the schedule for lunch and refreshments)?

Caterer's subcontractors: Are the caterer's subcontractor's reliable? (They showed up two hours late at the last picnic!)

As this example demonstrates, a strength of P/E diagrams is that they force you to recognize that it is not enough to investigate only internal sources of risk that arise from core processes. External sources of risk must be examined as well.

FLOWCHARTING PROJECT AND PROCESS MODELS

Flowcharts enable us to capture dynamic processes simply. If done properly, they are easy to build and easy to read. By reviewing a flowchart that describes a process, you are able to see how the process functions. You can work your way through the process step by step. As a consequence, because you are so close to the process, you may develop valuable insights about risks tied to the process.

To see how this works, look at Figure 4.4. This flowchart shows the steps that need to be taken to carry out a simple study. Recognizing that risk is inherent in conducting activities that lie outside our control, we shade the boxes that portray activities that are not under our direct control: "Get design approved," "Gather data (outside)," and "Conduct external review." These activities are now earmarked for special consideration—for example:

External Design Review

• Who on the outside will be approving our designs?

• Will we have direct access to them?

• Do they have a political agenda that they might pursue?

• Will they turn around our submitted designs quickly?

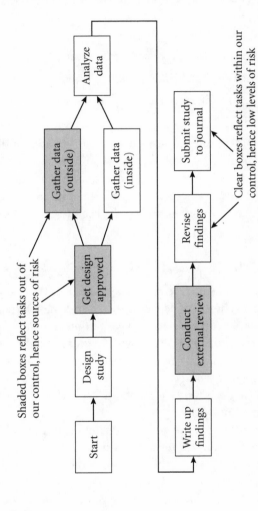

Shaded boxes reflect tasks out of our control, hence sources of risk

Clear boxes reflect tasks within our control, hence low levels of risk

Start

Design study

Get design approved

Gather data (outside)

Gather data (inside)

Analyze data

Write up findings

Conduct external review

Revise findings

Submit study to journal

Figure 4.4. Using Flowcharts to Identify Risks.

Gather Data (Outside)

- How accessible are the outside data?
- Do we need special clearances to access them?
- Are there access fees, and if so, how much are they?
- How can we check to see that the data are valid and reliable?

Conduct External Review

- Who will be sitting on the external review panel?
- Are they aware of our research goals?
- Will they be promoting a particular point of view that we need to be sensitive to?

By addressing these questions, we are better prepared to deal with curve balls thrown at us from players over whom we have no control.

A review of process flowcharts can surface risks in additional ways: highlight logical inconsistencies in the process, point out bottlenecks, and simply increase awareness of the degree of complexity of the project.

REGULAR MEETINGS

One of the best ways to surface risk issues is also the least sexy: hold regular meetings. When people get together and share experiences, they learn what others are doing and have an opportunity to provide others with information about their own experiences and viewpoints. During these exchanges, you can depend on the collective intelligence of the group to identify risk issues.

For example, George says: "We are about to purchase five thousand widgets from Beta Enterprises."

Marsha responds: "Haven't you heard? Beta is in financial straits and may be filing for bankruptcy any day now."

George: "Is that so? If that's the case, we had better look for a different supplier."

Meetings also provide an occasion where risk issues appearing in the risk log can be discussed. Risk-sensitive organizations set aside small blocks of time to go over the risk log during regular meetings. Through this exercise, the attendees at the meeting can collectively determine which issues need serious attention and which do not. For those issues that demand attention, attendees can even suggest ways of dealing with them.

CONCLUSION

In order to deal with risks, they must first be identified. The process of risk identification enables risk analysts to surface potential risk events so that they can be investigated and, if necessary, handled by means of an assortment of risk treatment strategies. As this chapter has demonstrated, several approaches exist to help surface risk events systematically. They range from humdrum methods such as holding meetings, to analytical techniques, such as developing fishbone diagrams, to more creative approaches, such as conducting brainstorming sessions. No one method is best. In fact, it is a good idea to combine the humdrum with analytical and creative approaches in order to view potential risk events from multiple perspectives.

Once risk events have been identified, their likelihood and impacts need to be determined. Are they likely to occur? If so, will they cause financial harm to the organization, or lead to slippages in the delivery of products, or result in low-quality deliverables? The matter of the impacts of risk events, both qualitative and quantitative, is the topic of the next two chapters.

CHAPTER FIVE

Assessing Impacts of Risk Events—Qualitative Impact Analysis

———— $\sim$ ————

With risk identification, we go through a systematic process of surfacing risk issues that can affect operations. As a consequence of this effort, we develop a good idea of things we should look out for when we do our jobs. Of course, not all risk events that we identify are equally significant. Those that we believe are highly significant are categorized as red zone risks. They require special attention. Those that are moderately significant are categorized as yellow zone risks, indicating the need for caution, and those that are insignificant are categorized as green zone risks.

Once risk events have been identified and classified, we turn our attention to answering the question: What are the consequences of the occurrence of the target risk events, particularly the red zone events? For example, if they arise, will this lead to major increases in expenses and decreases in revenue? (If so, by what amounts?) Will our clients face physical danger? (If so, what kinds of dangers?) Will we encounter delays in rolling out new products? (If so, how long will the delays be?)

The attempt to assay the consequences of the occurrence of risk events is called *risk impact analysis.* As a matter of convenience, we split risk impact analysis into two parts: qualitative analysis and quantitative analysis. With qualitative analysis, we attempt to examine the impacts of risk events primarily through the application of a logical reasoning process. For example, if we think Event A will happen, we speculate that it will lead to Consequence A. Consequence A, in turn, may give rise to Event B, which will result in Consequence B. And so on. Effective qualitative impact analysis is heavily dependent on experience, good logic, and good judgment. This chapter addresses qualitative risk impact analysis.

With quantitative analysis, we try to measure consequences numerically. For example, if a grinding machine breaks down on the factory floor, how much production will be lost? What is the dollar value of the losses? How long will it take before we resume production at normal levels? Answers to these types of questions provide insights to develop risk response strategies (see Chapter Eight). Let's say our quantitative analysis reveals that downtime of the grinding machine costs our company $30,000 a year in lost revenue. Let's say further that the cost of a new grinding machine is $50,000. The machine will likely pay for itself in less than two years. This information may lead us to conclude that we should purchase a backup grinding machine so that we don't suffer production losses. Quantitative risk impact analysis is handled in the next chapter.

Every now and then, people get caught up in a debate on which is better: qualitative or quantitative impact analysis. This is a fruitless debate. Both approaches are important, and both should be carried out. The two approaches address different things. The qualitative approach recognizes that experience coupled with hunches and good judgment enable people to develop insights that they cannot develop if they are constrained by the requirement that they work only with measurable phenomena. This is particularly true with a range of situations, including first-of-a-kind experiences, circumstances where politics reign, and situations where outcomes are determined through negotiations.

When you are able to assess impacts quantitatively, why not do so? Consider the situation where you are engaged in an impact analysis that addresses the following question: What are the financial consequences of a three-day interruption of business caused by a breakdown of equipment at the plant? Clearly, "A three-day interruption of business will lead to a $15,000 loss of revenue" is a far more informative response than "A three-day interruption of business will lead to a fairly serious financial loss." In general, an impact analysis based on valid and reliable quantitative assessments is more valuable than a corresponding impact analysis based on unsupported speculation.

In this chapter, we examine qualitative impact analysis and in the process investigate a number of tools that help us to engage in such analyses: scenario building, the likelihood-impact matrix, attribute analysis, and Delphi forecasting.

SCENARIO BUILDING

With qualitative scenario building, we bring together a group of informed people and ask them to apply their knowledge and imaginations to describe the state of affairs that will be achieved as a consequence of an action. While this statement sounds a bit foreboding, we should recognize that we engage in this type of activity all the time. To see this, consider the following dialogue:

GEORGE: If we leave the house at 7:30 A.M. and encounter no traffic, we can be at Sally's place by noon.

DOROTHY: That's right. But if there is traffic, it will delay us by at least a half-hour. We don't want to be late. So perhaps we should leave here at 7:00 A.M.

In this brief interchange, George and Dorothy create two simple scenarios: a good-case and bad-case scenario. Both scenarios are built on George and Dorothy's experience. Both entail the application of logical reasoning. By creating the two scenarios, George and Dorothy are even able to develop alternative courses of action. The conservative one would have them leave home at 7:00 A.M. to factor in the possibility of a half-hour traffic-induced delay in their journey. The optimistic one would have them leave home at 7:30 A.M.

George and Dorothy's scenario-building experience captures on a small scale the essence of what midsized and large-scale scenario-building exercises encounter. Big or little, scenario-building exercises are adventures in storytelling. The trick is to tell a story that will accurately reflect how things actually play out in the real world.

There are many ways that qualitative scenarios can be developed. We examine two approaches here: extrapolative and normative. The starting point for the extrapolative approach is recent history and where things stand now. Given this information, a future is built step by step, projecting forward from today. With the normative approach, the starting point of the scenario-building exercise is some imagined future state of affairs. Then stepping backward from the future, we develop a scenario in reverse order that gets us back to today.

Extrapolative Scenario Building

Extrapolative scenario building will be illustrated with a real-world example:

The senior management of Gamma Enterprises has decided that a major source of revenue growth for its line of garden tools is sales of the tools overseas. In attempts to identify risks and opportunities of expanding its operations abroad, one important source of risk that stands out is Gamma's inexperience with local market conditions in other countries. Although Gamma has great garden tools, it is obvious that the tools will not sell themselves. They must be marketed effectively.

Gamma's initial inclination is to adopt the marketing strategy it successfully employed in the United States and Canada: establish marketing/sales offices in a number of regions staffed by local people who know the markets well. Thus, in reviewing market expansion strategies overseas, Gamma's senior managers feel that Gamma should establish local marketing/sales offices in the target countries where Gamma intends to introduce its products.

The senior managers ask the head of their marketing/sales department to examine the consequences of setting up marketing/sales offices overseas. She puts together a cross-functional group of experienced managers from the marketing/sales department (Sally), legal department (Debby), human resource management department (Tom), finance department (Dick), and operations department (Harry). Together, these five people explore alternative scenarios of how things will play out if Gamma establishes marketing/sales offices overseas. Following is a portion of the dialogue they engage in:

SALLY [marketing/sales]: I'm a little nervous about assuming we can follow our North American expansion strategy overseas. I doubt that what has worked in Phoenix will automatically work in Beijing.

DICK [finance]: I agree. Let's see what would happen if we adopt our North American model in its entirety.

SALLY: Okay, let me start. Let's say we're in Beijing and want to set up a marketing/sales office there. What do we need to do?

HARRY [operations]: That's just the problem. We don't know anything about doing business in China in general and Beijing in particular.

SALLY: So we need to contact a local consultant who can guide us through the intricacies of local conditions.

DEBBY [legal): We need to be prepared for the fact that from the beginning, we will have a host of legal hurdles to contend with. I'm no expert about business law in China, but I know that we need to get a rash of approvals before we can begin operations.

SALLY: Good point, Debby. So let's say we've figured out the legal issues. What next?

TOM [human resources]: Obviously, we have to contend with human resource issues. For example, we will need to hire local staff. And one condition we must insist on is that they be bilingual, speaking both English and Mandarin.

DICK: How do you hire professionals in Beijing? Do they have headhunters there?

SALLY: Who knows? Let's assume we can do the job. Now what?

TOM: I'm not a marketing guy, but it seems obvious to me that we will have to develop a marketing strategy that addresses local conditions in Beijing. You know, a strategy that focuses on marketing's 4Ps.

HARRY: That raises an interesting issue. Are we sure that our gardening tools are usable in Beijing? Do they even have gardens there?

As Sally, Debby, Tom, Dick, and Harry continue their qualitative scenario-building exercise, it becomes obvious that the establishment of a local marketing/sales office in Beijing is filled with consequences that Gamma is not able to deal with given its total ignorance of local conditions in Beijing. Through the scenario-building exercise, a plethora of legal, marketing and sales, operational, and cultural consequences arise. When Gamma senior managers receive a write-up of the results of the scenario-building effort, they realize that copying their North American expansion model is too dangerous. Ultimately, they decide to launch operations overseas with a local partner. (Establishing local partnerships is fraught with risk as well, but we won't cover that topic here.)

A strength of extrapolative scenario building is that it forces people to work through the consequences of their proposed actions step by step. It is one thing to say, "Let's set up marketing/sales offices overseas; they have served us well here in North America," and another to think through the impacts of such an action. The very process of building the scenario surfaces a range of issues that need to be addressed and may even suggest strategies for handling them.

For extrapolative scenario building to work, it is important that the right group of people participate in the exercise. They need to be experienced and knowledgeable about the enterprise's business operations. They should also have a good understanding of developments in their industry. To make sure that the group has the knowledge needed to build workable scenarios, subject matter experts might be invited to participate in the scenario-building exercise. If the wrong people are working on developing the scenario, then the exercise is a waste of time or, worse, misleading.

Normative Scenario Building

The process of conducting a normative scenario-building exercise will be illustrated with an example that actually transpired as reported here. The names of the principal players have been changed for purposes of anonymity:

Epsilon Enterprises is an investment banker whose largest client is Kappa Capital, a substantial lending institution. Epsilon and Kappa often work together to structure merger and acquisition deals. Kappa has recently informed Epsilon that it would like Epsilon to be its principal partner in arranging mergers and acquisitions. In order to move toward this end, it needs Epsilon's information technology department to develop a software system that will allow Epsilon and Kappa to exchange financial data electronically, with no manual intervention. Epsilon creates Project Abacus to address this matter exclusively. The Abacus team prepares a project proposal that it plans to submit to Kappa Capital in one week, on September 15. In the section of the proposal document titled "Delivery Date," delivery of the solution is promised for November 30. The logic for this date is that the amount of programming necessary to deliver the solution would consume the efforts of three full-time analysts working two months.

Before the proposal can be submitted to Kappa, it must undergo a standard risk review to make sure that the proposed effort makes good business sense and the promises it contains can be achieved. The risk assessment group (RAG) that examines the proposal has a tough time believing that a deliverable of this complexity and importance can be delivered by November 30, so they request the Abacus team members to work with them in conducting a normative scenario-building exercise to test whether the project can be accomplished so quickly. One morning is set aside to carry out this exercise.

The future state of affairs that is used to launch the normative scenario-building effort is: "A fully developed and tested data interchange system will be delivered to Kappa Capital on or before November 30 that will enable Epsilon and Kappa to exchange financial data electronically, with no human intervention."

This is how the conversation goes:

RAG TEAM: For this delivery date to be achieved, what efforts need to be completed on Project Abacus two weeks before the final solution is delivered—roughly November 15?

ABACUS TEAM: The final tests of the system should be nearing completion by November 15.

RAG TEAM: If that is the case, when does final testing need to begin?

ABACUS TEAM: Two to three weeks before the tests are completed— roughly October 24.

RAG TEAM: For the final tests to begin on October 24, what development work needs to be completed on the system?

ABACUS TEAM: The system's five principal modules need to be coded.

RAG TEAM: And when can coding begin?

ABACUS TEAM: Roughly on September 30, about four or five weeks before the final tests begin.

RAG TEAM: And before coding can begin, what must be done?

ABACUS TEAM: The system must be designed.

RAG TEAM: And how long will the design effort take?

ABACUS TEAM: Probably three to four weeks. And by the way, in making our estimate for delivering the solution, we forgot to take into account that we need to work with Kappa's IT department and lending specialists to provide us with information on the data structure of their database. Those meetings will consume several weeks.

It turns out that there were many other requirements that the Abacus team overlooked when developing their estimate of the delivery date. For example, the system is being designed to function over the Web. Epsilon has a corporate policy mandating reviews by the legal department for all Web-based solutions. These reviews typically take six weeks. Furthermore, projects of this nature that are carried out with important partners require periodic senior management reviews, and scheduling such reviews can be a problem. A host of other time-consuming requirements emerge as a result of the normative scenario-building exercise.

At the end of the morning, when the exercise is done, it becomes clear that the earliest date that the product can be delivered to Kappa Capital is May, about nine months after the project's beginning. If Epsilon submits the original estimated delivery date of November 30, it will encounter a schedule slippage of at least six or seven months and will have generated plenty of ill will with Kappa Capital.

There is nothing magic about normative scenario-building exercises. Their strength lies in the fact that they have us looking into the other end of the telescope. The view we get is sufficiently novel that it helps us to question our operating assumptions. Risk consequences that can be lost through a conventional risk review might be obvious when looked at from a backward perspective.

Scenario-Building Case: Terrorist Attack on Washington, D.C.

Scenario building is particularly appropriate when trying to carry out risk analyses of unthinkable events. For example, in spring 2002, the Center for Strategic and International Studies developed a scenario for an attack on Washington, D.C., by terrorists with a dirty bomb, a conventional bomb wrapped in radioactive material. When it explodes, it disperses radioactivity into the community for an area of several square blocks. If there is a strong wind, the radioactive debris could be transported over a much wider area. The scenario development team concluded that while the immediate number of casualties of the explosion would be relatively small, the panic it would create in the community, coupled with cleanup costs, would make its impact very high. Consequently, disaster plans should focus heavily on addressing logistical issues to reduce the chaos that would ensue after a bomb has been detonated, for example, ensuring the free flow of traffic, to providing timely information to the public, and keeping businesses and government functioning.

LIKELIHOOD-IMPACT MATRIX

Risk comprises two components: likelihood and impact. When you say, "Getting hit by a bolt of lightning is not so risky, because it happens so rarely," you are emphasizing its likelihood aspect. Being struck by a bolt of lightning is not very likely.

Someone might disagree with you and respond to your statement in the following way: "I don't agree. Getting hit by a bolt of lightning is quite risky, because if you are struck, it can fry you alive!" This person is looking at the impact aspect of risk. If you are actually struck by lightning, it will harm you severely.

The two components of risk can be combined in a single chart called the likelihood-impact matrix. An example of this matrix is shown in Figure 5.1. A measure of the likelihood of an event is presented on the vertical axis. In our example in Figure 5.1, three levels of likelihood are noted: low, medium, and high. (If you want, you can

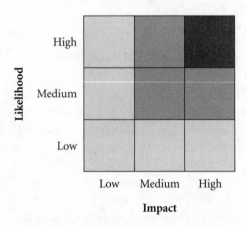

Figure 5.1. Likelihood-Impact Matrix.

picture more levels, for example, not likely, somewhat likely, moderately likely, likely, very likely.) A measure of impact is presented on the horizontal axis: low, medium, and high. (Again, you can employ more levels if you want to, for example, no impact, little impact, moderate impact, moderately high impact, high impact.)

The likelihood-impact matrix offers a good way to categorize risk events qualitatively in terms of their probability of occurrence and their consequences. Risk events appearing in the dark shaded cell in the top right-hand corner are called red zone risk events. Those appearing in the medium gray shaded cells are called yellow zone risk events. Those appearing in the light gray shaded cells are called green zone risk events.

Consider how each of the following risk events can be categorized according to the two dimensions of risk:

Encountering ants at a picnic in Maine. This event is very likely to occur, but its impact is low. That makes it a green zone event. The picnic planners shouldn't spend too much time worrying about dealing with it.

Earth is struck by an asteroid. This event is very unlikely to occur in the next ten thousand years, but if it does happen, it will have a catastrophic impact. Remember that such an event caused the extinction of dinosaurs 65 million years ago. As terrifying as the consequences of this event may be, the fact that it has a near-zero probability of occurrence makes it a green zone event. Earth's citizens should not lose too much sleep worrying about asteroid hits.

You are struck by a car while running blindfolded across a busy street. This is a red zone event. The probability of being struck by a car if you are crossing a busy street while blindfolded is very high. And if you are struck by a car, the consequences can be severe. The best way to handle this risk event is to avoid playing such a silly, dangerous game.

The likelihood-impact matrix is one of the most useful tools in the risk manager's toolbox. By categorizing risk events according to the two dimensions of risk, risk analysts can determine readily whether individual risk events warrant careful attention.

ATTRIBUTE ANALYSIS

Attribute analysis is a creative problem-solving technique that can be employed productively when exploring possible qualitative risk impacts. It was originally developed as a tool to generate new product ideas. When employed this way, what you do is take a product and visualize what it would look like and what it would do if you changed its attributes dramatically. For example, let's say you are the general manager of a company that makes tea bags and that you are trying to find new uses for tea bags and derivative products. You would raise a number of questions that force you to consider the consequences of changing some of the attributes associated with the teabags you produce—for example:

* *What if we change the content of the tea bag from tea leaves to something else?* This question triggers a number of possible responses. For example, if you want to maintain the tea bag's function as a delivery system for transporting flavors to beverages, you can reflect on different flavors that can be contained in the tea bag, such as coffee, fruit juice flavors, and herbs. The tea bags can also contain spices that can be used in the making of soups and stews. If you think about radically new applications, you might consider using the tea bag concept for prepackaging chemicals that students can use when conducting laboratory experiments ("Now dip the bag into a 50 percent alcohol solution for ten minutes").
* *What if you make the tea bags very large?* Possible uses might be that the large tea bags can be sold as disposable sacks for washing delicate fabrics in a washing machine or redesigned to serve as air filters (for vacuum cleaners). Or the tea bag material might serve as a filter for liquids, possibly to be used in manufacturing processes.
* *What if you make the tea bags very small?* In this case, they could serve as an alternative to capsules as a medicine delivery system or as filters on small mechanical devices.

The principal value of attribute analysis is that it requires you to examine something you are familiar with in different ways and to do so in a structured way. It enables otherwise noncreative people to develop creative solutions to problems by forcing them to look at things in an unconventional light.

The employment of attribute analysis in examining the possible impacts of risk events is a simple extension of its use in new product development. When examining a risk event, you can ask: What will its impacts be if it is magnified tremendously? If it is concentrated in a small area? If it plays out in reverse order? If it affects a nontargeted audience?

DELPHI FORECASTING

The Delphi technique was developed at the RAND Corporation in the 1960s. RAND was a think tank that thrived during the height of the cold war. Its principal function was to serve the U.S. Air Force by applying creative solutions to seemingly intractable problems.

The Delphi technique was developed as a forecasting tool. It was named after the ancient Greek Oracles at Delphi, whose job was to predict the future. Its principal purpose is to help a group of experts develop a consensus about some event. For example, a Delphi exercise might be set up to enable experts to predict when companies will establish operational space factories capable of producing flawless ball bearings in a zero-gravity environment. Thirty experts might be asked to participate in the exercise. For the Delphi exercise to work, it is important that the right experts are chosen. One consideration is to choose experts from a range of pertinent disciplines. In the space factory example, experts might be chosen from the following areas: metallurgists, payload specialists, industrial engineers, economists, political scientists, organizational behavior specialists, factory construction engineers, financiers, experienced factory hands, and users of precision ball bearings. This list of experts reflects the fact that building space factories has technical, economic, political, and business implications that need to be explored.

The experts who participate in the Delphi exercise typically do not know who their fellow panelists are. The rationale for this is to keep the experts from being unduly influenced by the reputation of their colleagues.

The exercise begins with each expert receiving a questionnaire. To keep the example simple, let's say that the questionnaire for the space factory exercise contains only one question: "In what year do you think fully functioning space factories capable of producing flawless ball bearings in a zero-gravity environment will be operational?" Each expert notes an answer and then returns the response to the Delphi administrator. The administrator tallies the responses. Of the thirty responses, the most optimistic predicts that space factories will be operational in ten years. The most pessimistic predicts that they will be operational in fifty years. The median response is twenty-five years.

The results are tabulated and portrayed graphically, as pictured in Figure 5.2. The peak of the asymmetric pentagon represents the median response of the experts. In statistics, the term *median* refers to the value where half the answers are larger and half smaller. So what this chart tells us is that the median response to the space factory question is twenty-five years. Note that the elongated pentagon shows only the results for the core 50 percent of the responses. This is called the interquartile range. The 25 percent most optimistic and 25 percent most pessimistic responses have been lopped off. In our example, the cutoff point for the bottom 25 percent of responses is twenty years and the cutoff point for the top 25 percent of responses is forty-one years.

Once the results have been tabulated, the Delphi administrator sends the questionnaire back to the experts, accompanied by a statistical summary of the results of the round 1 questionnaire distribution. Respondents are asked again when they think an operational space factory will come on line. However, they are further instructed that if their answer lies outside the interquartile range, they should write a brief explanation describing the rationale for their choice.

The experts state their estimates of the time frame for operational space factories and return their questionnaires to the Delphi administrator. As before, the administrator analyzes the results and carries

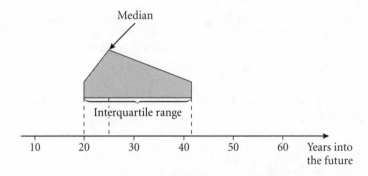

Figure 5.2. Summary Report in a Delphi Exercise.

out a statistical tabulation of the results. The round 2 results are returned to the experts for their consideration. This time, the rationales for outlier responses are supplied. The experts are asked to weigh their own judgments against those of their colleagues and offer once again an estimate of when they think operational space factories will come on line.

The objective of this methodology is to see whether experts can achieve a consensus on an issue after they have a chance to reflect on feedback provided by the responses of their colleagues. In a typical Delphi exercise, each round of questionnaire distribution leads to increased conformity in the experts' views on an issue. After several rounds, when it becomes clear that additional consensus will not occur, the exercise is ended.

In practice, people often approach the Delphi exercise in a less disciplined fashion than described here. The participants in the exercise may know who the panel members are. They might even carry out the exercise in a face-to-face setting. Whether implemented in a disciplined or loose fashion, the key feature of Delphi exercises is to have experts go through several rounds in their attempts to establish consensus on an issue.

The application of this approach for qualitative risk impact analysis is a natural extension of the process illustrated here. Participants in the exercise might be asked to "forecast" such things as the cost, schedule, and resource impacts associated with the occurrence of a risk event. The first round responses might be highly divergent. After several rounds of responses, however, the responses might show that a consensus has emerged on the impacts of the risk event.

CONCLUSION

All decisions that decision makers ponder have risk implications. The question is: Which of the innumerable risk events they surface require action and which do not? Clearly, not all risk events are equally significant.

Risk impact analysis helps answer this question. This chapter has examined how qualitative risk impact analysis enables decision makers to determine the consequences associated with the occurrence of risk events, using qualitative analytical tools such as scenario building, the likelihood-impact matrix, attribute analysis, and Delphi exercises. There are two advantages to the qualitative approach. One is that in contrast to highly disciplined and demanding quantitative approaches, qualitative approaches enable analysts to be as creative as they dare to be in exploring the consequences of risk events. The qualitative techniques discussed in this chapter share a lot with creative problem-solving techniques. With highly creative thinking, hard-to-predict consequences are more visible than when employing convergent-thinking, quantitative approaches.

A second advantage is that the impact analysis can be carried out even when quantitative data do not exist. This is particularly significant when dealing with new initiatives with which we have had little prior experience. The lack of quantitative data does not shut us down. Using a qualitative approach, we can employ experience and logic to determine the consequences of risk events.

To say that qualitative approaches to risk impact analysis are important is not to denigrate quantitative approaches. In an ideal world, we are able to employ both. If we are able to create reliable and valid models of the processes we work with, then we can simulate different risk scenarios to determine their dollar, schedule, and resource consequences. It is not necessary to actually experience failure to be able to determine its consequences. In the next chapter, we examine a number of approaches to conducting quantitative risk impact analyses.

CHAPTER SIX

Assessing Impacts
of Risk Events—
Quantitative Analysis

Quantitative risk impact analyses enable us to develop a solid sense of the tangible consequences of the occurrence of risk events. While risk analysts may not be able to predict the probability of a terrorist attack on an important target, or the death of the chief scientist of a major laboratory, or a flood in the industrial heartland, they can estimate with reasonable accuracy the consequences of untoward events. For example, they can determine that if five factories are shut down by a flood for three weeks, it will result in X dollars of lost production. Or if a building is destroyed in an earthquake, it will cost Y dollars to rebuild it.

In this chapter, we examine various techniques that risk analysts employ to help them assess the impacts of risk events quantitatively. For the most part, they do not need to have advanced quantitative skills to employ these techniques, because the data they are dealing with are so crude. In the risk arena, even mathematical adepts do not have a great advantage over people who are merely competent mathematically, because the data they work with are not good enough to put through sophisticated analyses. Garbage in, garbage out. Still, they must be mathematically literate. As mentioned earlier, the statistician

John Allen Paulos has written a number of best-selling books that detail the innumeracy of a typical "educated" person. The fact is (and this can be confirmed through many studies and practical experience) that many senior managers who make decisions that can make or break their organizations are mathematically innumerate.

In this chapter, we examine some of the quantitative approaches to investigating the impacts of risk that are employed by risk analysts. The perspectives and techniques we review are by no means comprehensive. A little thought suggests that there is no limit to the way that we can formulate risk impacts quantitatively. What we have done here is simply highlighted some approaches that have proved to be useful and are employed with some regularity in risk analyses in organizations.

MODELING RISK

A model is a simulacrum of reality. Aeronautical engineers build scale model aircraft whose aerodynamic properties can be tested in wind tunnels. Architects develop tabletop models of new building complexes in order to enable their clients to visualize what will be constructed for them. Meteorologists build computer models of weather systems, allowing them to predict actual weather patterns under different conditions. With models, you can simulate reality without directly experiencing it. The simulations enable you to understand what you are studying and to predict consequences associated with different scenarios.

Developing quantitative models can be helpful when trying to examine the consequences of risk events. The models may be as simple as a spreadsheet budget or as complex as a mathematical representation of a product, process, or project in all of its details. Simple or complex, models give analysts an opportunity to examine the outcomes of risk events when viewed according to different assumptions. You don't actually have to experience failure firsthand to understand it and its ramifications!

Table 6.1 provides an illustration of how a simple spreadsheet cost estimating model can provide useful information on project cost impacts resulting from changes in two cost parameters. Table 6.1a shows the original cost model. As often happens in life, the conditions that we initially believe will prevail soon change. In this case, we learn that the $300 per day engineers are not available to work on the job, and

	Cost	Cumulative Cost
a. Project Budget		

Labor costs

	Cost	Cumulative Cost
Engineers (50 days @ $300 per day)	$15,000	
Tech support personnel (100 days @ $200 per day)	$20,000	
Subtotal	$35,000	$35,000

Fringe benefits

Fringes (25% direct labor)	$8,750	
Subtotal	$8,750	$43,750

Overhead

Overhead (65% of labor + fringes)	$28,438	
Subtotal	$28,438	$72,188

Expenses

Materials consumed	$12,000	
Report reproduction	$7,500	
Subtotal	$19,500	$91,688

Fee (profit)

Fee	$7,500	$99,188
Grand total		$99,188

b. Revised Project Budget

Labor costs

Engineers (50 days @ $350 per day)	$17,500	
Effort extended by 20 days		
Tech support personnel (120 days @ $200 per day)	$24,000	
Subtotal	$41,500	$41,500

Fringe benefits

Fringes (25% direct labor)	$10,375	
Subtotal	$10,375	$51,875

Overhead

Overhead (65% of labor + fringes)	$33,719	
Subtotal	$33,719	$85,594

Expenses

Materials consumed	$12,000	
Report reproduction	$7,500	
Subtotal	$19,500	$105,094

Fee (profit)

Fee	$7,500	$112,594
Grand total		$112,594

Table 6.1.   Spreadsheet Cost Estimating Model.

the company is forced to employ more expensive engineers at $350 per day. Furthermore, owing to unanticipated technical difficulties, it appears that 120 days of technical support effort will be needed, as opposed to the original estimated 100 days of effort. After these changes have been factored into the spreadsheet model, we see in Table 6.1b that the project cost jumps from $99,188 to $112,594, an increase of $13,406. In addition, the extra twenty days of support effort will likely lead to an extension of the work effort's duration.

Figure 6.1 provides an illustration of an important modeling tool employed in project management: the PERT/CPM network diagram. (PERT stands for Program Evaluation and Review Technique. It was developed by the U.S. Navy in the 1950s to plan the Polaris missile project. CPM stands for Critical Path Method. It was developed by DuPont in the 1950s to plan large chemical engineering projects.) This diagram enables project planners to lay out tasks and estimate project durations. It is a systems diagram of sorts, showing how project tasks are tied to each other. Thus, the PERT/CPM network can detect the ripple effects felt throughout a project as a consequence of changes made to individual tasks. Beyond this, today's PERT/CPM software packages (several hundred are being sold) also capture resource and cost data, offering project planners a modeling tool that provides integrated cost, schedule, and resource information.

The project portrayed in Figure 6.1 is writing a four-chapter technical report. At the outset, only one resource is assigned to write the report: George. As the figure shows, the total effort should take twenty days and cost $6,000. However, the client for whom the report is being prepared insists that the report be completed in eleven working days. To meet the client requirements, an additional resource, Dorothy, is added to the project. George and Dorothy split the job: George writes Chapters One and Three, while Dorothy writes Chapters Two and Four. By doing work in parallel (called *fast tracking* in project management), the technical report can now be written in eleven days, saving nine days from the original schedule. However, using Dorothy has an impact on project cost. Because Dorothy's daily fee is $350, in contrast to George's $300, project cost increases from $6,000 to $6,450.

The next example shows how effective use of models can provide nonobvious results. Figure 6.2a portrays a PERT/CPM chart illustrating how John and Veronica plan to carry out a simple project to prepare for a picnic. The boldfaced path in the diagram shows the *critical*

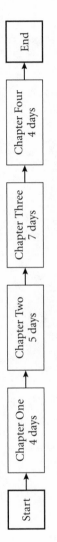

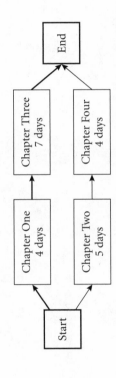

Start → Chapter One 4 days → Chapter Two 5 days → Chapter Three 7 days → Chapter Four 4 days → End

Facts: George will write the four-chapter report by himself. The effort will consume twenty days. George is paid $300 per day, so labor costs will be $6,000.

a. Model Before Change

Start → Chapter One 4 days → Chapter Three 7 days → End
Start → Chapter Two 5 days → Chapter Four 4 days → End

Facts: The client requires that the work be done in eleven days. Dorothy joins George and writes two chapters. She is paid $350 per day. The project will be completed in eleven days (George's path). Labor costs will now be $6,450.
Impact: Duration will be shortened by nine days, but costs will be increased by $450.

b. Model After Change

Figure 6.1. PERT/CPM Model of a Report Writing Project.

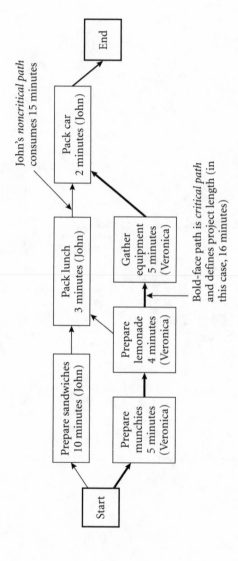

John's *noncritical path* consumes 15 minutes

Bold-face path is *critical path* and defines project length (in this case, 16 minutes)

a. Initial Preparations

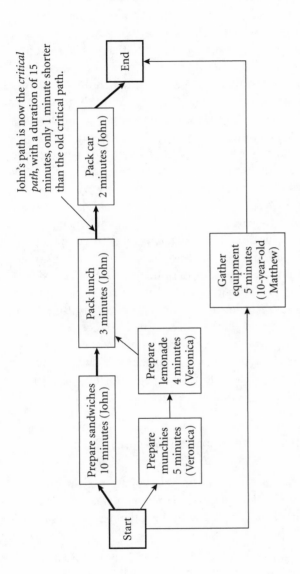

John's path is now the *critical path*, with a duration of 15 minutes, only 1 minute shorter than the old critical path.

b. Preparations After Adding Matthew

Figure 6.2. PERT/CPM Chart for Preparing for a Picnic.

path, that is, the path that consumes the greatest amount of time and defines the length of the project. (In the example, this is Veronica's path.) By adding up the durations of tasks on the critical path, you see that the project will take sixteen minutes to complete. Then John and Veronica realize that they should ask their son, ten-year-old Matthew, to participate in the picnic preparation effort so that he can feel good about making a contribution. They decide that the job he is most qualified for is to gather the equipment, a five-minute chore. Matthew's planned effort can be seen in Figure 6.2b.

Let's examine how including Matthew in the project effort affects the project schedule. Common sense suggests that if you add someone to a project to do five minutes worth of work, you will trim five minutes off the schedule. In this case, common sense is wrong. By adding Matthew to the picnic preparations, the new critical path is John's path, which is fifteen minutes long. That is, John and Veronica save only one minute. In general, it is unlikely that you will be able to intuit the correct schedule duration, particularly on more complex projects. In fact, your intuition is likely to lead you to wrong conclusions.

These examples provide simple cases of the use of PERT/CPM network models to carry out what-if analyses that can be important when trying to assess cost, schedule, and resource impacts resulting from changes to the project plan. On large, complex projects, where the number of tasks, resources, and budget items is overwhelming, PERT/CPM network models become indispensable in carrying out quantitative impact analyses. Among the types of what-if questions PERT/CPM network models can answer are these:

- What if the design engineers are a week late in joining the project effort? What will be the impact of this cost and schedule change?

- What if our client insists on our finishing phase 1 of the project two weeks earlier than planned? How many more resources do we need to apply to the project to meet the new schedule requirements? What are the cost implications?

- What if our project budget has been cut by 20 percent? How should we reconfigure the tasks in order to achieve the project goals? What are the schedule and scope impacts?

As the examples here show, an important value of models is that they enable analysts to conduct *sensitivity analyses.* That is, they show the outcome of events associated with different values we specify for variables and parameters. By adjusting these values carefully, we are able to identify how sensitive the process or project we are examining is to changes in the conditions it encounters. In some cases, major changes in conditions have little impact; in others, even minute changes affect the process or project strongly.

EXPECTED VALUE ANALYSIS

An important concept from statistics that is routinely employed in risk analyses is mathematical expectation. *Mathematical expectation* enables us to compute the expected value of an event, given that we know the values of specific outcomes associated with the event and their probabilities. For example, let's say that we have weighed 100 school children as part of a health awareness program. We find that 20 percent of them weigh 70 pounds, 30 percent weigh 75 pounds, 30 percent weigh 80 pounds, and 20 percent weigh 85 pounds. Given these data, we know that in this group, the probability of a child's weighing 70 pounds is 0.2, 75 pounds is 0.3, 80 pounds is 0.3, and 85 pounds is 0.2. The expected value of their weight is $(70 \times 0.2) + (75 \times 0.3) + (80 \times 0.3) + (85 \times 0.2)$, or 77.5 pounds. A little reflection shows that expected value is a measure of the mean of a distribution. In computing it, we are saying that the average weight of the children in the group is 77.5 pounds.

Mathematical expectation is employed frequently in financial analyses. To illustrate its application in making financial computations, consider the following simple example:

George is at the racetrack and wants to place a bet. He sees that five horses will be running in the fourth race. He is unfamiliar with these horses, so from his perspective, the probability of any given horse's winning is 0.2 (one in five). That means that if he bets on one horse, there is a probability of 0.8 that he will lose his money. He likes the name of one horse, Bright Star, so he decides to buy a $2 ticket to bet on Bright Star's winning the fourth race. Given the posted odds, George determines that if Bright Star wins, his ticket will be worth $12. While standing on line to place his bet, he overhears a couple of seasoned handicappers comment that any horse could win this race, so he feels confident that Bright Star's chance of winning is indeed 20 percent.

George has enough information to calculate the expected monetary value associated with this bet. If his horse loses, he will lose $2.

The expected value of this loss is 0.8 × 2.00, which is equal to $1.60. If he wins, he will pocket $10 (he needs to deduct the $2 for the bet from the $12 in winnings). The expected monetary value associated with winning is 0.2 × 10.00, which is equal to $2. When you take into account the expected value for winnings and losses, you can see that the winnings outweigh the losses by 40 cents (2.00 − 1.60 = 0.40). This tells us that given the probabilities and payoffs associated with this bet, if George were to play this race many times he would, on the average, be 40 cents ahead.

This example illustrates that in computing expected monetary value (EMV), you need to estimate expected gains and expected losses and then subtract the losses from the gains. That is:

EMV (Bright Star bet) = Expected gains − expected losses = 2.00 − 1.60 = 0.40.

What holds for gambling at the racetrack also applies to situations involving financial computations. For example, when trying to determine the EMV of profit associated with a defined investment, you need to calculate the expected value of the investment and subtract it from the expected value of revenues. In constructing a benefit-cost ratio, you need to compute the expected value of benefits and divide them by the expected value of costs. The important thing to note is that by adopting an expected value approach, you are able to account for risk (through the use of probabilities) when making financial computations.

When mathematical expectation is taught in the classroom, students duly study the material, carry out homework assignments, and answer questions on exams about it. Then when class is over, they forget everything they learned, because they do not see its connection to the real world. When you understand how mathematical expectation works, you can employ it to help make many day-to-day decisions. The following example illustrates how I used it to decide which route to take on a trip to New York.

My family agreed to have a family reunion at my younger sister's house over Thanksgiving weekend. My sister lives about 90 miles outside New York City, to the northwest of the city. I live in Washington, D.C., about 215 miles south of New York City. While I looked forward to reuniting with my parents and sisters, I dreaded the car trip to New York because the Thanksgiving holiday triggers the heaviest travel of the year. The traffic between Washington and New York is often terrible, so the trip can be enormously stressful.

Virtually all the automobile travel between Washington and New York is by means of Route 95 and the New Jersey Turnpike, so I decided to explore an alternative indirect route that few people use during Thanksgiving. The problem with this route is that it is a few miles longer than the regular route and makes more use of small roads with low speed limits. I used an Internet travel planner to check the amount of time it should take to get to my sister's house using both routes. The estimate I was provided stated that taking the regular route should get me to my sister's house in 4.46 hours, while the alternative route should take 5.07 hours. According to these figures, there is a small advantage to taking the regular route (about a quarter-hour savings of time). A problem with these figures is that they are based on the assumption that travelers are able to reach their destinations going at the posted speed limit. However, the reality over Thanksgiving is that there is so much traffic on the regular route that it is not likely that drivers will be able to maintain the posted speed limits.

Figure 6.3 shows a map that pictures the two routes that I explored. The eastern route is the regular heavily traveled route between Washington and New York. The western one is the out-of-the-way route. At this point, I decided to compute the expected values associated with traveling the different segments of my trip for both the eastern and western routes. Based on my experience in traveling to New York by car, I created five scenarios for each segment:

- Travel the segment in the scheduled time (computed by dividing the distance traveled by the speed limit)
- Travel the segment taking 10 percent longer than planned
- Travel the segment taking 20 percent longer than planned
- Travel the segment taking 30 percent longer than planned
- Travel the segment taking 40 percent longer than planned

Table 6.2 provides the worksheet I used to make my expected value computations. To see how it works, consider the Baltimore–New York City segment portrayed in the spreadsheet. The distance between Baltimore and New York City is 175 miles. The posted speed limit is 70 miles per hour. The estimated travel time based on these data is 2.5 hours (175 miles)/(70 miles per hour). Based on my experience traveling to New

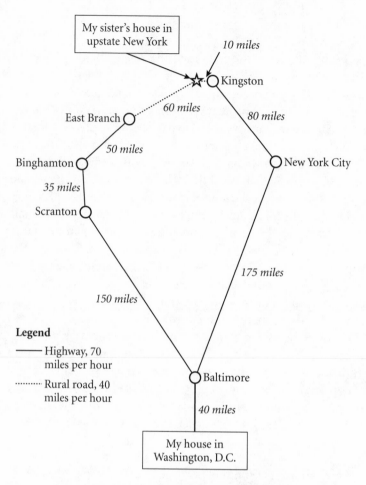

Figure 6.3. Two Routes to My Sister's House.

York during Thanksgiving, the probability of actually traveling this segment in 2.5 hours is zero; there is always traffic that slows the journey. By my reckoning, the probability of carrying out the trip 10 percent longer than scheduled is 0.1; 20 percent longer than scheduled, 0.2; 30 percent longer than scheduled, 0.5; and 40 percent longer than scheduled, 0.2. To compute expected time to travel the Baltimore–New York segment, we need to take each possible duration outcome and multiply it by the probability of its occurrence:

Route	Miles Traveled	Speed Limit (miles per hour)	Scheduled Time (in hours)	Probability Achieving Schedule	Probability 10% Longer Than Schedule	Probability 20% Longer Than Schedule	Probability 30% Longer Than Schedule	Probability 40% Longer Than Schedule	Expected Duration (in hours)
East route segment									
Washington–Baltimore	40	70	0.57	0.7	0.3	0.0	0.0	0.0	0.59
Baltimore–New York City	175	70	2.50	0.0	0.1	0.2	0.5	0.2	3.20
New York City–Kingston	80	70	1.14	0.1	0.2	0.3	0.3	0.1	1.38
Kingston–sister's home	10	40	0.25	0.8	0.2	0.0	0.0	0.0	0.26
Total	305		4.46						5.43
West route segment									
Washington–Baltimore	40	70	0.57	0.7	0.3	0.0	0.0	0.0	0.59
Baltimore–Binghamton	160	70	2.29	0.9	0.1	0.0	0.0	0.0	2.31
Binghamton–East Branch	50	70	0.71	0.9	0.1	0.0	0.0	0.0	0.72
East Branch–sister's home	60	40	1.50	0.8	0.2	0.0	0.0	0.0	1.53
Total	310		5.07						5.15

Table 6.2. Computing the Expected Value of Time Spent Traveling.

Expected duration = $(2.50 \times 0) + (2.75 \times 0.1) + (3 \times 0.2)$
$+ (3.25 \times 0.5) + (3.5 \times 0.2) = 3.20$ hours.

Note that in theory, the segment should take 2.50 hours to travel, assuming we travel the speed limit and encounter no delays. However, after I factor in the probability of delays, the expected duration grows to 3.20 hours. In the worst case, if delays add 40 percent duration to the scheduled 2.50 hour journey, traveling this segment could take 3.50 hours.

After applying this logic to all segments for both the regular and alternate routes, it turns out that the expected value of the eastern route is 5.43 hours (a full hour longer than the 4.45 hours estimated by the Internet travel planner). The expected value for the western route is 5.15 hours (only 8 minutes longer than the 5.07 hours estimated by the Internet travel planner).

Ultimately, I decided to take the western route. During the trip, there were no traffic jams at any point along the journey. In fact, traffic moved faster than the posted speed limit, and the trip to my sister's house took less than 5 hours. Traffic reports indicated that the eastern route was plagued with delays, and by my reckoning, the trip to my sister's house would have actually taken between 5.5 and 6 hours by this route.

BENEFIT-COST RATIO ANALYSES

For many years, economists and financiers have attempted to examine the degree to which management and policy actions generate benefits (or losses) by engaging in benefit-cost ratio analyses. These analyses enable decision makers to explore how benefits vary under different conditions. Benefit-cost ratio analysis is used most heavily for making investment decisions (including project selection decisions), but it can also be employed usefully to support quantitative risk impact analyses.

The conceptual grounding of benefit-cost ratios is simple: by taking some measure of benefit and dividing it by some measure of cost, you create a ratio that assesses the trade-off of one against the other. The most typical measure of benefit is revenue. Let's say that the market research department of a company forecasts that there is a market for a new widget, and once released, the new widget will generate $2 million in revenue. Let's say the operations staff estimate the cost of developing the new widget to be $500,000. Establishing a benefit-cost ratio is easy:

B/C = Benefit/cost = $2,000,000/$500,000 = 4.0.

This ratio provides us a measure of bang for the buck. That is, for each dollar spent, we anticipate generating $4.00 in revenue. When the measure of benefit is revenue, then the values of the benefit-cost ratios take on special meaning. To see this, consider the following three scenarios:

B/C = 1.0 indicates a break-even situation: benefits and costs exactly offset each other. For example, a $20,000 investment yields $20,000 in revenue. You are not making a profit, but neither are you losing money.

B/C > 1.0 indicates that benefits exceed costs. For example, a benefit-cost ratio of 1.32 indicates that for each dollar invested, $1.32 in benefits is generated. That is, benefits exceed costs by 32 percent. You are making a profit.

B/C < 1.0 indicates that costs exceed benefits. For example, a benefit-cost ratio of 0.85 indicates that each dollar invested generates only 85 cents in revenue. You are losing money.

In government projects and corporate infrastructure projects where no revenue is generated, benefits are usually measured as cost savings. For example, consider an information technology department that is trying to decide which customer relationship management (CRM) product to purchase and implement. It must make a choice from among three products: CRM-A, CRM-B, and CRM-C. Data on annual costs and annual benefits are offered in Table 6.3. The benefit-cost ratio analysis shows that only CRM-A has greater annual cost savings than expenses associated with purchasing and running the system. This fact is reflected in its benefit-cost ratio of 1.10. (The benefit-cost ratios for CRM-B and CRM-C are 0.97 and 0.92, respectively, indicating you are spending more money than you are saving.)

Benefit-cost ratios are valuable when they are carried out properly, but there are some obvious pitfalls associated with computing them. Three are examined here: losing sight of the absolute size of benefits and costs, not assessing when payback occurs, and measuring the wrong stuff.

	Product CRM-A	Product CRM-B	Product CRM-C
Costs			
Purchase price (annualized)	$25,000	$20,000	$30,000
Annual system operating costs	120,000	100,000	130,000
Annual system maintenance cost	60,000	30,000	80,000
Total	$205,000	$150,000	$240,000
Benefits			
Annual savings in reduced personnel	$120,000	$85,000	$120,000
Annual savings in reduced material consumption	90,000	50,000	85,000
Annual savings in storage facilities rental	15,000	10,000	15,000
Total	$225,000	$145,000	$220,000
Benefit-cost ratio	1.10	0.97	0.92

Table 6.3. Benefit-Cost Computations for Three Products.

Losing Sight of the Size of Benefits and Costs

As with all other ratios, benefit-cost ratios are size independent. A ratio of 2.70 can be generated in an infinite number of ways: 27/10, 270/100, 2,700/1,000, 27,000/10,000, and so on. When you divide one number by another number, the resulting ratio becomes dimensionless.

This means that when you are provided a benefit-cost ratio for a given investment scenario, you must ask: What are the absolute sizes of the benefits and costs that have gone into this ratio? This is particularly important when comparing ratios among investment alternatives. Investment A may have a ratio of 3.4, while investment B's ratio is 2.7. Investment A appears to be a clear winner until you learn that it reflects a $1,000 investment (with $3,400 in returns), while investment B entails a $1 million investment that generates $2.7 million in returns. We are not comparing apples and oranges here, but rather a grape with a watermelon. Knowing the absolute size of the values going into the computation will likely have an important bearing on how the ratio is interpreted.

This pitfall is not fatal. It is easily resolved if you make it a requirement to have reported benefit-cost ratios always be accompanied by the absolute values of benefits and costs.

Not Assessing When Payback Occurs

When comparing the investments, investment A's benefit-cost ratio of 3.4 appears more attractive than investment B's ratio of 2.7. Further exploration shows that investment A's benefit is an expected $3.4 million and investment B's is an expected $2.7 million, so you are comparing watermelons with watermelons here. A problem arises, however, when you learn that investment A will realize its $3.4 million return in five years, while B will realize its $2.7 million return in two years. Simple logic tells you that you are better recapturing your investment earlier rather than later and that investment B is more attractive than investment A from the perspective of payback.

Once again, you are not facing a fatal deficiency here. To deal with this potential problem, you must make it a habit to ask: "When will payback occur for the investment we are reviewing?"

Measuring the Wrong Stuff

The most serious possible shortcoming of a benefit-cost ratio is measuring the wrong stuff. This phenomenon often arises in the form of something called the *specification problem*. For example, in developing a model of the revenue stream associated with an investment, you may specify that growth will occur in a linear fashion, while in reality it will be nonlinear. Or your assessment of benefits may look at only immediate first-order benefits, while the true benefits may be second-order or third-order effects. Or in computing benefits, you may include only easily measured items, while the greatest benefits may be intangible.

If you measure the wrong stuff, you are dealing with a fatal deficiency. You will be making decisions based on the wrong assumptions and the wrong data and will likely be making the wrong decisions. There is no foolproof method for dealing with poorly specified models. The best you can do is to continuously review your assumptions and data for appropriateness and accuracy. You can also compute benefit-cost ratios for investments using different assumptions to see whether by changing assumptions, you will change your decision. If the different benefit-cost ratios tend to reinforce each other, then you can be reasonably comfortable that you have a sound basis for your decision making.

SUNK COST TECHNIQUE FOR MAKING GO/NO-GO DECISIONS ON INVESTMENTS

I was once teaching a class of project managers at the Defense Logistic Agency's enormous warehouse facility in Columbus, Ohio, when one of my students asked me, "David, can you show us how to kill the project that would not die?"

I asked the student to explain her question.

She responded: "About five years ago, after much deliberation, our senior managers chose to fund an information technology project to upgrade the management information capabilities of one of our business systems. So $500,000 was earmarked to carry out the project, which was supposed to be completed in a year. The next year, the project was still being executed, and $200,000 additional funding was requested and granted. In the following year and for two years after, the project limped along and was funded at $200,000 a year. By now, all the original players had moved on to other jobs, and no one was sure why the project was being carried out. Since so much money had been invested in the project, management was reluctant to kill it, even though they did not know what value it was bringing to our organization. It's coming up for funding again next month, and we on the project team want to know how to kill it."

The experience of this student is a common one. Projects often take on a life of their own, and no one is sure whether to continue them or kill them. On one side you have people saying, "We can't abandon this project. We have too much invested in it." On the other side, you have an equally vociferous group saying, "We can't keep supporting this loser. If we do, we are throwing good money after bad."

The problem with both arguments is that they lack any substance. The first statement is primarily concerned with the politics of budgeting. Its premise is that if our constituents learn that we spent a lot of money on a project and then abandoned it without showing any benefits, they will be angry with us. The second statement is concerned with wasting resources (a good concern), but its argument is articulated with empty words. What is "good money"? What is "bad money"? These are emotional terms and are no substitute for facts and solid financial reasoning.

One way to kill the project that will not die is to apply the sunk cost approach to making go/no-go decisions at the time of a project evaluation effort. The sunk cost approach employs the use of benefit-cost ratio analysis. The best way to explain how it works is by means of a numerical example.

The data for our example are found in Table 6.4. Table 6.4a shows the financials for a project. At the outset, during the project selection stage, it appears that if the project is funded with $100,000, it will yield revenues of $200,000. (To capture the risk inherent in these estimates, they can be generated using expected value logic. See the section on expected value above.) This means that the project has a benefit-cost ratio of 2.0. In the organization being examined, management insists that if a project is to receive financial support, it must have a benefit-cost ratio of 2.0 or greater. In this example, the project meets the minimum requirements and is funded.

Table 6.4b shows the project financials at the end of three months. Because the project has encountered some technical difficulties, it is experiencing financial problems. It has spent $60,000 to date, and the remaining expenditures are estimated to be an additional $80,000, for a total investment of $140,000. (The project budget is $100,000, so this reflects a cost overrun of $40,000.) Meanwhile, the marketing department determines that the anticipated revenues will be lower than originally estimated. They are now projected to stand at $120,000.

	Funds Expended	Future Expenditures	Anticipated Revenue	Benefit-Cost Ratio	Verdict
a. *Scenario A*					
Preproject	0	$100,000	$200,000	2.0[a]	Support
Month 3 of project	$60,000	80,000	120,000	1.5[a]	Kill
b. *Scenario B*					
Preproject	0	100,000	200,000	2.0[a]	Support
Month 3 of project	60,000	60,000	120,000	2.0[a]	Support

Table 6.4. Sunk Cost Approach to Decision Making.
[a]Required rate of return for the project to sustain support: B/C = 2.0.

Clearly, this project is in trouble. The question is: How do you decide whether to continue supporting it or to kill it? The sunk cost approach provides useful guidance. With this approach, you temporarily forget about the money you have spent on the project to date when reviewing a project's financial performance. The expended funds are given the name *sunk cost*. Their significance rests on the fact that those funds are gone and therefore are no longer under your control. What *is* under your control is the decision whether you should spend future monies to continue the venture. To determine the answer to this question, you need to calculate how much return you will gain by completing the project. If the gains are substantial in relation to the additional investment, then move ahead with the project. If the gains are small, then kill it.

In our example, sunk costs at the end of month 3 are $60,000. These monies have been spent and are out of your control. As the table shows, it is estimated that $80,000 is required to continue the project. The question management asks itself at this point is: If we spend $80,000 to finish the project, how much revenue will the $80,000 generate? In this case, the projected answer is $120,000. The benefit-cost ratio associated with the continued investment is 1.5 (120,000/80,000). Recall that this company requires that the benefit-cost ratios associated with an investment be 2.0 or greater. The B/C of 1.5 does not meet this requirement, so a recommendation is made to kill the project on financial grounds. The rationale here is that you should take the requested $80,000 and put it somewhere else where it can generate the level of return required. With a required benefit-cost ratio of 2.0, the $80,000 should be capable of generating at least $160,000.

The financials in Table 6.4b show a similar scenario, with one important exception: the estimated cost to complete the project at month 3 is now $60,000 (as opposed to the $80,000 in Scenario A). If this $60,000 is spent to complete the project, the organization will gain $120,000 in revenue. The benefit-cost ratio is 2.0, which meets the corporate investment requirement. You might as well complete the project, because you will not be better off spending the $60,000 elsewhere.

The sunk cost technique for making go/no-go decisions offers an important contribution to the logic of risk impact analysis: when examining the impacts of different risk scenarios, don't spend too much energy focusing on things you do not control.

CONCLUSION

We are not finished with quantitative assessments of risk impacts. What we have done in this chapter is to examine some commonly employed perspectives and techniques that help risk analysts do their jobs. We talked broadly about the role of quantitative models in assessing risk impacts and saw that models run the gamut from simple spreadsheet budgets to sophisticated simulations. We also examined heavily used techniques, such as expected value analysis, benefit-cost analysis, and the sunk cost approach to making go/no-go decisions.

In Chapter Seven, we will continue the investigation of quantitative impact assessments with a tutorial on probability and statistics that is designed to show their central role in effective risk management.

Assessing the Impacts of Risk Events

The Role of Probability and Statistics

*C*hapter Six offered an overview of quantitative risk impact analysis. It examined perspectives and tools commonly employed across a broad range of risky situations. Chapter Seven sets out a high-level treatment of the principles of probability and statistics; we zero in on the most important quantitative concepts and tools bearing on effective risk management.

In large measure, the core risk that managers face is making decisions in a state of ignorance. Probability and statistics are quantitative perspectives designed to reduce the level of ignorance we encounter when viewing the world around us. Unlike mathematics, they do not deal with *certainties*. Rather, their focus is on *tendencies*. In math, we ask the question: If X occurs, what will be the corresponding value of Y? In the arena of probability and statistics, we ask: If X occurs, what are the *likely* values of Y?

We have already dipped our toes into the waters of probability and statistics in Chapter Six, when we covered the statistical concept of expected value. With expected value, we look at some value that is being measured (for example, revenue generated by a project, the weight of students in a classroom) and multiply it by the probability that it will occur. The resulting number tells us what outcome we can expect to encounter *on the average*. In the treatment of expected value, we used probabilities to carry out expected value computations without explaining what they are. In this chapter, we examine systematically some principles of probability.

A PROBABILITY PRIMER

Having a basic knowledge of the rudiments of probability is important in a wide range of decision-making areas, particularly those where the course of action taken is contingent on certain things happening. Consider how helpful it is to know the probability that it will rain today when you try to decide whether you should lug your umbrella to work. If the probability is near zero, your decision is easy: don't bring the umbrella. If the probability is near 100 percent, again you face an easy decision: certainly, bring the umbrella, unless you don't mind getting drenched. It is in the in-between area where decision-making problems arise.

For most of us, the impact of getting dampened by rain is a matter of little consequence, so whether you know the probability that it will rain is not a momentous issue. But in your business life, knowing the probability that something will happen can make the difference between profit or loss, happy customers or angry ones, on-time deliveries or schedule slippages. For example, if your company has developed a database that tracks the time for installing widgets at customer facilities and if the data suggest that the probability of installing a widget in three days or less is a meager 5 percent, then never promise the customer that you can do the job in three days.

Managing risk is largely about making decisions in a state of ignorance. Knowing the probabilities of events reduces your degree of ignorance. If you have reliable information that the price of the stock of Globus Enterprises will drop 25 percent over the next week, you will certainly want to sell it right now. But you don't know that it will crash. In fact, you may be following the advice of some Wall Street analysts who are pushing Globus as a strong buy. In your ignorant enthusiasm, you decide to buy another five thousand shares of Globus and within a few days find that you have lost a small fortune. If you had reliable information that there was a 92 percent probability that Globus stock would lose a quarter of its value over the next week, you certainly would have made different choices.

The value of knowing statistics and the probabilities of events is often denigrated by well-intentioned math phobics. They brush away the value of statistics by pointing out (correctly) that while the statistics show that a typical household in the community possesses 1.87 automobiles, no one actually *owns* 1.87 automobiles. They downplay the value of determining the probabilities of events by emphasizing (correctly) that if there is a 60 percent probability that the Red Sox will win the pennant this year, there is no guarantee that the Red Sox will win.

What an understanding of statistics and probabilities offers is insight into the tendencies of events. Car ownership data suggest that the average household in a community tends to have multiple cars. The 60 percent probability that the Yankees will win the pennant suggests that there is a better than even chance that they will win the pennant. It's this matter of tendencies that keeps casinos in business. While the house might lose money on individual bets, the overall tendency, rooted in the laws of probability, is for the house to make bundles of money.

BASIC PRINCIPLES OF PROBABILITY

The knowledge base of probability is enormous. In this chapter, we cover only those principles that are reasonably easy to learn and contribute to conducting effective risk analyses. We start with five basic principles here and elaborate on these as the chapter progresses:

Principle 1: The "thing" that we are examining, whose probability we are trying to determine, is called an event. For example, when asking the question, "What is the likelihood of rain today?" *rain* is the event we are examining.

Principle 2: The probability of an event can be visualized as the relative frequency of the occurrence of the event. For example, when we say that the probability of flipping a coin and getting a head is 0.5, this implies that we should encounter approximately 50 heads when actually flipping the coin 100 times.

Principle 3: The probability of an event cannot be greater than 1.0 or less than zero. This point can be explained with a simple example. If you are visiting a Catholic seminary whose students are all male, the probability of selecting a male from a list of seminarians is 1.0. From a relative frequency perspective, if there are thirty seminarians on the list, you will find that thirty out of thirty entries, or 100 percent, are male. You cannot have a portion greater than this. Similarly, you will find that no entries, that is, 0 percent, are female. You cannot have a portion less than zero.

Principle 4: The probabilities of all events in a sample space sum to 1.0. The term *sample space* refers to all the possible outcomes that can be encountered in the situation you are investigating. For example, let's assume we are examining a jar full of 200 marbles colored red, blue, or yellow. Let's say further that 100 marbles are colored red, 60 are colored blue, and 40 are colored yellow. This information describes the sample space we are dealing with. If we are to choose one marble from the jar, where all the marbles are mixed together thoroughly and we are wearing a blindfold while selecting the marble, the probability of choosing a red marble is 0.5, a blue marble is 0.3, and a yellow marble is 0.2. Note that if you add together the probabilities of the three events covered by this sample space, they add up to 1.0.

Principle 5: Probabilities can be determined on an a priori or empirical basis. When we have a logical basis for examining the likelihood of an event, then we can compute an a priori probability. For example, we can logically deduce that in flipping a fair coin, it is just as probable that we get heads as tails. Consequently, we know the probability of obtaining heads when flipping a coin is 0.5. We can also calculate the probability empirically by conducting an experiment where we flip a coin, say, 1,000 times and compute what portion of the flips result in heads. The answer might not be exactly 500 owing to random variability, but it should be pretty close.

Before exploring additional properties of probabilities, let's take stock of what we have covered by means of a simple example.

PRACTICAL EXAMPLE: ATTENDANCE AT PARENT-TEACHER MEETINGS

When we try to calculate the probability of event A, we are attempting to determine the likelihood that event A will occur. If we have pertinent historical records of past occurrences of event A, we may have sufficient data to compute the probability of its occurrence empirically. For example, let's say we want to estimate the probability of encountering fathers attending parent-teacher meetings in our school district. Let's say further that we have perfect data on attendance at these meetings over the past ten years, and the data show that in

30,000 meetings, fathers and mothers attended together on 20,000 occasions; on 8,000 occasions, mothers attended alone; and on 2,000 occasions, fathers attended alone. Figure 7.1 portrays this graphically as a Venn diagram.

The data show that fathers attended parent-teacher meetings on a total of 22,000 occasions. On 20,000 occasions, they accompanied mothers. On 2,000 occasions, they attended the meetings alone. Assuming that the data are representative of the typical behavior of fathers and mothers in respect to attending parent-teacher meetings (and this is a rather heroic assumption), then we can say that the probability of encountering a father attending such meetings is 22,000/30,000, or 0.73. The probability of encountering a father who is attending the meeting alone is 0.07 (2,000/30,000), and with mothers it is 0.67 (20,000/30,000).

At this point, it is useful to introduce some simple symbolic notations that are commonly used in probability analyses. The statement "the probability of encountering a father attending such a meeting is 0.73" can be expressed succinctly as follows:

Pr(Encountering father at meeting) = 0.73

where, in general, Pr(A) reads: "the probability of event A occurring." The statement "the probability of encountering fathers and mothers attending meetings together is 0.67" can be expressed as:

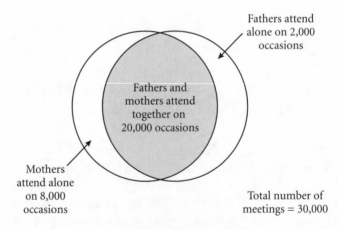

Figure 7.1. Venn Diagram: Attendance at
Parent-Teacher Meetings over Ten Years.

Pr(Fathers attend ∩ mothers attend [together]) = 0.67

where the symbol ∩ reads as "and" and is referred to as the *intersect* of the two events. On the Venn diagram, it is the shaded area where the two circles intersect.

The statement "the probability of encountering a father attending alone or a mother attending alone is 0.33" can be expressed as:

Pr(Father alone ∪ mother alone) = 0.33,

where the symbol ∪ reads as "or" and is referred to as the *union* of the two events. Note that the probability of the union of two or more mutually exclusive events occurring in a sample space is the sum of the probabilities of the individual events. In our example, Pr(Father alone) = 0.067 and Pr(Mother alone) = 0.267 Consequently,

Pr(Father alone ∪ mother alone) = Pr(Father alone) + Pr(Mother alone) = 2,000/30,000 + 8,000/30,000 = 0.067 + 0.267 = 0.334.

Note that this last result is predictable if we already know that the probability of mothers and fathers attending parent-teacher meetings together is 0.67. The rationale for this conclusion is offered in the following equation:

Pr(Father alone ∪ mother alone) = 1.00 − Pr(Fathers attend ∩ Mothers attend [together]).

This is saying that if there is a 0.67 probability of fathers and mothers attending together, then what is left over (1.00 − 0.67 = 0.33) is the probability of their *not* attending together, which is the same thing as their attending alone.

CONDITIONAL PROBABILITIES

The concept of conditional probabilities is an important one for risk analysts because it reflects the type of situation they frequently encounter when engaging in risk assessments. Examples of the logic of conditional probabilities are captured in the following statements:

• What is the probability of our software system's crashing, *given that* it is being forced to respond to 500 queries per minute and is designed to handle 400 queries per minute?

• What is the probability of a consumer's buying Scrub Free detergent, *given that* it is selling for $3.25 a box?

• What is the probability of our company's being profitable this year, *given that* revenue performance at the end of the third quarter is 80 percent of what we planned it to be?

The probabilities are called *conditional* because the information we seek is *conditioned* on information we already possess. The key words are *given that*: given that we know X, what is the probability of Y?

How do we know X? Someone has collected this information. For example, we have historical records that indicate that when our software system receives 500 or more queries per minute, there is a known likelihood that it will crash. Or we have conducted market research studies that describe buyer behavior for different price levels of our leading detergent. (Historical data suggest that given that we increase the price of a widget from $6.00 to $8.00, there is a 70 percent likelihood that the number of units sold will decrease by 5 percent.) Or we have historical records linking year-end financial performance for our company to end-of-third-quarter financial performance. (Historical data suggest that given that end-of-third-quarter financial data indicate that we have achieved only 75 percent of our target sales, then the likelihood of achieving our year-end sales targets is 65 percent.)

To see how conditional probabilities are computed, consider the following simple example: We want to compute the probability that it will rain by noon, given that it is cloudy at 9:00 A.M. The notation used to express this situation is:

Pr(Rain by noon|Cloudy at 9:00 A.M.),

where the vertical line is read as "given that."

To determine the conditional probability, we need to possess the following information:

• Based on historical data, what is the probability of encountering both rain by noon and cloudy conditions at 9:00 A.M.? A look at the records shows that the probability of this event is 20 percent. The notation used to express the event is: Pr(Rain by noon ∩ Cloudy at 9:00 A.M.), where the intersection symbol is read as "and" (that is, rain by noon *and* cloudy at 9:00 A.M.).

- Based on historical data, what is the probability of encountering a day that is cloudy at 9:00 A.M., regardless of whether it rains by noon? A look at the records shows the probability of this event to be 30 percent.

Given this information, the conditional probability can be computed in the following way:

$$\text{Pr(Rain|Cloudy at 9:00 A.M.)} = \frac{\text{Pr(Rain by noon} \cap \text{Cloudy at 9:00 A.M.)}}{\text{Pr(Cloudy at 9:00 A.M.)}}$$

$$= 0.20/0.30$$
$$= 0.67.$$

That is, if you find that it is cloudy at 9:00 A.M., you know that there is a 67 percent chance that it will be raining by noon. You better carry your umbrella!

The general formula for computing a conditional probability is:

$$\text{Pr(A|B)} = \text{Pr(A} \cap \text{B)/Pr(B)}.$$

Note that by rearranging this equation, we have $\text{Pr(A} \cap \text{B)} = \text{Pr(B)} \times \text{Pr(A|B)}$. This is a useful equation. In English, it states, "The probability of having both A and B occur is the probability of encountering A multiplied by the probability of encountering B, given that A has occurred." For example, if we know there is a 30 percent chance that it will be cloudy tomorrow at 9:00 A.M., and if we also know that when it is cloudy at 9:00 A.M., there is a 67 percent chance of rain by noon, we compute the probability of being cloudy at 9:00 A.M. *and* raining at noon as $0.30 \times 0.67 = 0.20$. Using standard probability notation,

$$\text{Pr(Cloudy at 9:00 A.M.} \cap \text{raining at noon)}$$
$$= \text{Pr(Cloudy at 9:00 A.M.)} \times \text{Pr(Raining at noon|cloudy at 9:00 A.M.)}$$
$$= 0.30 \times 0.67 = 0.20.$$

Example of Risk Analysis Using Conditional Probabilities: Events Plus Inc.

In Chapter Two, we briefly looked at the business activity of Events Plus Inc., a company that organizes seminars. In this section, we will discuss Events Plus in greater detail.

Each year, Events Plus holds some 120 seminars dealing with business management and public sector management themes. In order to encourage early enrollments to its seminars, Events Plus offers 20 percent discounts to participants who register for a class up to six weeks in advance of the date of the seminar offering. Because this is an attractive discount, popular classes usually experience heavy levels of sign-ups before the six-week preseminar cutoff point. Less popular courses experience weaker levels of sign-ups.

Table 7.1 shows data collected on 110 seminar offerings that were tracked by Events Plus over the past year and a half. Looking at the data, Events Plus finds that in 22 cases, enrollments were so strong at the six-week marker that they covered all anticipated seminar costs. Typically, these classes resulted in decent profits, although in two cases, the class had to be cancelled owing to instructor illness. In 33 cases, enrollments were reasonably good at the six-week marker and covered 70 to 95 percent of the seminar costs. The seminars tended to break even and usually experienced some profit, although on 10 occasions, classes could not be held owing to insufficient enrollments. In 55 cases, enrollments were weak at the six-week marker, covering less than 70 percent of anticipated seminar costs. Often these classes did not break even and in a number of cases resulted in substantial losses. On 22 instances, they were cancelled.

Events Plus uses the information contained in this table to track enrollment strength course by course. That is, decision makers use these historical data to determine the viability of current seminar offerings. At the six-week precourse marker, managers review enrollments and classify a seminar according one of three categories: break even as of today, almost break even as of today, and not near to breaking even as of today:

Break Even at Six-Week Marker?	Hold Seminar?	Overall Probability[a]
Yes, 22 times (20%)	Yes, 20 times (91%)	0.18
Yes, 22 times (20%)	No, 2 times (9%)	0.02
Almost, 33 times (30%)	Yes, 23 times (70%)	0.21
Almost, 33 times (30%)	No, 10 times (30%)	0.09
No, 55 times (50%)	Yes, 33 times (60%)	0.30
No, 55 times (50%)	No, 22 times (40%)	0.20

Table 7.1. Historical Data on Holding Seminars at Events Plus.
[a]Overall probability is computed by multiplying the probability associated with the event in the first column by the probability associated with the event in the second column.

"Given that" we break even as of today. The seminar is a go, because the probability of enrollments' being sufficiently high at the time of course delivery to warrant proceeding with the seminar is 0.91 (that is, "Given that the breakeven point has been reached by the six-week precourse marker, there is a 91 percent chance that the seminar will be held"). The data show that this eventuality—Events Plus reaches the breakeven point at the six-week marker and ultimately holds the seminar—is 18 percent probable.

"Given that" we almost break even as of today. The seminar is a likely go, because the probability of enrollments' being sufficiently high at the time of course delivery to warrant proceeding with the seminar is 0.70 (that is, "Given that the breakeven point has almost been reached by the six-week precourse marker, there is a 70 percent chance that the seminar will be held"). The data show that this eventuality—Events Plus nearly reaches the breakeven point at the six-week marker and ultimately holds the seminar—is 21 percent probable.

"Given that" we are not near to breaking even as of today. While the outcome of the seminar is doubtful, there is a better than even chance that it will be a go, because the probability of enrollments' being sufficiently high at the time of course delivery to warrant proceeding with the seminar is 0.60 (that is, "Given that the breakeven point is not close to being reached by the six-week precourse marker, there is a 60 percent chance that the seminar will be held"). The data show that this eventuality— Events Plus does not reach the breakeven point at the six-week marker but does ultimately hold the seminar—is 30 percent probable.

Picturing Conditional Probabilities with a Decision Tree

The data in Table 7.1 can be pictured graphically by creating a decision tree. The decision tree associated with Table 7.1 is portrayed in Figure 7.2. Conditional logic is readily apparent on the decision tree when you travel down a branch. For example, the top branch shows that the probability of Events Plus's reaching a breakeven point at the six-week preseminar marker is 0.20. Given this event, there is a 91 percent probability that the seminar will actually be held. The next branch

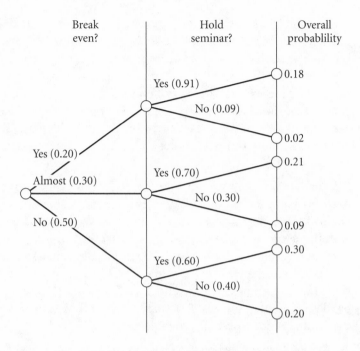

Figure 7.2. Decision Tree on Holding Seminars at Events Plus.

down shows that given that Events Plus reaches a breakeven point at the six-week marker, there is a 9 percent chance that the seminar will not be held (for example, owing to cancellations).

This decision tree enables us to answer a number of interesting questions about Event Plus's history of holding seminars. For example, when we begin the process of preparing to launch a new seminar, we know that the probability that it will actually be held is 0.69 (add together the overall probabilities of those branches that show we have held a seminar: 0.18 + 0.21 + 0.30 = 0.69). By the same token, we know that the probability of the seminar's ultimately being cancelled is 0.31 (1.00 − 0.69).

Guessing Probabilities

If you don't have historical data, you can guess probabilities. There are many ways this can be done, some more credible than others. Formal processes to guess probabilities subjectively often entail having a group of experts work together to see if they can develop a consensus on

Description of Condition	Probability
Nearly certain	0.95
Highly likely	0.85
Likely	0.70
Moderately likely	0.60
Fifty-fifty split	0.50
Moderately unlikely	0.40
Unlikely	0.25
Highly unlikely	0.15
Won't happen	0.5

Table 7.2. Subjective Probabilities.

what the target probabilities are. One of the most respected approaches is to guide experts through a probability-generating session using the analytical hierarchy process. This technique lies outside the realm of this book, but interested readers can learn more about it in Saaty (1999).

The most common approach to guessing probabilities is to have risk analysts look at verbal descriptions of likelihood and choose the one they think is most appropriate. Each item has a probability assigned to it. Table 7.2 provides an example of a matrix that matches verbal descriptions of likelihood with probabilities. For example, if a risk analyst believes that a particular event is "highly likely," the event is assigned a probability of 0.85. If the event is deemed "unlikely," it is assigned a probability of 0.25. There is nothing magic about the probabilities assigned by means of this mechanism. They are based on informed guesses. If risk analysts believe that a "highly likely" event should have a probability of 0.80 based on their experience, then the figure in Table 7.2 should be adjusted accordingly.

Is this a legitimate way to employ probabilities in risk impact analyses? Do the probabilities generated through this process have any value?

These are good questions. Regrettably, they do not have clear-cut answers. Mathematical statisticians might be distressed by the subjectivity of these probability estimates, whereas applied statisticians are less likely to be upset. Although you need to be cautious in using such crude measures, I believe that employing them is better than having people make decisions purely on the basis of unstructured gut feeling, which is the way most business decisions are made. Certainly, these estimates capture probabilities at the order-of-magnitude level. If analysts have reason to believe that an event is sure to happen, the probability of this event's occurring should be high, whether a figure of 1.0, 0.95, or 0.90 is used. If they believe another event is a fifty-fifty proposition, then the probability of the event should be in the middle range, whether the figure is 0.60, 0.50, or 0.40.

One way of dealing with this level of uncertainty in making estimates of probabilities is to conduct a sensitivity analysis, where different possible values of the probabilities are plugged into the risk model. If the same basic conclusions are supported for two or three different estimates of probabilities, then the risk analysts should be reasonably confident that they are on the right track. But if a small change in the probability estimate for an event results in different conclusions, then the risk analyst should be wary using subjective probabilities.

PROBABILITY DISTRIBUTIONS

One of the most useful quantitative tools in the risk analyst's toolbox is the probability distribution. Probability distributions offer the probabilities for all possible outcomes of an event. They are best explained by means of an example.

Jones Furniture Co. is trying to get a handle on how long it takes to paint its standard Kitchen Komfort Chair on the production line. A sample of twelve chairs is identified, and an analyst tracks how long it takes to paint each. The results of this experiment show:

8 minutes painting time	3 chairs
9 minutes painting time	4 chairs
10 minutes painting time	3 chairs
11 minutes painting time	2 chairs

A probability distribution can be easily developed from the data. Three of twelve chairs are painted in 8 minutes, so Pr(Paint chair in 8 minutes) = 0.25. Four of twelve chairs are painted in 9 minutes, so Pr(Paint chair in 9 minutes) = 0.33. Three of twelve chairs are painted in 10 minutes, so Pr(Paint chair in 10 minutes) = 0.25. And two of twelve chairs are painted in 12 minutes, so Pr(Paint chair in 11 minutes) = 0.17.

A probability distribution for the chair painting effort is given in Table 7.3. In addition to providing the probabilities of each possible event, the table offers summary statistics on the distribution's mean, mode, and standard deviation.

Painting Time	Frequency	Probability
8 minutes	3 chairs	0.25
9 minutes	4 chairs	0.33
10 minutes	3 chairs	0.25
11 minutes	2 chairs	0.17
Mean:	9.33	minutes
Mode:	9.00	minutes
Standard deviation:	1.03	minutes

Table 7.3. Tabular Probability Distribution for Chair Painting Times.

The *mean* of a distribution is the average value of all the items in the distribution taken together. In the chair painting example, we see that the mean is 9.33 minutes. That is, on the average, it takes 9.33 minutes to paint a Kitchen Komfort chair.

The *mode* of a distribution is the value that occurs most frequently. In the chair painting example, the mode is 9 minutes. It is possible to have multimodal distributions. A bimodal distribution, for example, looks like two humps on a camel's back.

The *standard deviation* of a distribution measures its spread. When the data points in a distribution cluster closely together, then the standard deviation is small. When they are spread out, it is larger. In the chair painting example, the standard deviation of the distribution is 1.03 minutes. Standard deviation is often referred to by the Greek letter σ (sigma).[1]

Figure 7.3 shows the probability distribution for the chair painting example in graphical format. The graph shows the probabilities for the different chair painting durations. A nice feature of graphical portrayals of probability distributions is that the mode stands out clearly: it is the peak of the distribution (in this case, at 9 minutes).

Probability distributions in either a numerical or graphical format are chock full of information that provides managers with answers to practical questions. Consider the following examples:

- What is the likelihood that it will take longer than 10 minutes to paint a chair?

  Answer: Pr(>10 minutes) = Pr(11 minutes) = 0.17 minutes.

- What is the likelihood that a chair can be painted in 9 or fewer minutes?

  Answer: Pr($\leq$ 9 minutes) = Pr(8 minutes) + Pr(9 minutes) = 0.25 + 0.33 = 0.58.

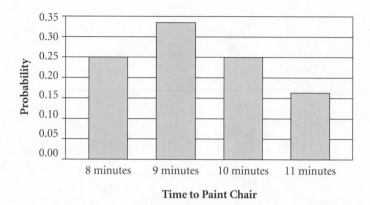

Figure 7.3. Graphical Probability Distribution for Chair Painting Times.

• What is the likelihood that a chair can be painted in less than 11 minutes?

Answer: Pr(< 11 minutes) = Pr(8 minutes) + Pr(9 minutes) + Pr(10 minutes) = 0.25 + 0.33 + 0.25 = 0.83.

Note that we could have approached this differently. We saw above that the probability of a chair's taking 11 minutes to be painted is 0.17. Consequently, the probability that it will *not* be painted in 11 minutes is 1.00 – 0.17 = 0.83.

The important point to remember is that if you can describe a phenomenon with a probability distribution, you can begin making powerful statements about the likelihood that events described by the distribution actually will occur. If you know the probability of an event, you can begin making informed decisions, thereby reducing risk.

COMMONLY ENCOUNTERED DISTRIBUTIONS

It turns out that in nature, business, and social affairs, a number of well-known distributions describe how things play out. We examine only two here: the normal and PERT beta distributions.

Normal Distribution

The normal distribution is also known as the bell curve. It is given that name because it takes on a bell shape when pictured graphically (see

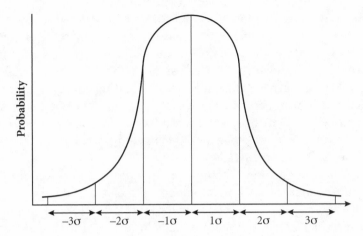

Figure 7.4. The Normal Distribution.

Figure 7.4). The importance of the normal distribution is that it arises over and over again in the physical, biological, and social worlds. Consider the range of phenomena that are accurately described by the normal distribution:

• The weight of eight-year-old Caucasian girls

• IQs

• The quantity of Coca Cola injected into a 12-ounce can

• Defects encountered in a production process

Because the normal distribution is encountered frequently, statisticians have studied it so thoroughly that they know all about its properties. For example, with the normal distribution, the percentage of events falling within ±1σ, ±2σ, and ±3σ are 68.3, 95.5, and 99.7 percent, respectively. Because IQ scores are distributed normally, we know that 68.3 percent of the population has an IQ score of 100 ±1σ. If σ = 17 (a typical value of σ for many IQ tests), this means that 68 percent of the population has an IQ that falls in the range between 83 (100 − 17) and 117 (100 + 17).

We also know that about 95.5 percent of the population has an IQ score of 100 ± 2σ—that is, their IQs fall in a range between 66 (100 − (2 × 17) and 134 (100 + (2 × 17)). Finally, we know that about 99.7

percent of the population has an IQ score of 100 ± 3σ. If we want to focus on only the top end of the scale, this means that only 0.15 percent of the population has an IQ greater than 151 (100 + (3 × 17)).

What holds true for IQ scores also holds for the weight of eight-year-old Caucasian girls, the quantity of Coca Cola injected in a can, and defects encountered in a production process. The point is that if you know that something is described by a normal distribution, you can determine the probability of different events occurring within the sample space you are investigating.

When is the normal distribution encountered in risk management? The answer is: Quite often. To a large extent, it depends on what you are looking at. If you are trying to predict the probability that a transistor will fail, you probably have an abundance of engineering data that show that the normal distribution is at work. In general, the normal distribution tends to kick in when you are dealing with fairly routine processes. For example, quality control charts used in manufacturing—where widgets are routinely being produced, one after another—assume that defects on the assembly line are normally distributed. However, when you are dealing with reasonably unique events, the normal distribution is not likely to be helpful.

PERT Beta Distribution

As we saw in an earlier chapter, in the late 1950s, the U.S. Navy developed a technique to plan complex projects, which they called the Program Evaluation Review Technique (PERT). This technique, which adopted basic flowcharting concepts from systems engineering, became the standard approach to scheduling project activities and is still used. Navy engineers knew how to portray the interrelationships among project tasks using flowcharting techniques, but they were not sure how to compute the duration of these tasks. Ultimately, statisticians provided guidance on estimating task durations. They employed an approach that today is called the PERT beta technique, based on a modified version of the beta probability distribution. To calculate expected task duration, you need to identify three parameters: the fastest time a task can be accomplished, the slowest time it can be accomplished, and the time most typically encountered. These values are then put into the following equation:

$$\text{Expected duration} = \frac{\text{Fastest time} + 4 \times \text{most typical time} + \text{slowest time}}{6}$$

For example, consider a project to install a piece of equipment in a factory. Let's say we have reason to believe that the fastest time the equipment can be installed is 3 hours. This duration can be achieved if the installation team is highly competent and everything goes perfectly. The slowest time to install the equipment is 7 hours. This is the duration that will be realized if the team is inexperienced and nothing works as planned. The most likely duration is 4 hours. This is how long it will take to install the equipment if everything goes fairly smoothly, with some small glitches developing here and there. Incorporating these numbers in the PERT beta formula, we have:

$$\text{Expected duration} = \frac{3 \text{ hours} + 4 \times 4 \text{ hours} + 7 \text{ hours}}{6}$$

$$= \frac{26}{6} \text{ hours} = 4.33 \text{ hours}$$

The expected duration we have calculated is an approximate value of the mean of the PERT beta distribution. The distribution itself is pictured in Figure 7.5. (Strictly speaking, this is not the standard beta distribution treated in statistics textbooks. It was called beta because its physical shape is similar to that of the classic beta distribution.) The general formula for approximations of its mean and standard deviation (σ) are:

$$\text{PERT beta mean} = \frac{a + 4 \times b + c}{6}$$

$$\text{PERT beta } \sigma = \frac{c - a}{6}$$

where a is the best case, b is the most typical case, and c is the worst case.

PERT beta is primarily employed as an estimation tool. As mentioned earlier, it arose initially to help project managers estimate the durations of tasks. However, because it is a general distribution, it can be employed to deal with other things as well. For example, it can be used to estimate costs and the number of workers needed to do a job:

$$\text{Expected costs} = \frac{\$3,000 + 4 \times \$4,000 + \$7,000}{6} = \$4,333$$

$$\text{Average masons} = \frac{3 \text{ masons} + 4 \times 4 \text{ masons} + 7 \text{ masons}}{6} = 4.33 \text{ masons}$$

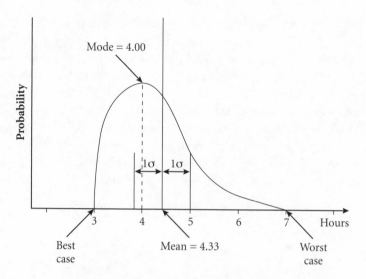

Figure 7.5. PERT Beta Distribution.

By employing the standard deviation figure we have computed for the PERT beta distribution, we are able to make rough probabilistic statements about the item under review. For example, it turns out that for the scenario we are examining, as pictured in Figure 7.5, about 20 percent of the values of the distribution lie beyond the 1σ point of 5 hours, and 20 percent lie before the −1σ point of 3.67 hours. Thus, if your manager asks you, "Can you install the equipment in three and a half hours or so?" you can respond, "Certainly, but with a probability of less than 20 percent."

Careful consideration of the PERT beta distribution suggests that it is a Murphy's Law distribution. Murphy's Law states, "If something can go wrong, it will." The PERT beta distribution states, "When doing a job competently, the most typical outcome is pretty close to the best-case scenario. But when things go bad, they can go terribly bad." In the equipment installation example, we find that usually it takes us about 4 hours to install equipment, which is just a little worse than the 3-hour best-case situation. However, if things don't go quite right (perhaps the site where the equipment will be installed has not been prepared properly), it can take up to 7 hours to complete the job.

We saw earlier that it is often appropriate to employ a normal distribution when dealing with routine phenomena and processes. The PERT beta distribution is often appropriate when dealing with non-routine processes, as when you are dealing with fairly unique phenomena or are inexperienced in doing a job. A nice feature of PERT beta and one reason that it is so popular is that all it requires is that you have a good sense of best-case, most typical, and worst-case scenarios. If you have an abundance of historical data to back up these figures, great. But even if you do not, you can still make reasonable estimates of task duration, or production costs, or resources required based on your informed guesses.

A Practical Note on Using Probability Distributions in Risk Analysis

Most people who operate at the periphery of risk analysis and are just beginning to study it don't know what to make of probability distributions. Even if they have a glimmer of understanding about their possible value, they dismiss their use for a number of "practical" reasons. Some say: "Frankly, I don't know if I am dealing with a normal distribution here, or a beta distribution, or something else. This is over my head, so I won't use it." Others say: "In our organization, we do not have historical data, so I haven't a clue about the probability of things happening around here." Along a related line, still others say: "Sure, I can see the value of using the PERT beta distribution to estimate task durations, budgets, and resource allocations. However, I don't think the data I am working with are accurate enough to justify employing it." Or finally: "It seems to me that using probability distributions is like trying to shoot mosquitoes with a twelve-gauge shotgun—a bit of overkill."

The concerns articulated here, as well as plenty of others not addressed, are legitimate. Our knowledge of the statistical distributions of events in the business arena is usually crude or nonexistent. In most organizations, we have not even tried to collect the measures that would enable us to establish the foundations of statistical distributions. When we do make an attempt to gather data, we find that the events we are looking at are largely unique, making it difficult to establish general distributions.

Even without access to good metrics, it is possible to make effective use of statistical distributions if you adhere to some basic guidelines— for example:

• *Are you examining a standard, repeatable process that is under control?* This is characteristic of manufacturing processes, where goods are routinely produced on an assembly line. It also characterizes the routine installation of equipment, the operations of a telephone call center, and the performance of students on a nationwide standardized test. If you are working with a repeatable process, chances are that the normal distribution is appropriate, since with controlled, routine processes, variations in performance tend to be characterized by the bell curve.

• *Are you inexperienced in doing something?* The PERT beta distribution is appropriate for new undertakings, such as the launch of a new product, estimating budgets for a first-of-a-kind project, and predicting the performance of inexperienced workers. With PERT beta, your best-case performance is usually only a little better than your typical performance. However, when things go badly (your worst-case situation), they go very badly indeed, leading to a distribution with an obvious tail. PERT beta is appropriate for new undertakings with which you are unfamiliar.

• *Are you dealing with events that occur with low levels of frequency?* Then you should investigate the employment of a Poisson distribution, which has been found useful in dealing with events that have a low probability of occurrence and is described in statistics textbooks.

• *Do you have reason to believe that the distribution you are examining has special traits that are not picked up by the normal or PERT beta distributions?* Could it be bimodal (that is, it has two peaks)? For example, studies of suicide suggest that suicide rates are highest for the young (teenagers) and the old. Studies of problems in managing project requirements show that they arise most heavily at the beginning of projects (Did we get customers' needs and requirements right?) and at the end (Does the customer believe we have delivered something that meets her needs?). Clearly, the normal PERT beta and most other distributions are unimodal and totally inappropriate for bimodal situations.

It is not just a matter of finding the right prepackaged distribution. The best statistical distributions are those that are based on data collected from real experience. Consider the Jones Furniture Co. example provided earlier in this chapter. In that example, we collected data on how long it takes to paint a chair. That required us to track the amount of time it takes to paint real chairs. Somebody had to look at the drying time history of a dozen chairs.

MONTE CARLO SIMULATION

Monte Carlo simulation is one of the most valuable tools in the risk manager's toolbox. The Monte Carlo simulation technique allows you to take a basic budget, or schedule, or inventory model—anything at all that can be represented in an electronic spreadsheet—and run it through a thousand iterations as if it were occurring a thousand times.

Back in the days when Monte Carlo simulations ran only on mainframe computers, learning the technique could be a formidable experience. In the late 1980s, however, a number of PC-based simulators that made it easy to carry out Monte Carlo simulations were introduced into the market. Most of these software packages were so friendly that a student could begin running reasonably sophisticated simulations after one or two hours of instruction. The best-known software package is @Risk.

The Basics

Table 7.4 shows the probability distribution for the cost of carrying out a design effort on a software development project. Three cost scenarios are pictured: a 20 percent probability that design cost will be $100,000, a 50 percent probability that it will be $110,000, and a 30 percent probability that it will be $120,000. In Chapter Six, we learned that we can calculate the expected value of design cost by multiplying each cost outcome by its probability and then summing the products of these computations:

Expected design cost = $100,000 × 0.2 + $110,000 × 0.5
+ $120,000 × 0.3 = $111,000.

The probability distribution in Table 7.4 enables you to compute the expected cost of design work on a software development project. What if you also have information on the probability distributions for software coding work and for testing efforts as well? How can you combine these individual distributions to come up with a probability distribution for total project costs? One answer is to solve the problem mathematically. However, that would require a knowledge of advanced statistics that even few experts have. Many of the problems you would want to examine are so intractable that expert mathematicians could not handle them. Another answer is to reveal the probability distribution "experimentally" by conducting a Monte Carlo simulation.

Cost	$100,000	$110,000	$120,000
Probability	0.2	0.5	0.3

Table 7.4. Probability Distribution and Cost Outcomes for a Design Project.

With Monte Carlo simulation, you "pretend" to compute a budget (or a task's duration, or the number of resources you want to use on a project) many times to see what happens. Each iteration gives different results because the numbers being computed are allowed to vary randomly. Then you review the results to see what the average, worst-case, best-case, and typical values are. You do all this by specifying a model for the phenomenon you wish to explore, describing the probability distribution of the data fed into the model and then letting a computerized simulator run through the model for, say, a thousand times.

The underlying methodology can be described easily with a numerical example. The example we use is the same one as captured in Table 7.4. We will use this probability distribution in tandem with a random number table to "pretend" to carry out the software design chore ten times and to calculate what expected design costs are.

Table 7.5 shows a random number table that contains seventy-five two-digit numbers that were randomly selected. This means that there is an equal probability of placing a finger on the table while blindfolded and hitting a 78, 00, 41, 12, or any other two-digit number. Note that if we put a blue marble in a jar any time a value ranging from 00 to 19 is encountered in the random number table, and a red marble in the jar when a value ranging from 20 to 69 is encountered, and a yellow marble in the jar when a value ranging from 70 to 99 is encountered, there is a 20 percent probability of selecting a blue marble from the jar randomly, a 50 percent probability of randomly selecting a red marble, and a 30 percent probability of randomly selecting a yellow model.

The same principle can be extended to estimating design costs in our example. Table 7.6 is a conversion table showing two-digit random numbers and the corresponding value of design cost. Thus, if you randomly "hit" 55, the table tells us this is the same thing as incurring a $110,000 charge to carry out a design effort. If you randomly "hit" 13, this is the same thing as incurring a $100,000 charge. And so on.

---

54 55 13 20 70 33 82 28 24 66 04 22 99 66 64
57 68 61 37 30 94 81 21 84 81 48 64 45 69 32
00 16 45 84 18 33 38 37 39 97 98 76 78 63 98
83 28 82 36 91 09 81 24 55 21 57 22 92 50 49
95 14 80 68 34 53 79 75 32 54 70 68 46 93 45

Table 7.5. A Random Number Table.

	Option A	Option B	Option C
If the random number is:	00–19	20–69	70–99
Then design cost is:	$100,000	$110,000	$120,000

Table 7.6. Linking Random Numbers to Cost Figures.

What we will do is to simulate the costs of doing design work ten times. We will start with the top left-hand corner of the random number table and work our way right until we have selected ten digits, which are: 54, 55, 13, 20, 70, 33, 82, 28, 24, and 66. (Note: Because this is a random number table, you can start at any point in the table.) These ten digits correspond to costs of: $110,000, $110,000, $100,000, $110,000, $120,000, $110,000, $120,000, $110,000, $110,000, and $110,000. The sum of these numbers is $1,110,000. Because there are ten numbers, the average value is $111,000, which tells you how much you would expect the design effort to cost. Note that in this specific case, the Monte Carlo simulation offers the same result as the expected value computation provided earlier. If you take the random numbers from a different row, you may get slightly different results. However, your answers will usually be very close to the $111,000 figure.

Let's use the principles described here to conduct a Monte Carlo simulation that is a little more complex.

In this example, we will estimate the total cost of a software programming effort when we know the probability distributions associated with design software, build software, and test software. These probability distributions are offered in Table 7.7. We will use random numbers from the random number table and compute total costs six times.

Table 7.8 converts random numbers for design, build, and test to the corresponding costs for doing the job. Table 7.9 presents the results of six rounds of the simulation, using random numbers from the

Design			
Cost	$100	$110	$120
Probability	0.2	0.5	0.3
Build			
Cost	$1,000	$1,200	$1,400
Probability	0.2	0.6	0.2
Test			
Cost	$50	$70	$90
Probability	0.1	0.5	0.4

Table 7.7. Probability Distributions and Costs for Design, Build, and Test of a Software System (000).

Design			
Cost	$100	$110	$120
Random numbers	00–19	20–69	70–99
Build			
Cost	$1,000	$1,200	$1,400
Random numbers	00–19	20–79	80–99
Test			
Cost	$50	$70	$90
Random numbers	00–09	10–59	60–99

Table 7.8. Linking Random Numbers to Cost Figures (in thousands of dollars).

	Round 1	Round 2	Round 3	Round 4	Round 5	Round 6
Design						
Random number	54	55	13	20	70	33
Cost	$110	$110	$100	$110	$120	$110
Build						
Random number	57	68	61	37	30	94
Cost	$1,200	$1,200	$1,200	$1,200	$1,200	$1,400
Test						
Random number	00	16	45	84	18	33
Cost	$50	$70	$70	$90	$70	$70
Total	$1,360	$1,380	$1,370	$1,400	$1,390	$1,580

Average cost: $1,413 (using total costs for the six rounds)

Table 7.9. Results of Six Rounds of Random Sampling (in thousands of dollars).

random number table. It shows that the average cost of developing software is $1,413,000. The best case is $1,360,000 and the worst case is $1,580,000. Note that with Monte Carlo simulation, we are able to create a "super" distribution that combines the results of individual distributions without resorting to a complex mathematical proof.

Case Example: Zelig Software Co.

The Zelig Software Co. example demonstrates the application of the Monte Carlo approach to a real-world business case. The Zelig simulation is simple. Monte Carlo simulations can become very sophisticated when applied to complex situations. Probably the most sophisticated employment of Monte Carlo simulations occurs in the defense community, where the technique is heavily used in simulating nuclear reactions. In this instance, the simulation must accommodate random perturbations of thousands of variables.

Usually Monte Carlo simulations of business scenarios are quite primitive. A significant constraint the analyst faces is that the low quality of the business data employed in most simulations does not warrant supersophisticated modeling. Another is that there is substantial uncertainty as to what variables should be included in the model and the interrelationship of these variables to each other.

How sophisticated should you be in developing Monte Carlo simulations? Clearly, the answer is tied to how much good data you have and how experienced you are in dealing with the process being modeled. Financial analysts who have developed sophisticated econometric investment models and have substantial reliable data on trades of securities can develop Monte Carlo simulations that parallel the simulations carried out in the hard sciences. A business analyst who is trying to determine whether to launch a brand-new product into a new market will use Monte Carlo simulations that are on par with the Zelig example provided here.

Zelig Software Co. produces and distributes accounting software that runs on desktop personal computers. The new product development group has just completed a study that examined how an existing product that Zelig produces can, with relatively modest adjustments, be converted into a new product with the code name Blitz. Market research shows that the introduction of this product is a bit risky, because similar products already are being sold by competitors. Blitz's chief advantage is that it employs the latest technology that makes the product easy to learn and use and is therefore vastly superior in this respect to any other product on the market. The big question is whether the public is willing to give up their existing software to acquire a fun and friendly software application.

Market research suggests that if Blitz takes off, it can sell more than 8,000 units in its first year. If it fizzles, it would be lucky to sell 1,000 units. The market research department decides to conduct a risk assessment examining the financial implications of producing and distributing Blitz given that it is not a guaranteed winner. The risk assessment is based on a Monte Carlo simulation of anticipated cost and sales data. These data are presented in Table 7.10.

130 MANAGING RISK IN ORGANIZATIONS

Item	Cost	Statistical Assumptions for Monte Carlo Simulation
Production costs		
Development costs	$270,833	Beta distribution, best case = $225,000, most likely = $250,000, worst case = $400,000
Promotion costs	$125,000	Normal distribution with mean = $125,000, σ = $12,500
Number of units produced	10,000	Fixed number of units produced under contract
Cost per unit	$12	Negotiated price determined under contract
Total	$515,833	
Sales		
Number of units sold	3,167	Beta distribution, least number = 1,000, most likely = 2,000, largest number = 10,000
Price per unit	$175	Price determined through market research study
Total	$554,167	
Profit	$38,333	

Table 7.10. Anticipated Cost and Sales Projections Developed for a Monte Carlo Simulation.

Monte Carlo simulations require the specification of statistical distributions in order to generate simulated data. Most Monte Carlo simulation software packages supply a number of standard distributions for this purpose, including the normal, log normal, beta, PERT beta, Poisson, uniform, and gamma distributions. The list of available distributions can be intimidating to nonstatisticians, but in practice, most simulations used in risk analysis can be carried out using either the normal distribution (for well-defined events whose outcomes are symmetric) or the PERT beta distribution (when all you really have a sense of is best-case, most typical, and worst-case outcomes).

Table 7.10 provides information on the statistical assumptions that were fed into the Monte Carlo simulator. For example, we assumed that development costs could be described by a PERT beta distribution, where the lowest cost is $225,000, the most likely is $250,000, and the greatest is $400,000. These figures were developed based on some careful budget analyses, which projected costs to be $250,000, accompanied by informed judgments on how good things can be ($225,000) and how bad ($400,000). The PERT beta formula reveals that given these parameters, expected development cost is $270,833.

We assumed that promotion costs can be described by a normal distribution, because Zelig has substantial control over what these costs should be. It has targeted $125,000 for promotion. The actual figure may be somewhat lower or somewhat higher. To capture the variability of the estimate, we employed a small standard deviation value of 10 percent ($12,500) of the expected value. This value was determined on the basis of experience.

Note that in our model, the number of units produced and per unit cost do not vary statistically because Zelig is contracting this effort out to a production company. The fixed-price contract specifies that 10,000 units of software will be produced at a cost of $12 per unit. The contractor is obligated to meet these conditions, so these values are set.

The cost and sales figures contained in Table 7.10 reflect what we expect to transpire. Currently, we believe that Blitz can generate a profit of $38,333 in its first year. However, if sales are lower than anticipated, Zelig can incur a substantial loss on this project. If Blitz is a success, profits can be very high. By taking the data in Table 7.10 and subjecting them to a Monte Carlo simulation, we can develop a reasonable idea of how good and bad things can get.

A Monte Carlo simulation of 1,000 iterations has been run on the data, and the results are offered in Figure 7.6, which pictures the distribution of profit resulting from the run. Note that the distribution has assumed the shape of a PERT beta distribution. Data accompanying the table tell us that out of 1,000 computations of profit generated by the simulation, the worst case is -$387,158. That represents a major loss to Zelig if it actually transpires. The best case emerging from the simulation is an impressive profit of $1,013,216. The average profit emerging from the 1,000 computations is $38,338. Of particular interest from a risk impact perspective are the data on how good and bad things can be. The good news is that the simulation suggests a 25 percent probability that Zelig can earn a profit of $201,701 or more on the venture. The bad news is that there is a 25 percent probability that it can lose $165,367 or more.

Given the information resulting from this Monte Carlo–driven risk analysis, what should Zelig do? The answer depends on the propensity for risk characterized by Zelig's senior management. If they are risk averse, the size of potential losses is substantial and may lead them

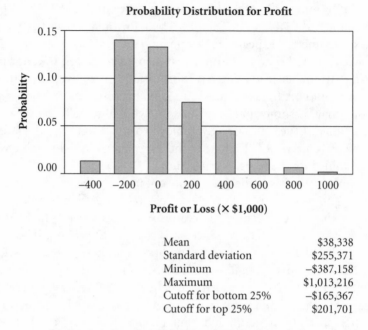

Figure 7.6. Results of the Monte Carlo Stimulation.

to abandon the project. If they are risk takers, the possibility of major gains may push them to proceed with the venture. Monte Carlo simulations do not tell managers what to do. Rather, they provide the information they need to make informed judgments.

CONCLUSION

Chapters Six and Seven provide the foundations for quantitative risk impact analysis. They cover core tools and principles that competent risk analysts should master:

- Model building
- Expected value analysis
- Benefit-cost ratio analysis
- Sensitivity analysis
- The sunk cost concept
- Probability operations

- Conditional probabilities
- Estimating probabilities
- Decision trees
- Principles of probability distributions
- The normal and PERT beta distributions
- Monte Carlo simulation

The ability to employ these tools and concepts requires serious study on the part of aspiring risk analysts. Beyond this it requires practice, practice, practice. Only by actually applying these tools and concepts, and thereby removing them from the realm of the theoretical, can their value be discerned.

Employment of quantitative techniques will not likely enable you to predict what in risk management we call the unk-unks (the unknown-unknowns, or total surprises). No quantitative model could have predicted the November 2002 outbreak of the SARS virus. However, models can predict the occurrence of known-unknowns (such as the likelihood of rain in April), and they certainly can assess the financial, social, and loss-of-life consequences of a generic catastrophic event occurring at the World Trade Center. Other things being equal, risk analysts who are able to employ quantitative tools can pursue far more options in conducting their risk assessments than those who cannot. Consequently, it is worth the effort to develop basic and relevant quantitative skills.

Note

1. Standard deviation is computed according to the following equation: $\sigma = \sqrt{\Sigma(X_i - \mu)^2/N}$, where Σ is mathematical notation indicating that you are summing values together, X_i is the ith data point, μ is the mean of all data points being examined, and N is the number of data points being examined. Consider the following numbers: 3, 4, 4, 6. In this case, $\mu = 4.25$, $(3 - \mu) = -1.25$, $(4 - \mu) = -0.25$, $(4 - \mu) = -0.25$, and $(6 - \mu) = 1.75$. The squares of these values are 1.56, 0.06, 0.06, and 3.06. The sum of these squares is 4.75. Standard deviation is the square root of this value, divided by 4, which is 1.09. Today, hardly anyone computes standard deviation manually because it can be computed easily on spreadsheets.

CHAPTER EIGHT

Planning to Handle Risk

Risk identification enables you to determine what good and bad things you might encounter when undertaking an effort to do something. Risk impact analysis, both qualitative and quantitative, provides insights into the consequences of the occurrence of the identified good and bad things. Now it is appropriate to ask: What can be done to deal with the identified risk events? The process of addressing this question is called *risk response planning*.

Risk response planning is concerned with how best to handle risk events that can arise. Its goal is to go beyond abstract analysis and to prepare people for action. If an untoward event arises and a plan has been developed to deal with it, handling it becomes a matter of implementing the plan. Having plans in place has advantages. First, it enables the people affected by a risk event to respond to it quickly, thereby minimizing damage that the risk event can cause. If you are prepared to put out a fire on your stovetop, you can arrest it before it grows into a conflagration. You can deal with it immediately.

Second, having plans in place to handle risk events enables people to deal with them intelligently. If a risk event arises that catches people by surprise, they are not sure what to do. They feel tremendous pressure to respond to it quickly but do not have enough information or time to reflect on the merits and demerits of alternative solutions. In this case, they may plunge into a situation that they are not equipped to handle, making poor decisions. Or this obvious lack of information needed for good decision making may cause them to hold off taking action. In this event, they may wait too long to handle the risk event, with disastrous consequences. In neither case are they prepared to make good decisions.

This chapter examines a risk response planning framework offered by the Project Management Institute in its *A Guide to the Project Management Body of Knowledge* (2000). This framework focuses on four broad categories of treatment: risk avoidance, risk mitigation, risk transfer, and risk acceptance. Other frameworks exist as well, although they largely replicate the PMI approach. For example, the British Prince2 project management methodology, which is heavily employed in Europe, breaks down risk treatment into the following categories (*Managing Successful Projects with Prince2*, 2002):

- Prevention, where countermeasures are put into place to stop the threat or problem from arising, or to prevent it from having any impact on the project or business. (This is the same as PMI's risk avoidance concept.)

- Reduction, where actions either reduce the likelihood that risk will develop or limit the impact to acceptable levels. (This is the same as PMI's risk mitigation concept.)

- Transfer the risk to a third party, for example, through insurance or penalty clauses in contracts. (This is the same as PMI's risk transfer concept.)

- Contingency, where actions are planned and organized to come into force as and when the risk occurs. (This is the same as PMI's risk acceptance concept.)

Standards Australia's *Risk Management: AS/NZS 4360:1999*, the national risk management standards adopted by Australia and New Zealand, divides risk treatment strategies into two categories: "actions to reduce or control likelihood" and "procedures to reduce or control consequences" (AS/NZS 4360:1999, 1999). Included in the first category are such actions as conducting audits; structuring contracts effectively; undertaking formal reviews of requirements, specifications, designs, engineering, and operations; preventive maintenance; implementing effective project management; implementing solid quality assurance efforts; training personnel; designing organizations to operate effectively; and implementing effective supervision.

Included in the second category are such procedures as implementing contingency plans, establishing clear contracts, implementing disaster recovery plans, planning to handle fraud, and establishing public relations strategies.

The details of the risk treatment framework are not particularly important. Most of the established frameworks address the same points. What is important is to possess a systematic perspective to handling risk events.

RISK TREATMENT METHODOLOGY

As Chapter Five demonstrated, risk has two components: likelihood and impact. When examining a risk event, one concern you should have is how likely it is to occur. For example, statistics suggest that the chance of an American's being murdered in a given year is 1 in 11,000. This figure indicates that despite the scare stories about violent crime in the United States that routinely appear in the news, the average American should not spend enormous amounts of energy planning to avoid death by murder. There are exceptions, of course. Murder rates of young men in the inner city are frighteningly high, and young men living or working in these areas should take precautions so that they do not wind up being homicide victims.

A second concern to address when examining a risk event is the level of its impact if it occurs. Will it be impact free? Will it lead to serious loss? When I lived in Montgomery County, Maryland, we regularly experienced power outages during summer thunderstorms. For me, the impact was low—just an inconvenience. If the power outage occurred at night before bedtime, I would light up several candles so that I could move around my house. Usually, power would be restored within one hour. But power outages could lead to serious consequences at the local hospital. That's why it is important for hospitals to have frequently tested backup generators.

In any planning to treat risks, attention should focus on these two dimensions. First, risk response plans should be developed to lessen or eliminate the likelihood of untoward events arising. For example, if you want to reduce the risk of being murdered, don't travel in high-crime areas. Second, risk response plans should be developed to lessen the impact of risk events. For example, if you don't want to miss your favorite TV shows during a power blackout, you can purchase a battery-operated tabletop television.

This chapter reviews four standard approaches to treating risk: risk avoidance, risk mitigation, risk transfer, and risk acceptance. When planning to respond to risk events, risk treatment strategies should be created that build on one or a combination of these approaches.

Risk Avoidance

Risk avoidance is concerned with lessening the likelihood that individuals and groups will encounter damaging risk events. Its underlying premise is not to do things that will get you in trouble. For example, if a risk impact analysis suggests that by adding a new module to a software routine you will increase the likelihood that the system will crash by 500 percent, don't add the new module.

If carried too far, risk avoidance has a negative side to it. It can lead to situations where individuals and organizations grow so risk averse that they won't make any decisions that can result in negative consequences. The problem with this approach is that for individuals and organizations to do well, they need to take occasional risks. Indeed, in today's fast-changing world, individuals and organizations that stick to the tried-and-true path soon find that they have grown obsolete. Their extreme caution may ultimately cause their demise, leading to the paradoxical conclusion that aggressive risk avoidance can be a risky path to follow.

Risk avoidance does not necessarily lead to inaction. If a review of a plan of action suggests that an organization is steering an unproductive course, a policy of risk avoidance does not mandate that the action be cancelled. Rather, it may suggest that the plan should be adjusted to eliminate the sources of problems. For example, a retail store may inadvertently schedule its grand opening at the same time that the World Cup soccer championship match is being held. If it goes ahead with its grand opening, it may find that customer traffic will be low, since many customers will be at home watching the World Cup finals on television. To deal with this problem, the retailer should reschedule the grand opening to a time when it does not conflict with a major event. Thus, risk avoidance is being practiced: don't do things that will get you in trouble. Specifically, don't hold a grand opening on a day when few customers will show up. Reschedule it for a more propitious moment.

Risk Mitigation

The word *mitigate* means to lessen. With risk mitigation, you try to lessen risks in two senses. First, you take steps to lessen the likelihood that a risk event will arise. Second, you take steps to lessen the negative impacts resulting from untoward risk events.

The following example illustrates both these approaches to mitigating risk.

> Robertson Eckhert, chief information officer at Paragon Medical Services, had a good relationship for years with Paragon's chief financial officer (CFO), Sherry Higgins. This good relationship enabled Paragon to revamp its financial systems smoothly, bypassing many of the frictions that often arise between information technology staff and their finance counterparts.
>
> Robertson was discouraged to find that Sherry's replacement as CFO, Mona Finkel, was cool and distant in dealing with him. At executive committee meetings, her disdain for the "patronizing ways of computer geeks" was evident. The cooperative environment existing between information technology and finance staff disappeared. At executive committee meetings, Mona argued that the information needs of the finance department could often be served better by using outside contractors rather than Paragon's information technology department.
>
> The sour relations between the IT and finance departments resulted in negative consequences for projects carried out jointly by the two groups. Schedules began slipping, cost overruns were common, and increasingly, the deliverables developed by the IT department were rejected by the finance department.
>
> At first, Robertson observed these developments with detached amusement. But when the executive committee launched Paragon's largest project ever, an enterprise resource planning (ERP) initiative to link Paragon's financial, sales, and production efforts, he grew concerned that the project would fail dismally in the current hostile environment. Robertson decided to initiate two steps to mitigate the risk of failure rooted in IT-finance hostilities. First, he would make an effort to meet regularly with Mona to strengthen communications channels with her. At these meetings, he would be friendly, even when Mona behaved in a hostile manner. In fact, he would take her to dinner and see if, in an informal environment, they could resolve any disputes that they had. By taking this step, he hoped to lessen the chance that conflict between his department and hers would create project prob-

lems. (Here we have risk mitigation where the likelihood of the surfacing of risk events is reduced.)

Second, he would see if Mona would agree to abide by a process where serious disputes that arose between his people and hers during the course of the ERP project would be mediated by a third party, Sally Kadith, Paragon's executive vice president, who was well liked by both Robertson and Mona and who also happened to be the sponsor of the ERP project. With such a mediation process in place, disputes could be resolved quickly and amicably and the project, he hoped, could meet its goals. (Here we have risk mitigation where the impacts of untoward events are reduced.)

Risk mitigation is commonly employed in quality management. Quality control processes surface quality problems that arise. Note that quality control techniques, such as control charts, serve a risk identification function. For example, quality control chart patterns might suggest a problem with a grinding machine. An inspection of the machine leads technicians to conclude that a loose drive belt is causing nonconformance of the product to specifications. Worse yet, the loose belt might ultimately tear and cause substantial disruptions to the production effort. To mitigate the likelihood of drive belt–based problems, the technicians tighten the belt and implement a policy of routinely tightening it once a month.

Risk mitigation is also the underlying premise of preventive maintenance. By taking routine steps to keep a piece of equipment in good working order—for example, by changing the oil in your automobile's engine every three thousand miles—the likelihood that it will break down diminishes dramatically. Consequently, preventive maintenance leads to the mitigation of equipment failure.

If you were to articulate a general rule of how risk mitigation works, it would be: once you have identified a source of risk, fix the problem. Thus, if a drive belt is loose, tighten it. If poorly maintained equipment breaks down, implement regular preventive maintenance procedures. If conflict with a colleague is making it impossible to work effectively, take steps to resolve the conflict.

When risk mitigation steps are taken to lessen the likelihood of untoward events arising, this assumes some of the characteristics of risk avoidance. The difference is this: with risk avoidance, you eliminate the source of the problem entirely. This may be done by refusing to carry out work that is risky, or it may entail replanning a work effort to eliminate risk sources. With risk mitigation, you temper it. Rather than bypass potential risk events entirely, you take steps to temper them with a view of reducing the probability of their occurrence or reducing their impact.

Risk Transfer

With risk transfer, you shift the burden of dealing with risk events to someone else. Thus, risk transfer is concerned with dealing with impacts of risk events once untoward events arise. There are various ways risk can be transferred. Three well-known risk transfer mechanisms are insurance, contracts, and warranties.

INSURANCE. With insurance, you pay a premium to protect yourself and your assets from unfortunate circumstances. For example, when you purchase insurance for your car, you have assurance that if your car is damaged in an accident, the bulk of the repair bill will be covered by the insurance company. Similarly, when you purchase life insurance, you are assured that your heirs will receive financial compensation upon the event of your death.

Just about anything can be insured. During World War II, Betty Grable, the pin-up queen, took out insurance on her legs, which were her chief income-generating asset. In the event that her legs were disfigured, she would receive payments from the insurance company that would partially compensate her for loss of income resulting from unemployment. Shipping cargoes can be insured. This was a major source of business for insurance companies over the past few centuries. They can even gain special insurance in war time. For example, during the Vietnam War, boats taking supplies to Phnom Penh along the Mekong River paid 25 percent the value of their cargoes as premiums for war risk insurance.

Some standard areas of insurance coverage include these:

- *Direct property losses*—for example, losses to property caused by fire, flood, and earthquake
- *Indirect property losses*—for example, loss of income tied to interrupted business operations and costs associated with implementing disaster recovery procedures
- *Liability*—for example, dealing with lawsuits from the public for personal injury or property damage

- *Personnel-related losses*—for example, expenses incurred in relation to injuries suffered by employees on the job
- *Performance-related losses*—for example, loss of income when a job is not completed

CONTRACTS. Contracts rank among the oldest risk management tools employed by humans. They were used in the Middle East back in the time of the Sumerians and Babylonians, four thousand years ago.

When most people think of contracts, they focus on the fact that they are agreements between two or more parties, defining the roles and responsibilities of each party. A little deeper reflection shows that contracts also are risk-apportioning tools. For example, contracts typically contain the following type of provision: "If contractor does not deliver 1,000 widgets to buyer by April 13, contractor will pay a penalty of $2,000 per day for each working day of delay in delivering all 1,000 widgets." The contract may also contain a provision putting some burden of risk on the shoulders of the buyer, as the following provision makes clear: "If buyer does not supply contractor by March 10 with the necessary specifications defining the performance requirements of widgets, contractor will not be required to pay penalties for late delivery of the 1,000 widgets."

The way contracts are structured has powerful risk management consequences. This is evident when you look at the two dominant ways contracts are structured. One approach is called the *firm fixed-price contract* (it is also called a *lump-sum contract*). With this approach, the contractor agrees to supply defined goods or services to the buyer by a specific date and for a specific price. For example, the contract may specify that the contractor will deliver 1,000 widgets to the buyer by April 13 at a price of $120,000.

With a firm fixed-price contract, the contractor bears the bulk of the risk. If it costs her $130,000 to produce the 1,000 widgets, she will lose $10,000 on the contract. But if she is able to produce and deliver 1,000 widgets at a cost of $90,000, she will make a profit of $30,000.

The firm fixed-price contract is not entirely risk free for buyers. One significant problem they may encounter is when the contractor gets in trouble and starts losing significant amounts of money on the contract. In the worst case, the contractor may go out of business. In this instance, the buyer cannot recover moneys spent thus far and also will not get the widgets ordered.

The second standard approach to structuring contracts is called the *cost-plus* (or *cost-reimbursable*) *approach*. This approach is commonly employed on work efforts that are hard to define, such as IT projects and research and development projects. With this approach, contractors are reimbursed for expenses they incur. Clearly, buyers assume the principal burden of risk with this structure, because if contractors experience cost overruns, the buyers pay for them.

A number of variations on cost-plus contracts have emerged to provide incentives to contractors to keep costs under control. The best-known examples are cost-plus incentive fee contracts (CPIF), cost-plus award fee contracts (CPAF), and cost-plus fixed fee contracts (CPFF).

With CPIF contracts, a written cost and time schedule is laid out where the contractor is provided bonuses for early delivery of goods on or below budget. For example, if a contracted software program is delivered a month early, the cost and time schedule may indicate that the contractor is entitled to a $10,000 bonus. If the software program is delivered late, $5,000 per month may be deducted from the negotiated profit for each month of delay.

With CPAF contracts, an award fee pool is set aside for the purpose of rewarding the contractor for good performance. Unlike the CPIF structure, where the link between performance and bonuses is laid out in black and white, allocation of bonuses with the CPAF structure is made by means of an award fee panel. In deciding the size of the bonus, the panel members can take into account such subjective factors as the cooperativeness of the contractor. For example, contractors who do not respond to telephone inquiries from the buyer and behave in a surly fashion may have their bonus reduced accordingly.

With CPFF contracts, buyer and contractor negotiate a profit (that is, a fee) to be paid for the work before any work has begun. For example, the buyer may agree to pay a fee of $70,000 on a $1 million contract. If the contract is executed for $900,000, the contractor is paid the $70,000 fee. If it is executed for $1.1 million, the contractor is paid a $70,000 fee. The point is that with this structure, there is no incentive for contractors to spend excessively. CPFF contracts are heavily employed on research and development projects.

In recent years, there has been a drive to make contracts as "performance based" as possible. With performance-based contracting, the statements of work contained in the contract document focus on defining what the contracted effort should be producing. Statements on how deliverables should be produced should be avoided. The idea is to focus on writing contracts that have clearly defined deliverables and work effort so as to avoid the confusion and conflict that invariably accompany vaguely stated documents.

WARRANTIES. Warranties are a type of contract. With a warranty, the seller warrants that her goods or services will perform according to specifications for a defined period of time. The warranty agreement specifies the obligations of the seller in the event that the goods or services do not perform properly. For example, when you buy a toaster, you may find that it comes with a ninety-day warranty: the seller agrees to replace a defective toaster if it is returned in the ninety-day time frame. Car tires usually come with a sliding-scale warranty: you will be refunded for a defective tire according to the amount of wear it has experienced. When a systems integrator delivers a customer relationship management system, it may agree to fix cost free any bugs that arise during its first six months of operation. What warranties do, then, is transfer risk from the buyer to the seller.

Risk Acceptance

With risk acceptance, we acknowledge that life is filled with risk and that we need to move on with our lives and go about our business, risky or not. Certainly, a trip to New York to attend a family reunion at Thanksgiving is likely to encounter major traffic backups. Because we want to see our family and because we are willing to accept hassles getting to the reunion site, we give ourselves an extra hour of travel time, grit our teeth, and head down the road. Thus, we accept the risk of hassles and delays.

The most common way to handle risks in a risk acceptance situation is to establish contingency reserves to deal with untoward events. For example, we add an hour to the travel time to get to the family reunion so that we do not arrive too late. (If the traffic is fine, then we arrive early, which presents no problem.) Also, we know from experience that our car consumes three-quarters of a tank of gasoline to travel to New York, but we fill it up just in case delays and detours cause us to use more gasoline than planned. We thereby have gasoline reserves to serve us in case of an emergency.

When we establish contingency reserves, we have an idea of what we need to contend with. In our family reunion example, we know that we may face delays, so we add an hour to our expected travel time as a buffer. Contingent on our facing traffic delays, we are still able to arrive at the reunion site on time. We also add extra gasoline to the tank, so that we have enough fuel in the event of an emergency: Contingent on the need to consume more gasoline than planned, we have plenty of fuel to arrive at our destination.

With contingency reserves, we are dealing with what are called *known-unknowns*. That is, we know that a particular risk event can occur but do not know the details about its occurrence. Still, simply knowing what the risk event is that we can encounter allows us to prepare for it. For example, two hundred years of weather data tell me that it will rain in Washington, D.C., in April. So I know it will rain. However, I don't know exactly when the rain will fall. Nor do I know whether it will be a light drizzle, a downpour, or steady rain. My contingency reserve is to carry a small umbrella with me during April. Contingent upon rain, I can pull out my umbrella and stay dry.

Nevertheless, situations may arise that can throw off our best plans. I am talking here about the total surprises we occasionally encounter in our lives—for example:

- An earthquake strikes a geologically stable zone, causing loss of life and severe damage to buildings and roads.

- Just before a young high-tech company goes through an initial public offering, its CEO announces that he is leaving the company to join ranks with a competitor.

- A week after signing a $40 million joint venture agreement with the Slovobian Ministry of Post and Telecommunications, a coup d'état deposes all Slovobian senior leaders, including the minister of post and telecommunications.

- During year three of a five-year program to develop a next-generation fighter aircraft, politicians cut back funding that is needed to support testing efforts of prototype fighters.

These total surprises go by the name of *unk-unks*, an abbreviation of *unknown-unknowns*. Unlike the situation with known-unknowns, we cannot earmark contingency reserves to deal with them. Instead, what we can do is to set aside what is called a *management reserve*. Management reserves usually take the form of funds set aside to deal with surprises. For example, on large U.S. defense projects, it is common practice to establish a management reserve of 5 percent of the contract price to cover unanticipated problems that lie within the scope of work.

A significant challenge facing risk managers is to determine what level of contingency or management reserves to set aside. Clearly, there are practical and economic constraints on how much reserves should be established. Each dollar dedicated to such reserves is a dollar that is unavailable for directly productive uses, so there is pressure to keep backup reserves as low as possible. If a serious problem arises and insufficient reserves are available to deal with it, an organization may face catastrophic consequences. Thus, there is countervailing pressure to fatten reserve pools to the extent possible.

The level of reserves that should be established is tied to the consequences of not being able to meet one's obligations in the event of the occurrence of an untoward event. This fact is illustrated in disaster recovery plans established by IT departments in organizations. Typically, IT operations are backed up through one of three mechanisms: hot sites, warm sites, and cool sites.

With *hot sites,* an organization fully replicates its on-site operations at an off-site location. Everything that transpires at the principal site is replicated instantly at the off-site location. If the principal location experiences a catastrophic event, operations can be shifted fully and instantly to the off-site location with no interruption of service. The downside of hot sites is that they are enormously expensive to maintain. They require a complete duplication of equipment, software, and personnel used in the organization's main office operations. Their upside is that they provide the organization with a high level of confidence that its business operations will not be interrupted. This is very important in financial organizations, where the failure of information systems can result in unthinkable chaos. It is also important for operations where systems failures can lead to injury and loss of life. NASA's manned space missions are filled with redundant systems, where if the primary system fails, a backup system can seamlessly take over operations.

When the impacts of untoward events are less than catastrophic, organizations may decide to maintain a *warm site* for backup purposes. In this case, limited off-site operations are carried out. For example, rather than have off-site operations running concurrently with the main office operations, data may be backed up twice a day. Usually, with warm sites, equipment and software employed at the main site are replicated. However, their principal purpose is to be available for use when needed, not to provide seamless backup to the primary systems. If the main site shuts down, operations can be resumed fairly quickly, though not instantly, as with hot site backup.

The cheapest form of providing some measure of continuity of operations is to maintain a *cool site*. This may entail nothing more than establishing an arrangement with another organization to store important files at its facilities and to use its facilities in the event of troubles at the main office. Cool site backup is probably all that is needed for most organizations engaged in routine business transactions.

The significance of establishing some sort of backup capabilities is often overlooked in organizations. Most managers cannot envision their operations experiencing a catastrophic shutdown. This fact is highlighted dramatically when disaster strikes. For example, a major New York City law firm that was located in the World Trade Center had no off-site backups of its physical documents and information systems. As a consequence of the September 11 terrorist attack, all of its client records, as well as its own records, were lost. Clearly, this law firm's lack of risk management precautions created serious problems for its clients and jeopardized its own viability as an organization. I suspect that this law firm is not atypical and that most organizations have not taken steps to implement disaster recovery plans.

CALCULATING CONTINGENCY RESERVES

Two types of contingency reserves will be discussed here. The first is *budget contingencies*. Establishing budget contingencies has planners computing how much money should be set aside to deal with unanticipated slip-ups that drive up project and operations costs. The second is *schedule contingencies*. With schedule contingencies, attention focuses on how much padding should be put into the estimates of task duration.

Budget Contingencies

Most contingency reserves for project budgets are ad hoc. Many organizations simply set aside a standard percentage of project budget, say, 5 or 10 percent, to handle contingency needs. Thus, if a realistic estimate of the cost of a work effort is $120,000, the organization may tack on an additional $12,000 for contingency reserves.

Organizations that are serious about computing contingency reserves take a more scientific approach. The most frequently employed approach makes use of the statistical concept of expected value, which is covered in Chapter Six. The following example illustrates the logic of using expected value analysis to compute contingency reserves:

> Synex Scientific Devices Co. is planning to launch a small project to upgrade its chemical analyzer product. A series of tasks will involve the use of skilled machinists during the second week of October. Regrettably, the machinists are heavily committed to work on other projects at this time. It is estimated that there is a 25 percent probability that outside contractors will be hired to carry out some of the work in the event that Synex's machinists are not available. If they are hired, they will cost Synex $8,000 more than originally planned for the project. Using expected value logic, it is decided that $2,000 of contingency funds should be included in the project to deal with the possibility of using the outside machinists. (Computation: Contingency reserve = [additional cost] × [probability of incurring additional cost] = $8,000 × 0.25 = $2,000.)

Table 8.1 extends this principle to four tasks, each of which faces a possibility of a defined cost overrun. The conclusion is that the $37,000 four-task work effort should set aside an additional $1,665 as a contingency reserve.

Schedule Reserves

The usual practice in estimating task durations is to estimate a reasonable expected duration and then to add safety to the estimate to make sure that the task does not encounter schedule slippage. Eliyahu Goldratt, author of the best-selling work, *Critical Chain* (1997), makes

Task	Budget	Possible Overrun	Probability of Overrun	Contingency (Overrun × Probability)
Task A	$15,000	$3,000	0.20	$600
Task B	10,000	2,000	0.30	600
Task C	2,000	300	0.30	90
Task D	10,000	2,500	0.15	375
Total	37,000			$1,665

Table 8.1. Computing Contingency Reserves.

a convincing argument that this approach does not work and increases the risk of carrying out work efforts using more time than necessary. Goldratt's point is simple. His argument is based on Parkinson's Law, which states that work expands to fill the time available to perform it.

Applying Parkinson's Law to everyday work efforts, you will find that if you give a worker 4 days to do a 3-day job, he will likely complete the job in more than 4 days (to keep things simple, let's say 4.5 days). If you had given him 3 days to do the exact same job, he would likely complete it in a little more than 3 days (let's say 3.5 days). If you had given him 5 days to do the job, he would likely complete it in a little more than 5 days (let's say 5.5 days).

The explanation of this behavior requires a little armchair psychology. Workers who find themselves overscheduled in their jobs tend to put off tasks until the last possible moment, because they are already occupied trying to meet other impossible deadlines. Those who do not have much work to do tend to drag out work assignments to look busy. They too begin work on their chores at the last moment. For both overworked and underworked employees, in holding off doing a job until the last minute, they tend to underestimate how much time is needed to complete the effort. Consequently, this contributes to small schedule slippages in executing their chores.

These points have important scheduling implications that are illustrated in Figure 8.1. Figure 8.1a shows the typical way planners schedule work efforts. Let's say it is estimated that tasks A, B, and C should take 3 days each. A 1-day contingency buffer is added to each task to increase the likelihood that the three tasks will not experience schedule slippage. Thus, 12 days are scheduled to do the job. Goldratt would maintain that owing to Parkinson's Law, the task workers will use up all 12 days available to them.(They may even use more than 12 days if they hold off executing tasks until the last moment.)

Figure 8.1b shows what can happen if a schedule buffer is added at the end of a sequence of tasks. According to Parkinson's Law, the workers will execute the three 3-day tasks in 9 days (or slightly more). The workers may then consume some of the 1.5-day buffer to accommodate whatever schedule slippage they encountered in executing tasks A, B, and C. The whole effort is likely to be carried out in 10.5 days. By adding a buffer at the end of a sequence of tasks, the workers do the job 1.5 days more quickly than by adding buffers to each individual task. That is, they get the job done in 10.5 days rather than 12 days.

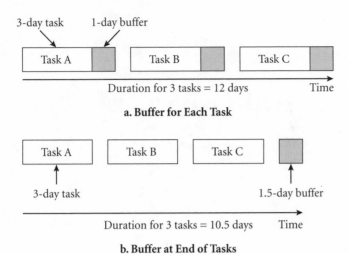

Figure 8.1. Where You Put Schedule Buffers Affects Schedule Length.

Is this the way the world really works? Absolutely. Throughout the late 1990s and into the early 2000s, a number of experiments were carried out to see whether the way schedule reserve (the buffers) is added to work efforts has an impact on schedule duration. They found consistently that adding schedule reserves task by task increases the overall length of work efforts.

Therefore, in establishing schedule reserves, the smart thing to do is to schedule work to be carried out according to expected duration (for example, how much time it should take to do a task on the average), and then at the end of the string of tasks to add half the reserves you would use had you added reserves task-by-task.

CONCLUSION

By identifying risk events, studying their potential impact, and developing strategies to handle them, you have carried out the basic steps that constitute risk assessment. You are now prepared to deal with life's curve balls. But you should be aware that until this point, risk management has largely been an intellectual exercise. As you will see in Chapter Nine, which examines risk monitoring and control, your great insights and plans will not amount to much if you are not able to deal with risk events as they actually unfold. It is one thing to be prepared to handle risk. It is another to handle it effectively in the heat of an ugly event.

Monitoring and Controlling Risk

=◆◆◆=

The last process of risk management is *monitoring and control.* This is the action phase of risk management. The earlier processes—risk planning, identification, qualitative analysis, quantitative analysis, and response planning—entail cerebral activities. I call them the *might* phases, because they have risk managers speculating on what bad (and good) events *might* happen, what the consequences of these events *might* be, and what steps *might* be taken to deal with them.

With risk monitoring and control, we descend from the heights of speculation and plant our feet in the real world. As the term *monitoring and control* makes clear, we are dealing here with two components. *Monitoring* has risk managers continually scanning the risk horizons to see what untoward risk events are looming. Monitoring risk events is like making periodic checks of the pressure gauge on the boiler in the basement. So long as the needle is in the green zone, everything is okay. When it is in the yellow zone, we need to prepare for action. When it is in the red zone, we need to take physical steps to reduce the pressure.

Control refers to the actual actions we take to handle the risk event. If there is a fire in the kitchen, we put it out with a fire extinguisher or throw baking soda on it. If a computer system breaks down, we immediately switch all computer activities to the backup system. If the press reports that we are manufacturing defective products, we launch a public relations effort to minimize the damage to our organization's reputation.

This chapter examines monitoring and control efforts in some detail. When discussing control, it focuses special attention on crisis management—steps that need to be taken when dealing with worst-case situations that can harm people's health and lives or can seriously threaten the well-being of the organization.

MONITORING RISK

Risk monitoring is an information-gathering effort, carried out during the normal course of business, with a view to determining whether any risk events have surfaced and, if so, whether they are serious enough to warrant action. Unlike risk identification, which is carried out in the context of a specific undertaking, such as launching a new project or exploring an investment opportunity, risk monitoring is an ongoing, almost routine process. Nothing specific is triggering the monitoring effort. In a sense, it is a preventive maintenance activity. Just as smart car owners change the oil in their automobiles every three thousand miles, smart organizations routinely conduct risk monitoring activities in order to avoid nasty surprises.

A large portion of risk monitoring is informal. As people are doing their jobs, they should be sensitive to things that don't seem to be quite right. An order taker at a call center who has five customers in a row complaining that they waited five to ten minutes before having their call answered, when the mean waiting time is one minute, should recognize that something may be wrong with the call-in system and should alert his supervisor to the pattern of complaints. An editor who notes that the stockpile of xerographic paper in the copy room is down to nothing the day before an important report is to be printed should check with the stock clerk to see if the organization is truly out of paper or whether supplies are being stored elsewhere. If each employee in an organization is sensitive to anomalies or potential problems, the level of risk the organization faces is greatly reduced through their informal monitoring efforts.

In this chapter, we are concerned primarily with formal risk monitoring. We examine four commonly employed formal risk monitoring activities: the employment of status reports, the use of issues logs, the conducting of evaluations, and the use of periodic risk audits.

Status Reports

Status reports are the most commonly used mechanism to assess progress on projects and operations. They are usually issued monthly. For the most part, they follow a prescribed format. For example, they describe budget performance for the past month or identify milestones achieved and missed. In production environments, they describe how many widgets were produced.

A common feature of status reports is that they focus on variances from the plan. For example, a review of cost and schedule status for a project may indicate that it is 10 percent over budget and 12 percent behind schedule. The combined data suggest the project is in trouble. An important question is: Will these variances continue to grow, or are there steps we can take to bring the project back on track?

Typically, unfavorable cost and schedule variances indicate that a project is encountering a standard set of problems. Some of these may be related to poor implementation of the project plan, as when inexperienced workers are used on tasks, or needed materials arrive late. Some are related to excessively optimistic plans, as when the salespeople promise clients that the project team will deliver a ten-month job in six months. These standard problems can be handled in various customary ways. For example, if the cause of overruns is employment of inexperienced workers, more experienced personnel can be put onto the project. Or if a project is based on overly optimistic assumptions, the plan may be "rebaselined," that is, adjusted to capture reality.

But cost and schedule variances may also be rooted in nonstandard problems that portend the surfacing of new sources of risk. For example, an investigation of persistent schedule slippages for a project may reveal that they are triggered by changes in local government regulations that require that the project's deliverables undergo unanticipated government inspections at frequent intervals. Thus, changes in government regulations leading to increased inspections are a new source of risk that has been surfaced by the risk monitoring effort.

Issues Logs

In Chapter Four, issues logs were discussed as a tool that assists in risk identification. They are filled out monthly and are presented as part of the status report for projects or operations. They typically are divided into two portions: *pending issues* and *resolved issues*. The pending issues portion lists possible items of concern. Issues are not risk events per se. They are discussion points that need to be addressed because they might ultimately be sources of problems. An item on the pending issues list can be something as innocent as, "Employees are upset that the thermostat is set too low in the canteen eating area," to something as significant as, "Our principal client has just filed for Chapter 11 bankruptcy."

The resolved issues portion of the issues log itemizes previous pending issues that have been taken care of. The date when each issue was resolved should be noted, so that management has an idea of how much time is being spent dealing with issues. Ideally, the pending issues portion of the issues log is quite short, and the list of items in the resolved issues portion should be growing longer and longer. This circumstance reflects the fact that as issues arise, they are being handled quickly. A lengthening list of pending issues indicates that the issues are not being handled expeditiously.

The use of issues logs is quite popular today. They have two important advantages. First, they provide a systematic way for employees to highlight concerns they have about how things are going in the business. In a sense, the employees are being asked regularly: "Is there anything happening now or in the future that might adversely affect our operations?" Consequently, the possibility of untoward risk events' arising is kept in front of them.

Second, issues logs place pressure on employees to handle risks promptly. Nobody wants her issue sitting in the pending issues portion of the issues log month after month. At best, it reflects ineptness in resolving issues. At worst, it reflects a lack of commitment to solving problems. Neither of these characterizations helps an employee's career prospects in the organization.

Evaluations

Evaluations are exercises in periodic stock taking. They are sanity checks that are conducted to see whether the fundamental objectives of an undertaking are being achieved. I have had many people tell me that their organizations do not conduct evaluations, but they are mistaken. Actually, most organizations conduct an abundance of evaluations; it's just that they do not call these efforts "evaluation." Examples of evaluation include preliminary design reviews, critical design reviews, pink and red team reviews, walk-throughs, audits, management-by-objectives (MBO) reviews, and performance appraisal reviews.

Preliminary and detailed design reviews are commonly used approaches toward technical evaluation. They are conducted to gain assurance that the design that is being formulated for a product is on target. Pink and red team reviews are evaluation efforts carried out during the process of writing important proposals that will lead, everyone hopes, to project funding. The pink team review is held early in the proposal writing effort, when a group of colleagues plays the role of the customer and critiques the nascent proposal from a customer perspective. The red team review is held later in the proposal writing effort; as with the pink team review, the proposal is critiqued from the customer's point of view.

With walk-throughs, customers or technical team members review the merits (or demerits) of a product in great detail. The walk-through concept is familiar to anyone who has purchased a new home. One of the last things a home purchaser does before handing over a check to acquire a property is to walk through the property carefully, looking for flaws that need to be fixed.

Like walk-throughs, audits entail a detailed review of a product or process. Many audits are financial reviews, as when auditors from the tax authorities review a company's books, looking for irregularities. Other audits are reviews of an organization's processes, for example, when a university is undergoing an accreditation review or a factory's operations are being audited to see whether they are in compliance with ISO 9000 standards.

MBO reviews are classical management evaluations. Employees and their managers agree that the employees will achieve a well-defined set of objectives by a particular time. When that point is reached, the employee's performance is evaluated to see whether the objectives have been achieved.

Finally, performance appraisal reviews are a form of evaluation. They address the effectiveness of employee performance according to a number of defined criteria. Their importance rests on the fact that they help determine whether employees become promoted, win bonuses, and gain salary increases or whether they are relegated to the organization's internal gulag.

Clearly, evaluations serve a risk monitoring function. Although it is not popular to say this, when evaluations are held, the evaluators are fundamentally looking for trouble. Evaluations are seldom carried out for the purpose of patting people on the back. However, it should be noted that evaluators are looking for trouble *not* for the purpose of punishing employees but for the purpose of identifying problems when they are still small and manageable. In this respect, standard evaluations and risk monitoring have a lot in common.

Risk Audits

As organizations have grown sensitive to the need to implement good risk management practices, the employment of risk audits has increased dramatically. Risk audits are conscious, systematic attempts to examine an organization's projects, processes, and risk management procedures to determine whether things are progressing smoothly or whether problems lurk in the shadows. They are conducted by risk audit teams of highly experienced men and women who are trained on good risk management practices. Risk assessment groups used in organizations such as IBM, Hewlett Packard, and NCR are examples of risk auditors. As Chapter Four points out, one important function they play is to review contract terms and statements of work to make sure that they are realistic. If a new initiative is promising more than the company can deliver, the risk assessment group identifies this problem before formal agreements are signed and funds are released, preventing the organization from launching itself down a path that is preordained to result in failure.

PERILS OF RISK MONITORING

For risk monitoring to be successful in surfacing risk events, three conditions need to be met:

1. *The monitoring effort must be focused on the right sources of information.* This is an obvious point. If you want to anticipate the arrival of a rainstorm, you should monitor atmospheric pressure on a barometer rather than check the temperature in your living room. History is filled with examples of risk events that were missed because

people were looking at the wrong things. For example, the Central Intelligence Agency (CIA) did not anticipate Ayatollah Khomeini's revolution in Iran because its channels of information came principally from Iranian government sources and it was unaware of the activities of the opposition forces.

2. *The information must be timely.* Even the best information is not useful if it arrives too late. A famous example was the cable warning Washington of an impending attack by the Japanese on Pearl Harbor. By the time the cable had been processed and gone through channels, the attack had already occurred and U.S. entry into World War II had begun.

3. *The people reviewing the information must be able to make sense out of it.* We are all inundated with data. When we log on to check our e-mail in the morning, we are sometimes overwhelmed by the number of messages that have reached our in-box since we logged off the previous evening. If we are typical, we know that the majority of the messages is junk mail. So we delete obvious junk mail candidates, open messages we know are real, and put questionable messages aside to deal with later.

People who monitor risk face a similar situation, only much worse. They come across heaps of data but have trouble separating signal from noise. If they don't know what they are looking for, they cannot see patterns in the data that reveal potential threats.

A look at the terrorist attack on the World Trade Center in 2001 demonstrates how even well-funded, experienced risk monitoring experts cannot do a good job if they are weak on one or more of the three factors. A review of the monitoring efforts of the principal intelligence-gathering agencies in the United States—the Federal Bureau of Investigation, the CIA, and the National Security Agency (NSA)—shows that they performed well on the first factor but poorly on the second and third.

Since the mid-1990s, each agency has targeted members of the al Qaeda network for special attention. Consequently, the agencies identified the right players who pose a serious threat to the security of the United States.

However, they did not interpret the information they had in a timely fashion, partially because they could not make sense out of it. In at least one case (the case of the NSA), crucial information was delayed in getting processed because the NSA had an insufficient number of Arabic-speaking translators translating intercepted messages into English. It turns out that fairly specific information about activities on September 11 had been gathered electronically by the NSA—information that might have enabled the United States to prevent the terrorist attacks—yet this information surfaced only after the attacks were carried out owing to delays in translation.

Probably the greatest shortcoming was with the third factor. In retrospect, we see that the FBI, CIA, and NSA together had substantial amounts of information that could have enabled them to anticipate the terrorists' actions. For example, the CIA had been tracking two of the September 11 terrorists, Khalid Almihdhar and Nawaf Alhazmi, since an al Qaeda meeting in Kuala Lumpur, Malaysia, in January 2000, but did not share this information with the FBI until August 23, 2001, after the two terrorists had already entered the United States. For its part, FBI headquarters ignored strong warnings from its Phoenix field office, which had noted unusual numbers of Middle East nationals taking flight training courses at U.S. schools.

No one who is experienced in managing risk should be surprised that U.S. intelligence agencies were unable to unveil the plot of the al Qaeda terrorists. The fact is that the agencies receive a continuous stream of warnings about threats to the United States, most of which do not pan out. In fact, many of the warnings are planted by enemies of the United States to confuse its information-monitoring efforts. Thus, a major challenge that risk managers face when conducting their risk-monitoring activities is to identify which information is credible and which is not. Even then, their job is not over, because once they possess credible information, they must work out its meaning.

CONTROLLING RISK

Risk control, which is often called risk handling, refers to the steps that are taken to get risk events under control once they arise. If a newly released product fails to sell in the marketplace, a control action might be to implement a backup marketing plan. If a project experiences severe schedule slippage, a control action might be to trim back on its scope. If the battery in your car is dead, a control action might be to jump-start the car using a neighbor's vehicle.

Ideally, your previous risk assessment efforts leave you well prepared to deal with the risk event. To control the risk, you implement the risk-handling actions you identified during the risk response planning exercises you carried out earlier. That is, you draw funds from your contingency reserve accounts (risk acceptance), or you now fix the problems that you anticipated would arise (risk mitigation), or you contact your insurance company to be compensated for the damage you experience (risk transfer).

Quite often, the way risk events play out does not match what you anticipated during the risk assessment effort, however. There is often a large gap between theory and practice. In this case, the risk response team has to make some tough decisions. Follow the plan, even though its relevance is questionable? Abandon the plan and improvise? Do something else?

The following case study illustrates Robert Burns's sentiment that "the best laid schemes o' mice an' men gang aft a-gley." It examines a catastrophe that befell a major metropolitan area and shows how in the case of one risk-sensitive company, its best risk planning efforts were only partially helpful in dealing with the emerging crisis. What saved the company ultimately was the fact that it employed a number of intelligent, well-trained risk managers who maintained their cool demeanor during the crisis and figured out what to do by applying basic management and technical principles that they had been trained to employ.

One of the greatest calamities to befall a modern city during peacetime occurred in Auckland, New Zealand, in mid-February 1998. Four power cables that provided Auckland's central business district (CBD) with power failed, and the CBD suffered a power blackout that lasted three weeks. Even then, power was only gradually restored. Many enterprises had to move their operations out of the CBD in order to continue their activities. Retailers, of course, could not and suffered severe economic damage.

COMPANY X'S PROBLEM

A New Zealand telecommunications company (Company X) found itself in a situation where it could not provide telecom service to its customers in the CBD. A crisis management group at Company X worked diligently to restore service as quickly as possible. For years, Company X had been committed to implementing good risk management practices. It regularly carried out risk identification exercises, engaged in risk impact analyses, and had risk-handling plans in place. It even established an emergency response group that held regular meetings and created an emergency management protocol. Although most of the emergency response team members were employees from different parts of the organization who worked part time on emergencies, the company also had a full-time risk management team headed by a risk management expert who had received extensive training on handling telecommunications risk events while serving with the army.

DETERMINING WHAT'S GOING ON

Once it became apparent that a major crisis was unfolding in Auckland, Company X's emergency response group went into action. One of the first items covered in the emergency management protocol was: "In the event of an emergency, the emergency response team should assemble immediately." There was a problem, however. The power outage was total. Even telephone service was lost. So the matter of how to contact emergency response group members when there was no telephone service became an issue. Fortunately, most of the team members had enough good sense to assemble at their usual meeting place. The emergency response team also discovered a fact that many of us already know: people have become so mobile that contact information for about one-fourth of the people who needed to be contacted was out of date.

Another early challenge was to determine the extent of the power outage. Was Company X merely experiencing a local outage, or was this citywide? Would power be lost for an hour or two, or was this something more serious? The principal risk manager, Tony F., was able to contact key engineers at two power companies that served Auckland. When asked how bad the situation was, the engineer at the first company responded: "It's very bad. We are likely to be without power for a few days." The engineer at the second company responded: "It's very bad. We are likely to be without power for a couple of weeks." Tony had been trained in the army to take the worst estimate and double it. He concluded that Auckland could be out of power for four weeks (which turned out to be close to the mark). He planned his company's recovery efforts accordingly.

COUNTING ON MURPHY'S LAW

As with any other well-managed company, Company X tested its backup generator once a month: an engineer would trek down to the basement, start the generator, and run it briefly. When Auckland lost power, Company X's backup generator kicked in, a source of comfort to Company X's management. However, a few hours into the crisis, the backup generator failed. Although monthly tests had demonstrated that it could start properly, the fuel that ran the generator had not been changed in years; debris that accumulated in the fuel caused a filter to clog, which caused the generator to crash. When Company X tried to purchase another backup generator, it learned that it would be weeks before a new generator could be acquired.

During the month-long power outage, many of Company X's customers relocated to Auckland's suburbs, which still had power. Company X needed to adjust telephone circuits to serve customers who had temporarily moved. Following good risk management practice, changes to circuits were carefully documented once a month. Unfortunately, the crisis occurred just a day or two before new changes were to be noted, so the existing documentation on circuits was out of date by one month, a substantial deficiency in view of the continual changes made to circuitry. This made it difficult to determine the exact state of the circuits that affected each customer.

THE VALUE OF EXPERIENCE

During the crisis, Tony recalled an important lesson he had been taught in the army signal corps. His training highlighted that if telecommunications capabilities go down, a typical organization can survive data losses for one to three weeks. However, it simply cannot function with loss of voice telecom capabilities. Consequently, Tony instructed the recovery team to focus all of its early efforts on rebuilding voice transmission capabilities for its clients. Later he learned that a competing organization devoted equal attention to restoring voice and data communications, with the result that it was much slower than Company X in providing customers with crucial voice service.

LESSONS LEARNED

Six months after the crisis had ended, Tony was asked what he had learned from the power outage experience. He said there were three lessons that stuck with him. The first is that in a crisis, nothing unfolds the way it is supposed to. Consequently, although extensive risk preparations may be made to contend with a particular scenario, in reality the scenario you encounter is quite different from the one you are prepared to deal with. You need to be flexible.

The second is that flexibility in responding to a crisis should be rooted in the application of intelligent general principles. For example, in the army, he had been taught as a general principle that when restoring telecommunications service, always focus on getting voice transmissions up as quickly as possible.

Finally, Tony said that perhaps the most important lesson he had learned is that during a crisis, it is important to keep a cool head. For example, during the power outage, Tony and his team felt tremendous pressure to restore telephone service to their clients as quickly as possible, at any cost. Tony resisted the temptation to jump in and start restoring service. He had been trained that when taking actions to respond to a crisis, you should always look to the time when the crisis is over. Don't get caught up in the passion of the moment and do things that you will regret later. Following this principle, Tony recognized that even as Company X's technicians rerouted telecom transmissions to Auckland's suburbs, they should meticulously record all the actions they undertook. In the short run, this slowed down the recovery effort a little. However, in the long run, this policy paid for itself handsomely. The technicians at Company X's competitor did not document their efforts and paid the price later for this shortcoming. It turned out that this documentation was crucial for a number of reasons: (1) when power returned to Auckland, Company X was able to employ the documentation to return customers' circuits to their original state, (2) the documentation provided Company X with a basis of charging clients for services it rendered during the crisis, and (3) the documentation was important to recover costs through insurance.

Risk Control Issue: What's Happening?

As the Auckland power outage case illustrates, the first reality that a risk response team must contend with is: "Are we facing a serious problem? If so, what is its nature?" Think about the conditions encountered by the people working at Company X. They are going about their business in a routine way when suddenly the electric power to their building is lost. The backup generator kicks in, so there is no need to panic. But what is going on? Has the local transformer blown? This is not an unusual circumstance. If there is a problem with the local transformer, presumably it can be fixed in a few hours. Is the problem more serious? Of course, in the early stages of the power outage, no one conjectured that all power would be lost to the city for a long period of time, because this type of event had never befallen a modern city.

Thus, the most important risk control issue facing managers in the earliest stages of a significant risk event is to determine what is happening. When Johnson & Johnson's senior managers were informed in 1982 that seven people had died in the Chicago area after consuming arsenic-laced Tylenol capsules, their first reaction was one of disbelief. "Could this really be happening? Is someone so mentally unbalanced that they would kill innocent people this way?" When the reality of the horror sank in, the next question they grappled with was: "How pervasive is the poisoning? Is this a local Chicago phenomenon, or has the terrorist poisoned Tylenol capsules in other cities as well?" Clearly, answers to these important questions would shape the strategies that Johnson & Johnson should pursue to deal with the crisis. In the end, Johnson & Johnson's senior managers realized that they could not afford to wait to learn the answer to the second question, since lives were at stake: they agreed to withdraw all Tylenol products from the shelves of pharmacies and convenience stores at a cost of $100 million.

A sad story emerging from the World Trade Center terrorist attack tells of how one company asked its employees over its public address system to remain calm and stay at their desks until senior managers could determine what threat they faced. This request seems reasonable. The vision of panicky employees filling the stairwells is a frightening one. Unfortunately, senior management proffered bad advice, and all the employees who dutifully stayed at their desks awaiting further instructions died when the building collapsed.

Risk Control Issue: The Need for Flexibility

When an anticipated risk event translates into a real incident, there is a good chance that it will not follow the script defined during risk planning exercises. This means that the people responding to the risk event need to be flexible. When they see that things are not playing out as planned, they should be able to improvise. It is important to note that the improvisation must be rooted in knowledge, experience, and good judgment, because poorly conceived improvisation can create more problems than it solves.

Knowledge means that the people handling the risk event have a thorough understanding of what they are working with. For example, a person who is an expert on using a particular database is more qualified to deal with problems affecting the database than an amateur who has no knowledge of its workings. The amateur will be slower in dealing with the problems than the expert. Furthermore, the amateur is likely to make mistakes and add to the problems rather than alleviate them.

Experience means that the people handling the risk event have dealt with similar circumstances previously. The experienced person is one who can say, "Been there, seen it, done it." Experienced people are less likely to panic when they encounter adverse situations. Also, their experience may provide them with significant insights into how to handle particular problems.

Good judgment means that the people handling the risk event operate logically and ethically and employ good sense. Good judgment may require the risk handlers to go against established procedures. For example, there once was an occasion when large numbers of Melbourne school children were engaged in field trips in the bush when a prairie fire arose. The standard school safety rules required the school bus drivers to return to home base in the event of an emergency. But in view of the fact that the fire raged between the school buses and home base, the school bus drivers wisely decided to ignore standard procedure. Another example is that in developing rules for dealing with leaks of toxic gases, the safety committee at one company instructed employees to run away from the leak. A little thought showed that this instruction might not be smart if a breeze was blowing from the direction of the gas leak, since employees would be running with the toxic cloud surrounding them.

CRISIS MANAGEMENT

Managing crises is a special case of risk control that has become a study area unto itself. In view of the mishandling of notable crises over the past few decades, many organizations have developed crisis management centers. Certainly, poor crisis management capabilities have led to the downfall of many prominent politicians.

President Nixon was driven from office in shame because of his inability to deal with the Watergate scandal. In the 1990s, a stream of Japanese prime ministers were forced to resign because they mishandled scandals. Helmut Kohl, one of the most venerable post-World War II European statesmen, left his office in disgrace for similar reasons. President Bill Clinton tarnished his reputation with the Monica

Lewinsky scandal and created serious legal problems for himself by swearing under oath that Lewinsky's accusations were false. In each of these cases, the politicians initially denied culpability; some went further by attempting to cover up their misdeeds. Through their words and actions, all of them exacerbated their problems. In retrospect, it is clear that the employment of solid crisis management principles would have helped the politicians to deal with their problems more effectively.

Business has its share of mishandled crises. Union Carbide's cold response to the disaster at Bhopal led ultimately to its demise. Firestone's denial of defects in its Wilderness tire not only brought sales of its products to a standstill, but also led to a rupture in its relations with its number one client and long-standing business partner, Ford Motor Corporation. Arthur Andersen's poor auditing of its Enron client and subsequent illegal shredding of documents sealed its fate and put it out of business. As with the case of politicians, effective crisis management could have defused the crises these companies faced and helped them sustain their long-term viability as business enterprises.

In this section of the chapter, we examine three crises that reflect common occurrences encountered when organizations experience unfortunate events that lead to crises.

A Crisis Management Lab Experiment: Sydney Water

In the Sydney Water crisis, we see that what really was not a crisis turned into one because of inept communications on the part of the chief protagonists:

Sydney Water is a government-tied company charged with supplying Sydney, Australia, with its drinking water. In July 1998, routine tests of water samples indicated that levels of certain parasites in the drinking water supply (*Giardia lamblia* and *Cryptosporidium parvum*) could possibly be high enough to warrant concern. Following prescribed procedures, Sydney Water notified the health department of these findings and escalated decision making to the highest levels of the organization.

Although the presence of the parasites caused some concern, it was not evident that they presented a health hazard. Initial lab tests did not firmly establish whether the levels of the parasites were above an acceptable threshold. Tests of the water supply often produce false positives. That is, they often indicate there is a problem when in fact there is not. Consequently, a number of tests are typically run to see whether a problem truly exists. The senior managers of Sydney Water did not want to take any actions publicly to deal with the problem until it was ascertained that a problem did indeed exist. There was even concern that a premature release of information about parasites in the water supply could cause public panic. The initial tests occurred on a Thursday. The senior managers decided to wait until Monday before taking action. This would give them time to review additional test results.

Regrettably, the news media learned about the potential problem and featured it heavily in news reports. The story was released over the weekend, when Sydney Water employees were away from their offices. The emerging crisis was exacerbated by the intervention of politicians. To show their attentiveness to public issues, key politicians immediately leaped into action and took over the principal decision-making authority at Sydney Water. Scare warnings were issued. People were told to cease using water from the tap, or if they used it, to boil it thoroughly.

The image emerged that Sydney Water was inept and insensitive to the public good. All of the top managers left the organization soon after the crisis, and the organization's operating authority was severely curtailed (for example, authority over dams and catchments was taken away). Ironically, subsequent tests of water quality suggested that the water met standards of potability. There was no problem.

The Sydney Water case provides a good example of how crises emerge and can get out of hand quickly. I carried out interviews with some of the principal employees of Sydney Water and asked them what lessons they had learned from their experience. Their insights are interesting and apply to a wide range of crises.

One major lesson they learned was that the crisis was primarily rooted in poor communications. The parasite problem turned out to be a nonproblem, yet it blossomed into a full-blown crisis because of ineffective communications. For example, Sydney Water should have dealt with the report of parasites immediately. The decision to wait until Monday to draw conclusions about water quality was disastrous for a couple of reasons. First, Sydney Water appeared unconcerned about the public well-being. If in fact high levels of cryptosporidium existed in the water supply, this would have serious consequences; some one hundred people died of cryptosporidium-tainted water in Milwaukee in 1993. The perceived lack of urgency in dealing with a potentially serious situation caused great anger to be directed at Sydney Water. Second, the delay in dealing with the test results created a situation where Sydney Water lost the opportunity to take the initiative in handling the emerging crisis. Once the newspapers and politicians stepped into the fray, Sydney Water found itself reacting to the barbs of its critics. Its posture became defensive, which contributed to the sense that the water authority was incompetent and trying to cover up the facts.

An examination of policies employed by water authorities in other cities shows that many of them regularly publish the results of water quality tests. Such a policy of open communication makes it impossible for critics to accuse a water authority of hiding the truth. It also reduces the level of surprise in the event that evidence of poor water quality arises, since people can see trends that may indicate a gradual deterioration in water quality.

Another communication-related lesson that the employees of Sydney Water learned is that the organization was harmed by the fact that it did not have a single point of contact that the public and politicians could deal with. This was especially troublesome in dealing with the press. When they learned of the possible contamination of Sydney's drinking water, reporters began calling a range of Sydney Water employees and got different messages from different employees. As a consequence, it was not clear what the water authority's responsibility and position were with regard to any potential problem with parasites.

Another major lesson learned by the employees of Sydney Water was that they were unable to deal with the crisis because the organization did not have an adequate approach to managing risk. The risk management plan they developed focused narrowly on engineering issues. Their number one concern was dealing with interruptions to the water supply caused by broken pipes. The plan did not deal with broader issues, such as water quality, handling the press, and dealing with politicians. Consequently, the Water Authority was not prepared to handle problems that lay outside the realm of the interruption of water service.

How Not to Handle a Crisis: Union Carbide in Bhopal

In the Bhopal tragedy of 1984, we see how a company's obsession with delivering good financial performance and developing world-class technology (admirable qualities by themselves) created a situation that made possible one of the worst industrial accidents in history:

On December 2, 1984, over 40 tons of a poisonous gas, methyl iso-cyanate (MIC), leaked into a residential community in Bhopal, India. Reports indicate that from four thousand to six thousand people died in the immediate aftermath of the leak, half a million people were exposed to the gas, and some fifty thousand people suffered serious consequences, experiencing damage to eyes, lungs, kidneys, liver, in-testines, brain, and reproductive and immune systems. The leak orig-inated in a chemical facility owned and operated by Union Carbide of India, Ltd.

When word of the disaster first reached Union Carbide's Danbury (U.S.) headquarters, the initial report was that ten people had died, then thirty, and then within forty-eight hours, a thousand. Union Car-bide chairman Warren Anderson immediately flew to the disaster site, where he was arrested by Indian authorities. While Anderson's initial response was focused on helping the victims of the gas leak, it is re-ported that within a week, his chief concern shifted to limiting the company's financial liability. Eventually, Union Carbide liquidated as-sets and made large payouts to shareholders in order to reduce its pay-outs to victims. In the end, Union Carbide agreed to pay $470 million in damages. The average compensation settlement per victim worked out to $300.

According to Indian sources, when victims began arriving at local hospitals with serious symptoms, Union Carbide's management assured them and medical personnel that the gas they were exposed to was not poisonous and would not result in serious damage. The company also did not provide information to medical personnel on the composition of the gas that leaked and did not share insights into how patients should be treated in order to deal with their exposure to toxic gas.

Union Carbide's safety record at its Bhopal facility was poor. In the three years prior to the MIC leak, the following safety problems had been documented:

- A plant operator was killed by a phosgene gas leak in 1981.
- Twenty-eight workers were seriously injured in January 1982 owing to another phosgene gas leak.
- Four workers were exposed to MIC in 1982 when a broken valve caused an MIC gas leak.
- A safety audit carried out in May 1982 identified sixty-one hazards, thirty of them major and eleven in the dangerous phosgene/MIC units.

When a small-scale leak occurred eight months after Bhopal in Union Carbide's Institute, West Virginia, plant, resulting in the hospitalization of 120 people, it became apparent that people living near Union Carbide facilities anywhere, even in the United States, were at risk.

Over the long term, the Bhopal incident seriously tarnished Union Carbide's reputation. Its workforce was cut from 98,400 people in 1984 to 12,000 in the late 1990s. Between 1980 and 1992, its sales were cut in half. Its stock price plunged. Morale within the company dropped tremendously.

In order to resurrect its reputation, Union Carbide took a public stand where its new chairman, Robert Kennedy, indicated that the company would be second to none in its environmental, safety, and health standards. The position of corporate vice president for safety, health, and the environment was created, and a staff of twenty people were charged with developing corporate-wide safety policies and conducting safety audits of Union Carbide plants worldwide. Most critics of Union Carbide believed this action was too little and came too late.

The Union Carbide legacy lingered for years under the cloud of Bhopal. In November 1999, a class action suit was filed against the company, charging that it "demonstrated a reckless and depraved indifference to human life in the design, operation and maintenance of [its Indian facility]." The suit further charged that "the defendants are liable for fraud and civil contempt for their total failure to comply with the lawful orders of the courts of both the United States and India." This last charge was directed at Union Carbide's successful effort to resist extradition motions by the Indian government directed at senior managers. Ultimately, Union Carbide ceased to function as an independent entity after it merged with Dow Chemical in 2001.

As with most other people and organizations that face crises, Union Carbide was not sure that there was a serious problem when reports first trickled in about the gas leak. The earliest reports from India suggested a small problem. Then reports suddenly indicated that thousands of people were dying. With the conflicting reports, it was difficult to know what was really happening in Bhopal. The initial response of Union Carbide's management was humane. Chairman Warren Anderson immediately flew to India to witness what was happening firsthand and to offer assistance. However, his arrest upon arriving in India was a major shock. It convinced him of the seriousness of the problem. It also made him less willing to cooperate with the Indian government. He became concerned about the legal implications of what was transpiring in Bhopal, and this legal orientation colored all of Union Carbide's future actions.

Union Carbide's communications policy was a public relations disaster. The company's public stance was to deny that anything serious had happened in Bhopal. Spokespeople consciously avoided saying anything that could be interpreted as an admission of guilt. They became the poster boy of the bad citizen. Their future was doomed.

In part, Union Carbide's approach to dealing with the tragedy of Bhopal reflects a corporate philosophy that is totally oriented toward the bottom line. In its mission statement, it identified its principal goal to be wealth creation. In its vision statement, it emphasized its desire to be technically excellent and to perform well financially. Although it was a chemical company that produced highly dangerous substances, it identified "safety and environmental excellence" as a single bullet point under the rubric of "corporate values." If vision and mission statements are built on core values and enable us to predict corporate behavior during times of duress, then Union Carbide's response to events in Bhopal is not surprising.

How to Handle a Crisis: Johnson & Johnson and Tylenol

Johnson & Johnson's handling of the poisoning of Tylenol capsules in Chicago in 1982 possibly the most successful crisis management incident in business history:

> Johnson & Johnson encountered a nightmare situation when someone in the Chicago area laced Tylenol capsules with cyanide. Seven people died as a consequence. After they were notified of the poisoning incident, the company's senior managers held an emergency meeting to decide what to do. They had little information upon which to make a decision. The most significant question facing them was: Is the poisoning limited to Chicago, or is this a nationwide problem? If it was simply a local problem, the obvious step would be to remove Tylenol products from the shelves of Chicago stores and recall outstanding stocks. If it was a national problem, the recall would cost the company an estimated $100 million. The senior managers decided the right thing to do would be to recall *all* Tylenol products throughout the

United States, even though there was no evidence that tampering had occurred outside the Chicago area.

While Johnson & Johnson's actions resulted in a major financial hit, its quick and ethical response turned a disaster into a public relations victory. Johnson & Johnson followed up on its initial actions by taking a leadership role in creating tamper-proof packaging for food and drug products. Virtually all textbooks that deal with corporate ethics cite the Johnson & Johnson case as the exemplar of how a company should behave in the face of bad news. In the long run, the morally responsible stance paid off, and Johnson & Johnson's financial performance exceeded precrisis levels quickly.

To understand why Johnson & Johnson was able to respond to the Tylenol crisis the way it did and to respond quickly, it is helpful to understand its corporate values. These values are contained in a document titled "Our Credo," written by Johnson & Johnson president Robert Wood Johnson in 1943:

We believe our first responsibility is to the doctors, nurses, and patients, to mothers and fathers and all others who use our products and services. In meeting their needs everything we do must be of high quality. We must constantly strive to reduce our costs in order to maintain reasonable prices. Customers' orders must be serviced promptly and accurately. Our suppliers and distributors must have an opportunity to make a fair profit.

We are responsible to our employees, the men and women who work with us throughout the world. Everyone must be considered as an individual. We must respect their dignity and recognize their merit. They must have a sense of security in their jobs. Compensation must be fair and adequate, and working conditions clean, orderly, and safe. We must be mindful of ways to help our employees fulfill their family responsibilities. Employees must feel free to make suggestions and complaints. There must be equal opportunity for employment, development, and advancement for those qualified. We must provide competent management, and their actions must be just and ethical.

We are responsible to the communities in which we live and work and to the world community as well. We must be good citizens—support good works and charities and bear our fair share of taxes. We must encourage civic improvements and better health and education. We must maintain in good order the property we are privileged to use, protecting the environment and natural resources.

Our final responsibility is to our stockholders. Business must make a sound profit. We must experiment with new ideas. Research must be carried on, innovative programs developed and mistakes paid for. New equipment must be purchased, new facilities provided, and new products launched. Reserves must be created to provide for adverse times. When we operate according to these principles, the stockholders should realize a fair return.

What is remarkable about this statement of core values is that financial issues are secondary to concerns for customers, employees, and the community. Johnson & Johnson's response to the Tylenol tragedy demonstrated it practiced what it preached.

LESSONS LEARNED FROM CRISES CASES

The cases discussed in this chapter, coupled with the experiences of many other crises, lead to clear conclusions on what good crisis management requires.

Develop a Communication Plan

A review of mishandled crises shows that one thing they have in common is bungled communications. Sydney Water, for example, responded too slowly in dealing with the potential problem of parasites in the water supply. Union Carbide refused to acknowledge any culpability for the disaster at Bhopal. During sworn testimony, Bill Clinton denied having sexual relations with Monica Lewinsky. Communications problems can be mitigated by developing a communication plan that prepares the organization for handling communications issues. There are a number of things the plan should focus on, including:

• *Establish a single point of contact.* It is always important for organizations to present themselves cogently to the outside world. During a crisis, this need is doubly important. Everyone who works in the organization should be instructed that during the course of an emergency or crisis, if they are asked questions by clients, government authorities, or newspaper reporters, they should direct the questions to a single individual who is authorized to be the spokesperson for the organization. In most organizations, this person resides in the public relations or communications department. By following this procedure, the organization can speak with a single voice. Without it, a gaggle of employees will provide the public with contradictory messages, some of which might carry legal liabilities.

• *Maintain regular relations with the news media.* The news media should not be viewed as the enemy. It is important to recognize that reporters are simply looking for a story. Their goal is not to destroy reputations, but to discover an interesting story that sells newspapers. If your organization maintains good relations with the press corps by providing them with news stories and making personnel accessible to reporters when appropriate, then the reporters are more likely to present an informed, sympathetic story during the course of a crisis.

• *Prepare public responses to different types of situations.* Most organizations recognize that there are predictable types of crises they will encounter. Companies that handle hazardous substances always face the possibility that employees and members of the public will suffer injury from such substances. Companies that engage in e-commerce realize the substantial likelihood that their order processing systems will crash from time to time. Companies that ship perishable goods to customers know that shipping delays may cause some of their products to spoil en route to clients. Because these types of risk events are predictable, companies can prepare a public statement to deal with them before the predicted events occur. By making such preparations, the company is able to think through its response in a relaxed environment and is not issuing statements under duress. It is also able to respond quickly, which shows the public that it cares about what they think and that it is on top of the situation.

Communicate Effectively Once the Crisis Is Underway

Obviously, planning a communication response to crises is important. But even good plans will not be worth much if they are not implemented effectively once the crisis is underway. Organizations should do two things to ensure that they communicate effectively during the crisis:

• *Respond quickly.* As a crisis is unfolding, a great frustration that crisis managers face is a lack of information to make good judgments. This is particularly true when the event puts the organization in a bad light. The temptation is to hold off taking action until the circumstances are better understood. The rationale goes: "Let's not make hasty judgments. If we wait a while, we may even find that the bad things will go away."

Experience shows that with real crises, slow responses make things worse. At best, you look as if you are insensitive to the problems that are arising. In fact, your initial denials that there is a problem make you appear dishonest. At worst, you lose the initiative in dealing with the crisis and are put into a reactive posture. Ultimately, circumstances control you rather than you controlling them.

To say that you should respond quickly is not to suggest that you should roll out a fully developed plan of action. Clearly, you do not have enough time to put together a well-conceived plan at this point. However, you should be prepared to make a statement that demonstrates that you take the crisis seriously and are pursuing a course of action to resolve it. The statement, "There is no problem," will invariably get you in trouble. The statement "There may be a problem, and if there is, we plan to deal with it rigorously," is more credible and enables you to maintain the initiative in handling the crisis.

• *Be honest, and get your facts straight.* When post mortems are conducted on mishandled crises, one of the most common mistakes surfaced is that the people handling the crisis did not provide honest information early in the life of the crisis. Then as the crisis pursues its inescapable course, the misstatements stand out and the organization suffering the crisis appears dishonest and incompetent. Most times, the misleading statements are not made in a attempt to lie to the public. Rather, they reflect wishful thinking. However, when their falsity becomes manifest, the misstatements become lies in the mind of the public.

Balance Short-Term Demands Against Long-Term Needs

One of the smartest things the crisis managers of Auckland's Company X did was to resist the temptation to come up with quick fixes, which would not be viable in the long run. They recognized that one day, the crisis would pass and they would have to live with decisions made in the heat of the moment. They needed to make sure that the cure did not become more dangerous than the disease.

The advice to be temperate in solving the problem can come into conflict with the earlier offered guidance to respond quickly. On the one hand, the emerging crisis demands action. On the other, after the crisis is over, you may regret the actions you have taken. There is no correct answer to the question: Which of the two approaches should take precedence when they are in conflict? Clearly, when deciding what to do, you must balance the need for short-term action against the realities of long-term consequences.

Establish and Then Follow
Solid Guiding Principles

Because risk events seldom proceed as predicted, it is hard to develop response plans that are perfectly relevant to real events. The plan might say, "In the event of an emergency, contact all the members of the emergency response team, and bring them together at the emergency response center." But what if a total power failure, as experienced in Auckland, knocks out telephone communication? Or what if a fourth of the team members' telephone numbers listed in the telephone directory are no longer valid? Or what if the emergency response center is located in a facility that has been destroyed or damaged by the disaster event, which renders it inoperable and greatly complicates efforts to handle the disaster?

Responding to a risk event requires flexibility. When you are improvising a response, it is important that your actions are not arbitrary, because an ill-conceived response may create more problems than it solves. That's why appropriate improvisation should be based on knowledge, experience, and good judgment. In view of the discussion of Johnson & Johnson's effective response to the Tylenol tragedy, we will add another item to this list: follow solid guiding principles that define how the organization should function during an emergency. At Johnson & Johnson, one guiding principle was clear: in the event of an emergency, people come first, then profits. At Auckland's Company X, Tony F. followed a guiding principle that he learned in a telecommunications class: when a telecommunication system crashes, first get voice communications working; then turn to fixing data communication problems.

By establishing and following guiding principles, you don't need detailed instructions on how to deal with a crisis. Rather, you identify appropriate actions that are in harmony with your guiding principles.

The trick is to establish guiding principles that work. The test of whether a guiding principle is any good is whether it enables the organization to survive the crisis. Some guiding principles save you in the event of a jam, while others get you into deeper trouble. A good example of the latter was Union Carbide's overriding guiding principle, as captured in its mission and vision statements: management's first and foremost job is to strengthen the financial position of the company. In the case of Bhopal, this translated into profits coming before people—the opposite of Johnson & Johnson's perspective. What is interesting is that the Union Carbide view reflects what was taught in business schools from the post–World War II era through the 1980s. During this time, virtually all textbooks dealing with business management preached that the principal responsibility of a company's senior management team was to increase financial returns to the stockholder. In order to protect the stockholder, Union Carbide carried out policies that were later viewed as reprehensible. The irony is that these policies so damaged Union Carbide's reputation that the company's long-term well-being was ruined.

Establish an Emergency Response Team

History is filled with stories of organizations that perished because they were not prepared to deal with unexpected crises. Life is risky business. Few individuals with means and good sense avoid paying for health and life insurance. By doing so, they know that in the event of illness or death, they or their heirs will be cared for.

As with individuals, organizations should consider insuring themselves against disasters. One way to do this would be to establish an emergency response team. The team should be fairly small, with representatives from key parts of the organization—for example, from the information technology, operations, marketing and sales, finance, and legal departments. As a group, they should identify in what ways the organization is vulnerable to crises. They should develop plans for dealing with different types of crises and establish guiding principles to provide decision makers with a rough map of what paths they should travel during trying times. They should meet regularly to discuss possible threats to the organization and to clarify and modify procedures that the organization can follow to handle crises. They should maintain a close relationship with the organization's communication department to establish an intelligent crisis communication plan.

Emergency response teams I have encountered take their duties seriously. Members are on twenty-four-hour call. They carry beepers or cellular phones so that they can be contacted in the event of an emergency. When members go on vacation, backup players are added to the team to assume the role of the missing members. To their chagrin, the backup team members find that they inherit the vacation takers' beepers or cell phones.

Organizations with emergency response teams are prepared to handle crises as soon as they arise. Without such teams, days may be lost in an attempt to organize a response to a crisis. Once an ad hoc crisis team is brought together after a crisis arises, it is likely that its members will need time to learn something about each other so that they can function effectively as a team. Meanwhile, more time is lost as the members of the newly assembled team try to discover what procedures the organization has in place to deal with emergencies.

In today's risky world, it is a good idea for most organizations—large or small, high tech or low tech, retail or government—to invest in an emergency response team. As with health and life insurance, its chief value is that it provides managers with a sense of comfort that in the event that an untoward event befalls their organization, they are prepared to deal with it.

CONCLUSION

Risk monitoring and control are where the rubber meets the road. Organizations can establish superlative risk identification, risk impact analysis, and risk response planning processes, but if they cannot actually handle risk events effectively once they begin experiencing bad things, then their overall risk management approach is worthless.

As this chapter makes clear, the gap between what you plan to deal with and what actually happens can be enormous. This fact should not be surprising, since when dealing with risks, you are dealing with unknowns. If you have good risk management processes in place, you can make educated guesses about what risk events you might encounter, and you can even establish steps to deal with them. However, you should recognize that your best guesses can be dramatically off the mark. The test of a good risk manager is that when reality differs from the expected scenario, he or she can improvise and deal with the surprises effectively.

CHAPTER TEN

Business Risk

—⁓⁓— I n the final analysis, business management is about managing risk, because in running a business, the business professional is operating in an environment filled with uncertainty. Every decision made—choosing a project, hiring an employee, investing in a new product, upgrading operations—has risk implications that decision makers must take into account consciously. Will the chosen project be delivered on time and within budget? Will the new employee, who shined during the interviews, perform competently when on the job? Will anyone buy our new product once it is on the market? Will the benefits of the recently installed customer relationship management system offset its great expense? The point is that in the arena of business, nothing is certain.

PRINCIPAL COMPONENTS OF BUSINESS RISK

Simply put, business risk is the risk people face when they run a business. What distinguishes business risk from insurable risk is that it carries with it the opportunity for gain as well as loss. People launch and run businesses to make money. In general, if they enter into a safe business—for example, running an established convenience store— they are not likely to make great incomes, but neither are they likely to lose much. If they develop a technology breakthrough, they have a chance to make a fortune, as well as an opportunity to lose their life savings.

All decisions that businesspeople make are risky to some extent. For example, each time you hire new employees, you are taking a risk. There are no guarantees that you have made a good choice. What if the employee does not work out? What if he can't follow instructions and continually makes errors in doing his job? Hiring employees can be expensive. If ultimately they are fired after several unsatisfactory months, crucial work has not been done and you find yourself back at square one. As another example, advertising a new product in the newspaper can be expensive, and there are no guarantees that it will generate revenue. Will your $10,000 advertisement reach the customers you are targeting? What if the ad is buried in the back pages of the newspaper? What if it does not generate even one customer inquiry?

Business risk can be visualized in different ways. The approach taken here is captured in Figure 10.1, which shows business risk as

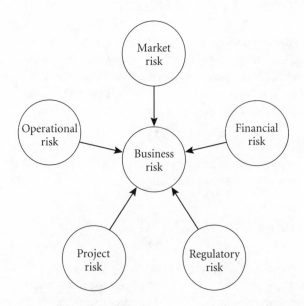

Figure 10.1. Principal Components of Business Risk.

comprising five components: market risk, financial risk, operational risk, project risk and regulatory risk.

Market Risk

All businesses that sell goods and services are concerned with market risk. Market risk is captured in the following basic question: When we put a product into the marketplace, will it sell? Clearly, this issue is of utmost concern to companies that introduce new products. The problem with new products is that they have no track record. We don't know whether customers will find them attractive. The more innovative the new product is, the greater the risk is that is associated with its introduction. What may seem like a surefire-can't-lose idea during a brainstorming session in the new product development shop may prove to be a dismal failure once it is released. But new products that succeed can be big moneymakers. If they are first to market, the company may be able to create a temporary monopoly and practice cream-skimming pricing strategies. One blockbuster may be all a company needs to establish itself as a major player.

Mature products face market risk as well. For example, once a product becomes commoditized—that is, it has become indistinguishable from products produced by competitors—its success in the marketplace is largely determined by price. As with pork bellies, the cheaper the price of the commodity (be it a desktop computer or a generic drug), the greater is the volume of its sales. The ability to reduce price is determined by operations, not by the marketing department. Can the company increase the efficiency of its operations, enabling it to lower production costs? If it can, then it can offer its products at a lower price and still be profitable.

Financial Risk

The finance department of any business is concerned with two big questions:

1. How much money are we spending?
2. How much money are we making?

If you want to stay in business, you should be making more money than you spend. Following up on this logic, it is clear that the principal financial risks that businesses face are spending too much money and not making enough income.

Cash outflows can be excessive for a variety of reasons. For example, if a company has poor financial control systems in place, it may be spending more money than it can afford to spend. One way to handle the risk of this happening is to establish tight financial controls. Or if an expensive piece of equipment breaks and needs to be replaced, this may cause a surge in cash outflow. This can be handled by implementing preventive maintenance procedures, to reduce the likelihood of equipment breakage, and establishing contingency reserves to cover the expenses of breakdowns when they occur. Other contributors to cash outflow problems include launching programs based on bad cost estimates, spending at Mercedes Benz levels when Hyundai-level spending is good enough, and dealing with discontinuities arising in the environment, such as radical changes in government regulations.

Cash inflows can be deficient for a number of reasons. For example, your product fails in the market, or you produce low-margin goods and services, or your accounts receivable efforts are weak so that you are not collecting the money owed you by your clients. These risks can be handled, respectively, by conducting effective market research studies, shifting production efforts to a mixed portfolio of low- and high-margin products, and strengthening your accounts receivable capabilities.

Often the financial risks that businesses face are rooted in the timing of cash outflows and inflows. That is, a company runs out of money before revenues cover expenses. Cash flow problems are the number one source of small business failure. Without access to cash, a company cannot meet payroll or pay vendors. Consequently, it has to shut down operations—often, just before the big payoff to its investment is realized.

Operational Risk

Operational risk arises as a consequence of carrying out basic business operations in an enterprise. That is, the very acts of using equipment, maintaining an order processing system, hiring new personnel, packing items to be shipped, and so forth create risk. If not maintained properly, the equipment may break down; if not properly tested, the order processing system may crash; if the hiring system is insensitive to promoting racial diversity, discrimination lawsuits might ensue; if there is an insufficient inventory of products, there may be no items to pack and ship.

Operational risk (covered in detail in Chapter Eleven) is typically handled by strengthening business processes. The goal is to implement procedures that lead to consistent results and that move the organization away from ad hoc management. The whole arena of quality management is oriented toward reducing operational risk and its consequences.

Project Risk

Murphy's Law is the governing law of project management. It states that if something can go wrong, it will go wrong. Because of the prevalence of Murphy's Law on projects, a significant component of project management is risk management.

The governing imperative of project management is to get the job done on time, within budget, and according to specifications, leading to customer satisfaction. Project risk management addresses the threat that the project won't get done, or that it may encounter schedule slippages, or that it may experience cost overruns, or that it may not achieve the defined specifications, or that it is rejected by customers.

As more and more business activity becomes project based, it becomes important that enterprises get a handle on project risk. Otherwise, they will find that the projects they launch will seldom achieve their objectives. (Project risk is handled in detail in Chapter Twelve.)

Regulatory Risk

All businesses are regulated. Most are regulated at the local, state or provincial, and national levels. They also can be regulated by professional bodies. For example, in the United States, good accounting practice is defined by the Financial Accounting Standards Board. The types of regulations that businesses face are overwhelming, ranging from rules governing occupational safety and health, to instructions prescribing the proper way to store hazardous substances, to requirements to report the details of business activity for tax collection purposes.

Interestingly, the principal risk of regulations is not the fact that regulations exist. Businesses recognize that a measure of regulation is necessary to provide an environment that allows business transactions to be carried out smoothly. Rather, the principal risk associated with regulations is sudden changes in the rules. You may find that basic procedures you carry out in your organization become illegal overnight with the stroke of a regulator's pen. Or you may discover that to garner the resources needed to comply with a change in regulations, you must divert them from uses that are crucial to your growth strategy. In the 1970s, DuPont Corporation was so concerned about the impact of government regulations on its business that it made Irving S. Shapiro, a lawyer, its CEO. This was the first time a nontechnical person was put in charge of the company. Shapiro's appointment reflected the fact that the most important challenges DuPont faced in the 1970s were not technical but rather regulatory—specifically, in the areas of antitrust and compliance with environmental regulations. Given this reality, it was more important to have a lawyer at the helm of the organization than an engineer.

Because regulations are compulsory, businesses find that responding to them must be a high priority. For example, if the tax authority changes the way taxes should be computed on mutual fund stock portfolios, financial firms must respond to the requirement quickly, or else they will be put out of business by the government.

RISK AND THE PRODUCT LIFE CYCLE

The job of a business is to produce goods and services that customers in the marketplace purchase. These products go through standard stages over their lives, called the product life cycle. A typical product life cycle is pictured in Figure 10.2. The life cycle is broken into four phases: investment, growth, maturity, and decline.

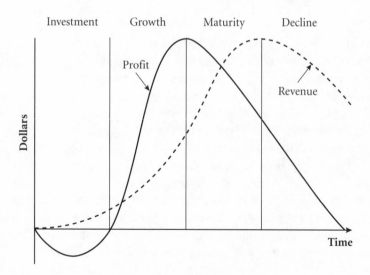

Figure 10.2. Product Life Cycle.

The risks a product encounters vary dramatically over its life. For example, risks encountered in the investment phase are quite different in content and impact from those encountered in the maturity phase. The effective management of a product over its life requires managers to be thoroughly familiar with the different kinds of risk encountered during the different life cycle phases. To see how this works, we will look at the life cycle for a hypothetical physical product from a risk perspective.

During the investment phase, where the future is a big unknown, overall risk is greatest for the product. Market risk is high, because you are not sure whether buyers will find the product attractive. Financial risk is high, because you know that you are incurring substantial costs, but it is not clear that revenues generated by the product will be sufficient to cover them. Technical risk may be high, particularly if you are engaged in a first-of-a-kind undertaking, because you are inexperienced in producing this type of product. Finally, operational risk will be high, because you have not yet begun producing the product on a large scale. It is a common experience to find that although a prototype might be easy to build, producing the product on a grand scale may be tricky.

During the growth phase, market risk diminishes as the product is accepted in the marketplace. Maintenance of market dominance may be solidified if the product is patented, because patent law prohibits others from making, using, or selling the product without the owner's permission. If growth occurs rapidly, this will strain the organization's capacity to produce enough units of the product to satisfy demand, so operational risk remains high. In its early years, AOL faced a situation where demand for its services grew faster than the company's ability to meet it, with the near-disastrous consequence that users experienced terrible e-mail and Internet access for a few months. In the early 1980s, IBM's inability to meet customer demands for its new personal computers enabled a brand-new company, Compaq, to go from zero dollars in sales to $1 billion in sales in its first year of operation. Technical risk diminishes at this stage, because the product is now developed and fully tested.

During the maturity phase, market risk may increase again, particularly if competitors figure out how to create competing products without infringing on the product's patent. Although the company may be in a good financial state because its revenues are high, competition puts pressure on profit margins. Consequently, the risk of not

184   MANAGING RISK IN ORGANIZATIONS

meeting profit objectives increases. One way to keep profits strong is to reduce production costs, so great strides are usually made in the operations area during the maturity phase, allowing the enterprise to produce the product cheaply. Mastery of the production effort results in a reduction of operational risk. At this point, technical risk is low, because the product is now mature and the technical challenges of dealing with something new are gone.

During the decline phase, the principal risk the company faces is that the cash cow is moribund. Sales of the product drop, often because it is growing obsolete or because competition is attracting customers to their products. Unless there are a host of other products in the product portfolio, the company will be dealing with a cash crunch. To forestall the death of a good product, many companies conduct research and development (R&D) activities earlier in the product life cycle with a hope of developing incremental innovations that will add zip to it, extending its appeal in the marketplace. As with any other investment, there is no guarantee that the additional R&D will pay off. However, without an attempt to extend the product's life, its imminent demise is certain.

Discussions of business risk have a certain abstract quality to them. A statement like "all business is risky" is too broad to provide insights into what business risk is really about. So is the following generic cure to dealing with business risk that I recently heard: "The best defense against business risk is good management. If you manage your affairs properly, then things tend to work out well." At a visceral level, I agree with this statement because well-managed organizations make fewer mistakes than poorly managed ones, and they are better prepared to deal with life's curve balls. However, the statement lacks sufficient substance to be useful.

The best way to gain an understanding of the origins and challenges of business risk is to look at stories of organizations that actually faced specific risky situations. In this section, we offer a number of thumbnail sketches describing a variety of real business risk situations. The examples presented are not comprehensive. However, taken together, they demonstrate some of the basic dimensions of business risk.

RISK IN REAL ESTATE INVESTMENTS

Timing can be an important determinant of risk. When the economy is doing well, it is relatively easy to launch new business ventures. But when the economy is down, even the best-conceived business initiatives struggle. Certainly, the timing of real estate investments can make the difference between creating fortunes or generating large losses.

In 1999, Excelsior Land Development Co. bought an office building that fronts the Potomac River on the Arlington, Virginia, side of the river. Excelsior paid $12 million for the structure. The site has an excellent view of the Potomac River and Washington, D.C. The office building, called Potomac View, was built in the 1960s. Although it was showing the signs of its age and required steady maintenance, it was still serviceable. In fact, it had maintained 90 percent occupancy for the ten years up to 1999. It had upscale tenants, including the Washington office of one of America's leading venture capital firms, the training arm of the U.S. Department of State, a leading jewelry retailer, and political lobbying groups.

Excelsior planned to raze the fourteen-story building and construct a thirty-story multiuse property called Capitol Star that would house a retailing operation, a hotel, business offices, and residential apartments. The cost of constructing this property was estimated to be $90 million. The project would be financed through a consortium of institutional and individual investors. Excelsior submitted a development plan to Arlington County, indicating that it would begin preparing the property for the new construction effort in nine months. Current tenants began moving out of Potomac View.

A few months after Excelsior purchased Potomac View, the stock market collapsed, and the economy began a slide into recession. As companies tightened their belts to weather the recession, they cut back on the office space they rented. Consequently, a glut of office space quickly developed in the Washington area. Plans for new construction efforts in the region were put on hold. Excelsior's management realized that this was not a good time to build its Capitol Star center. For one thing, they were unable to get the needed financing in these bad times. For another, forecasts suggested that the commercial real estate market in Washington would be soft for the foreseeable future.

As their leases ran out, more tenants abandoned Potomac View. Because Excelsior still hoped to move forward with Capitol Star at some point, it would not accept new leases and instead rented its space on a month-by-month basis. Occupancy in the building dropped to 40 percent eighteen months after Excelsior's purchase of the structure. Tenants who stayed negotiated reductions in their monthly payments. It was not clear when, if ever, the Capitol Star project would be resuscitated.

This case illustrates a common situation that arises in the real estate industry. When times are good, there are great fortunes to be made. Some of the world's richest denizens—in America, Europe, Hong Kong, and Korea—made their billions in real estate. However, when times are bad, fortunes can be lost as quickly as they were made. The biggest threat facing property owners is running out of cash, so that the hefty carrying charges associated with property ownership (such as maintenance costs, mortgage expenses, and tax levies) cannot be covered. During recessionary and uncertain times, occupancy levels and rental rates drop. Revenue generated by a property may be inadequate to cover carrying charges. If economic troubles persist over a protracted period of time, the investment in the property may experience financial hemorrhaging.

RISK IN NEW PRODUCT DEVELOPMENT

Whenever you introduce a new product, you are traveling down a risk-filled path. When deciding whether to finance a new product, you are at the earliest stage of the product life cycle and faced with limitless unknowns—for example:

- *Market risk:* Is there a market demand for our product? Will anybody buy it?

- *Technical risk:* Are we technically able to design and build working models of the new product?

- *Operational risk:* Will we be able to produce the product efficiently on a large scale?

- *Financial risk:* Will the new product be profitable?

- *Regulatory risk:* Will the new product be in compliance with government regulations?

An answer of no to any one of these questions anticipates product failure. In this section, we look at three well-known, high-risk new product introductions that initially seemed like winners but ultimately failed: DuPont's Corfam synthetic leather, Ford's Edsel automobile, and Coca-Cola's New Coke.

DuPont's Corfam Synthetic Leather

Consider the following unnerving fact: new product failure can occur even when you do everything right. A good example of this was DuPont's development of Corfam:

In the 1960s, there was a belief that world demand for leather would outstrip supplies, leading to leather shortages. So DuPont and other companies conducted research to develop synthetic leathers as a leather substitute. DuPont's Corfam product was the most ambitious attempt in this arena. Ultimately, Corfam failed miserably in the marketplace, making DuPont look as if its executives had flunked Business 101. How could such a rich, experienced, and powerful company produce such a loser as Corfam?

Actually, DuPont did its homework before committing itself to developing and producing Corfam. Before investing heavily in Corfam products (such as shoes), DuPont's market research group tested them extensively among consumers. They asked basic questions, such as, "Is this Corfam product attractive to you?" and "Would you buy it?" and received positive responses from customers. However, when the product was finally released, it was universally rejected by consumers.

I was one of a small number of Americans who actually bought a pair of Corfam shoes in 1968. When I saw them at the shoe department at Sears, I thought I was buying brown shoes. But when I stepped outside, they assumed a greenish cast. They were downright ugly. Furthermore, the synthetic leather did not breathe, so that wearing Corfam shoes was uncomfortable. When I reflect on the comments of members of DuPont's consumer focus groups who answered that they found Corfam products attractive, I can only surmise they lied.

DuPont's experience with Corfam shows that even after careful testing and preparation, there is no guarantee that a new product will be successful in the marketplace.

Ford's Edsel

When dealing with new products, a big question is, "How innovative should we be?" On the one hand, an innovative product that is well received and seen to be progressive can capture an entire market. On the other hand, a conservative buying public is limited in how much innovation it is willing to accept. Ford's introduction of the Edsel illustrates the dangers of not correctly gauging the innovation readiness of the market.

In 1956, Ford announced that it was introducing a new line of Ford automobile. The new car, to be named the Edsel (after Edsel Ford, chief executive at Ford Motor Corporation from 1919 until 1943), was intended to offer a radical change of design from traditional automobile offerings and also to employ new marketing strategies. It was a midpriced car, geared to attract a broad swath of the market. More than twenty editions were produced, ranging from basic lower-priced models to higher-priced sports versions. Five factories were dedicated to produce the car. First-year sales were projected to be greater than 200,000. Ford's senior managers were convinced they had a winner.

Production and sales began in early 1957. It became immediately apparent that the car was a flop. The short-term problem was that its radical design was considered ugly by the critics. As soon as it was released, it became the butt of jokes. People flocked to the showrooms, but they did not buy the car. Rather, they came to see this curiosity, much as if they were visiting a newly discovered space alien at the zoo. At the outset, Ford had to deal with bad publicity about the car. After all, who would buy a car that was widely viewed as a joke? Sales were so low that Ford discontinued production of the Edsel only three years after it was introduced. Business books rate the Edsel as one of the all-time great business fiascoes.

The Edsel's long-term problem was rooted in a failure of marketing. Two issues stand out here. First, American car buyers were enormously conservative in the 1950s. In choosing a car, you would likely buy the same brand of car your parents bought. So you had Ford families, Chevy families, Chrysler families, and so forth. Any new line of car would have to contend with the reality of strong buyer loyalty to a particular brand. To introduce a product that defied pigeonholing into a brand category was a dangerous proposition.

Second, the attempt to produce a car that was all things to all people was disastrous. With more than twenty editions of the Edsel, customers were confused about what was being sold. Why would customers purchase an expensive high-end sporty edition of the Edsel when their neighbors owned a low-end work horse?

The need for a right marketing focus was highlighted a few years later when Ford had one of its greatest product successes with the introduction of the Mustang. The source of the Mustang's success was that it was geared to a narrow segment of the market: young adults aged twenty to thirty. Its message was simple: the Mustang is a modestly priced car, with few options, geared toward pleasing the young and the young at heart. Interestingly, the decline of the Mustang began a few years later when Ford started offering several versions of it, increased its overall size, gave it the traits of a standard sedan, and tried to convert it into a luxury car. As soon as the Mustang lost its market focus, its popularity diminished.

When reviewing the history of the Edsel, it is tempting to ask, What kind of fools would launch a product that was doomed to failure? The response to this question is simple: the Edsel's corporate sponsors did not see the venture as doomed. All of their projections suggested that it was a bold new product that would capture the fancy of the public. This was, after all, the booming 1950s, the era of *Sputnik,* and the glorification of innovation and progress. They gambled, and they lost.

To learn from past risk events, it is important that you not fall into the trap of becoming an ex post facto prophet to whom the future is crystal clear—once it is past. The point is that the future is always unknown in some measure. If you are taking an action, such as introducing a new product into the marketplace, the more radical it is, the higher the risk you face and the greater the possibility of failure. The good news is that innovative, breakthrough ideas can be real moneymakers when they work out. The bad news is that you don't know whether *your* particular product will be the one that makes it big.

In the case of the Edsel, the true source of problems was not that its design was too strange for the public to accept. Look at the couture of the 1950s, and you see some of the strangest hats, veils, and crinoline-supported dresses imaginable. You develop a sense that the folks of the 1950s would buy just about anything, no matter how bizarre, if it were marketed properly.

The Edsel's failure was a marketing failure. Critics of the car took the initiative and made it a laughing stock in the press and comedy circuit. No one wants to be branded a fool for buying something that is publicly labeled as ridiculous. The Edsel marketing team clearly did not take the right steps to make purchase of an Edsel a prestigious act.

In addition, with more than twenty editions of the Edsel being marketed, customers did not know what they were buying. A starter car for the new buyer? A quirky high-range car for the adventuresome buyer? Something else? It appears that the Edsel marketing team made an error that is covered in introductory marketing courses: keep your product focused. Market it toward a defined segment of customers. Don't try to be all things to all people. In retrospect, the best risk management step the Edsel team could have taken was to follow the rules taught in introductory marketing courses.

New Coke

One approach to managing risk is to do your homework. In the case of new product introductions, you need to talk to your customers and get to know them well. Unfortunately, even when extensive market research is carried out, there are no guarantees that the fact-based business decisions you make are the right ones. This reality is illustrated in the case of New Coke's introduction.

At the outset of the 1970s, Coca-Cola had four times as many people drink its cola product exclusively as its archrival, Pepsi Cola (18 percent for Coke versus 4 percent for Pepsi). A decade later, Pepsi had drawn nearly equal to Coke in sales despite the fact the Coke greatly outspent Pepsi in advertising its product (in the early 1980s, 12 percent of beverage consumers drank Coke exclusively versus 11 percent for Pepsi). Market researchers at Coke carried out a number of studies to determine why Pepsi was successful in closing the gap. Their research focused on the taste of Pepsi versus Coke. They determined that Pepsi was sweeter than Coca-Cola. They then conducted a massive experiment involving fifty thousand subjects in ten geographical regions. Subjects were asked to sample a number of beverages without knowing what product they were tasting (this is called a blind taste test). Subjects of the experiment consistently favored a sweetened version of Coca-Cola over Pepsi. Interviews with a sample of Pepsi drinkers suggested that a portion of them would switch from Pepsi to a sweeter version of Coke.

Senior management at Coca-Cola Company decided it was time to revamp the Coke formula to reflect the tastes of modern consumers. After all, the formula had been around since the beginning of the twentieth century, and it was time for a change. In 1985, New Coke was introduced into the market, and Coca-Cola headquarters announced that the old Coke was being withdrawn. There was a near instant outburst of outrage among the public. Coca-Cola was seen as an American icon, and its abrupt dismissal by corporate bean counters was viewed as disgraceful. New Coke was soundly rejected in the market, forcing the Coca-Cola Company to resurrect the old Coke under the name Classic Coke. Interestingly, after the dust settled from the public relations debacle, Classic Coke sales increased substantially toward the end of the 1980s, once again making it the dominant product in the cola market. Although New Coke was an obvious failure, it is not clear that its introduction harmed the Coca-Cola Company in the long run, since it refocused public attention on Coca-Cola's role as cultural icon and resulted in increased sales.

Risk managers can take away at least two lessons from the New Coke episode. First, when you want to determine the risk consequences of an action, make sure you are addressing the right issues. The market researchers at Coca-Cola were convinced that sales of Coke were diminishing because their product was not sweet enough to satisfy the contemporary palate. All the scientific market research tests they conducted supported the hypothesis that consumers preferred a sweeter soft drink to what Coca-Cola offered. They naturally concluded that they needed to make Coca-Cola sweeter to boost sales. Unfortunately, they did not realize that soft drink consumers were really buying a brand. It turns out that the image of a soft drink product is more important than its taste. Old Coke was a venerable brand; New Coke was an alien introduction rejected by consumers.

A second lesson is that the scientific investigations you carry out in your risk analyses must be tempered by good sense. I am sure that the market researchers at Coca-Cola were stunned by the immediacy and hostility of the public outcry against the introduction of New Coke. Every bit of evidence they garnered in their carefully conducted studies suggested that the public demanded a sweeter drink. Blind taste tests conducted on tens of thousands of subjects proved the point. The unremitting confirmation of this finding blinded them to other factors that contribute to buyer preferences. Within one or two days of New Coke's introduction, scores of commentators raised the question: "What's going on at Coke's Atlanta headquarters? How can they be so out of touch with their consumers? Why would they even consider retiring the venerable old Coke formula?" The consistency of the criticism directed at the actions of the Coca-Cola Company demonstrates that the decision makers in Atlanta were indeed out of touch with their consumers.

TECHNOLOGY RISK: COMPUTERIZING PATENT FILES

Dealing with state-of-the-art technologies provides its own special risk issues. When something has never before been developed, a whole range of issues arises: Is our technical solution feasible? Is it economical? How do I plan a development effort when I am not sure of what technologies will be available for incorporation? These are just some of the questions facing the U.S. Patent and Trademark Office when it decided to upgrade its document storage capabilities using brand-new technology.

Until the mid-1980s, patent files in the U.S. Patent and Trademark Office (USPTO) were processed much the same way as they were handled in the late eighteenth century, when Thomas Jefferson served as America's first patent administrator. The patent documents handled by USPTO patent examiners were all paper based. When examiners wanted to examine the contents of a patent, they needed to get hold of a paper copy of the patent. By the mid-1980s, the USPTO had search files of more than 25 million patents, all printed on paper.

In 1983, the USPTO was ready to automate. After a competitive bidding process, it awarded a $289 million, eighteen-year cost plus fixed fee (CPFF) contract to Planning Research Corporation (PRC). PRC proposed to develop a state-of-art data storage system, where patent text and images would be stored on optical disks and indexed by two large mainframe computers. Patent examiners could retrieve patent data at workstations equipped with high-resolution screens.

From the outset of the contract, things went badly. Almost immediately, when work had just begun, the USPTO asked PRC to stop work and carry out an extensive review and evaluation of the system it had proposed. This action added a year to the development effort. Another problem was that at this time, optical storage technology was in its infancy, so there were many technical uncertainties that the PRC project team had to contend with. These problems were compounded by a government requirement that all procurement of supplies, equipment, and subcontractor services be conducted competitively. This made it impossible for PRC to create a reasonable estimate of the cost of developing the system because PRC was not sure what technology would be available to incorporate into the system one or two years down the line and what price vendors would charge to supply the undefined technology.

By 1988, the development effort was in serious trouble. It was estimated that cost overruns on the $289 million project would reach $159 million. Furthermore, no key milestones had been reached, and it was not clear when the USPTO would find itself in possession of a usable system. The contract had caught the attention of the congressional watchdog agency, the General Accounting Office (GAO), as well as the

House Government Operations Committee. These two players strongly criticized how the contract was structured, pointing out that with an eighteen-year CPFF contract, PRC had no incentive to save money. Ultimately, PRC was willing to renegotiate the terms of the contract, agreeing to break the contract into shorter segments and accepting a cost plus incentive fee contract structure (with incentive fees, it would make bonuses only if it performed as planned or better than planned).

PRC's experience with the patent automation project is fairly typical of advanced technology projects that have not been carefully thought through. For example, contracting experts would agree that the USPTO's acceptance of an eighteen-year CPFF contract was a high-risk decision that actually increased the likelihood of poor performance. The cost-plus aspect of the contract meant that PRC would be reimbursed for whatever costs it incurred, so it had no incentive to save money. The fixed fee aspect meant that PRC would be paid a fixed profit (negotiated to be $13.6 million for the life of the contract) regardless of whether the project achieved its cost, schedule, and performance goals. Again, the contract offered no incentive to perform well. The eighteen-year term of the contract meant that the USPTO was stuck with PRC as the prime mover on the automation project for a very long time.

Procurement experts with substantial experience in issuing contracts for acquiring advanced technology goods and services would never enter into a contract like this. To lessen risk, they routinely break large contracts into smaller pieces. For example, they could issue a one- or two-year contract to design a patent automation system. Because advanced technology design projects like this are highly speculative and immersed in unknowns, it is legitimate to structure the contract as a CPFF contract. Once the design work is done, they could then issue a one-year stage two contract to demonstrate the viability of the design. This second contract should be awarded competitively, which means that the contractor who carried out the design work will not necessarily win the award to demonstrate the viability of the design. The second contract could be structured as a cost plus incentive fee contract, meaning that the contractor would be given bonus incentives to do a good job. A stage three implementation contract could then be awarded competitively. This contract would have a contractor actually build the patent automation system. Incentives could be written into the contract that provide the contractor with bonuses when it delivers deliverables on time, within budget, and according to specifications. Finally, the experienced experts would award the maintenance contract separately from the development work.

When dealing with advanced technology, you often encounter substantial risk because you are traveling down unblazed trails. However, as this case makes clear, you can still manage the development effort to reduce the level of risk you encounter.

The patent automation case also illustrates regulatory risk. One of the constraints facing PRC was that it was required to acquire goods and services competitively because it was working on a government contract. That means that if it wanted to buy equipment or supplies, it needed to get at least two vendors to submit cost proposals and select the cheaper offering. The intent of this requirement is good: contractors working on cost-reimbursable contracts should take steps to keep costs low. When dealing with routine projects, the requirement that goods and services be purchased through competitive means is not very burdensome administratively and will likely lead to cost savings.

However, the consequences of this regulation for contracts dealing with new technology may slow work and drive costs up. When technology is just emerging, there usually is no clearly defined standard of technical performance, so comparing the costs of goods and services across vendors is often meaningless. Furthermore, implementing competitive procurement procedures will slow progress on work efforts (requests for proposals must be generated, bids must be reviewed, disputes must be resolved) and drive up costs, with no assurance that cost savings will ultimately be realized.

RISK MANAGEMENT IN FINANCE

In business schools, finance majors devote a substantial amount of their studies to examining the role of risk in financial decision making. They are taught, for example, that when the debt-equity ratio for a firm is above a threshold level or when net working capital is low, the firm is operating under seriously risky conditions. When investing in common stocks, they recognize that stocks with volatile prices are riskier investments than those with stable prices. They acknowledge that for most companies, the largest component of the cost of capital the firm faces reflects risk. They know that in creating an investment portfolio, you should focus on the overall risk to the portfolio rather than the risks associated with individual investments.

This section examines two important risk concepts that finance majors learn: assessing the riskiness of a firm's common stock by examining the stock's beta value and computing the risk component of cost of capital estimates. The treatment of these topics is intentionally cursory. The objective here is simply to provide a sample of the kinds of risk issues and risk reasoning that financial experts contend with routinely.

Assessing the Volatility of Common Stock Prices with Beta

In finance, an important measure of risk is the variability of a stock's price. As noted in Chapter Four, a commonly used measure of variability is standard deviation. If a stock's price experiences no variability— for example, if its price remains exactly $11.20 a share each day over a one-year period—standard deviation is zero. If the price is something like $11.20 ± 2.00, where the $2.00 is the computed standard deviation, then investment in the stock is low to moderately risky. If the price is something like $11.20 ± $7.00, then investment in the stock is quite risky. You have an opportunity for tremendous gain, but also a corresponding chance of major loss.

By itself, the standard deviation of a stock's price provides a sense of how much the price is likely to fluctuate over a period of time. An obvious question at this point is: "Okay, so I know the standard deviation of a stock's price. But is the variation in price greater than, less than, or equal to variations of other stocks in its industry?" To address this question, financial analysts employ a measure called beta, which looks at the volatility of a stock's price and compares it with the overall volatility of the whole portfolio of stocks of companies working in the industry. Technically,

$$\text{Beta} = \text{Covariance}(X, M)/\text{Variance}(M)$$

where covariance (X,M) is a measure of how much the price of common stock X varies in relation to variations of the price of other common stocks in industry M's portfolio, and variance (M) is a measure of the overall variability of the price of common stocks in industry M's portfolio. Thus, a beta of 1.6 tells you that the price of common stock X is 60 percent more volatile than for the overall industry. A beta near 1.0 tells you that the stock price has average variability, while a beta of 0.7 tells you that the price of common stock X is 30 percent less variable than for the portfolio of common stocks in industry M. Thus, stocks with beta greater than 1.0 are higher-risk common stocks, those with beta equal to 1.0 are average-risk common stocks, and those with beta less than 1.0 are lower-risk common stocks.

Assessing the Risk Component of the Cost of Capital

If a company wants to come up with a measure of risk associated with its overall financial performance, this measure can be estimated with the following formula:

$$\text{Risk} = \text{Beta} \times (k_m - r_f),$$

where k_m is the return of an average stock in the industry, r_f is a risk-free rate of return, usually measured as the rate of return of U.S. treasury bills, and as we have just seen, beta is a measure of the volatility of a company's common stock price. Knowledge of the risk-free option is important in assessing financial risk, because it identifies a guaranteed rate of return on an investment. Treasury bills constitute the risk-free option because the U.S. government has never defaulted on interest payments on treasury bills. If the treasury bill rate is 2.5 percent, you are guaranteed to receive a 2.5 percent return on your investment. Thus, the gap between k_m and r_f is a measure of risk associated with the performance of an average company in an industry. If the return of an average stock in your industry is 5.5 percent and the treasury bill rate is 2.5 percent, then the gap between k_m and r_f is 3.0 percent.

Furthermore, if within that industry, your company has a beta of 1.6, then by multiplying the 3.0 percent figure by your particular beta value, you obtain a measure of risk associated with your company's efforts: $1.6 \times 3.0\% = 4.8\%$. This value is the risk premium you need to address when trying to compute your cost of capital, where cost of capital is a measure of the rate of return you should expect to encounter in your investments based on your risk profile. Your cost of capital, then, is:

$$\text{Cost of capital} = r_f + \text{beta} \times (k_m - r_f).$$

This formula tells you that your required rate of return when investing in a new business opportunity is the zero-risk option, plus the measure of risk associated with your business operations.

Using the data in our example:

Cost of capital = 2.5% + 1.6 (5.5% − 2.5%) = 7.3%.

This approach to computing cost of capital is called the *capital asset pricing method* (CAPM) and is taught in all basic finance courses. The resulting estimate of the cost of capital is used in conducting discounted cash flow analyses of different investment options the company can pursue.

Real Option Approach to Project Selection

Financial investors routinely buy options either to purchase or sell a stock by a certain date (referred to as *calls* and *puts,* respectively). Options provide investors with time to see how well a stock performs before committing their full resources to purchasing or selling it. For example, for a price of $5 a share, you may be able to buy a call option to purchase Globus stock at $60 a share by a given date. If Globus stock rises to $80 a share, you can exercise your option and pocket a respectable profit. If it does not rise sufficiently, you will elect not to exercise the option. Note that use of these options serves a risk management function. By purchasing an option, you are buying time to gain information on a stock's performance.

The options approach to investing in stock can be generalized to cover investments in physical assets as well. In this case, you are said to be dealing with *real* options. For example, managers at a chemical company can view investment in research and development (R&D) as a call option. By carrying out R&D, the managers can gain valuable information on what kind of production line they should build to produce and market the chemical that emerges from the R&D effort. Thus, they are in a better position to make a major decision on whether to build a new production line and what it should cost to lead to profitable results. By taking a real options perspective on making the R&D investment, they try to determine whether the "price" of the option (that is, the anticipated R&D expenses) is worthwhile in view of the added investment information it provides.

A numerical example helps to clarify how the real option approach can be used to manage the risk associated with selecting projects. Let's say that Globus Enterprises is thinking about expanding its capacity to manufacture the chassis used to house personal computers. The expansion would require building new production facilities. Before launching the expansion project, it would conduct a feasibility study estimated to cost $800,000. Preliminary thinking suggests that Globus should expand in one of three ways: conduct a major expansion at a cost of $6 million, a moderate expansion at a cost of $4 million, or a minor expansion at a cost of $2 million. Is there a market for the additional chassis? The marketing department sees two possible revenue scenarios: a high volume of sales of $6.5 million and a low volume of sales of $2.5 million. The alternatives facing Globus are pictured as a conventional decision tree in Figure 10.3.

CONVENTIONAL PROFITABILITY ANALYSIS. At this stage, the question Globus management is wrestling with is whether the financial prospects of the potential project are sufficiently good to justify investing $800,000 to conduct a feasibility study. They carry out a conventional financial analysis to see whether anticipated return on investment justifies spending $800,000 on a feasibility study. (For a review of the expected value analysis employed here, see Chapter Seven.)

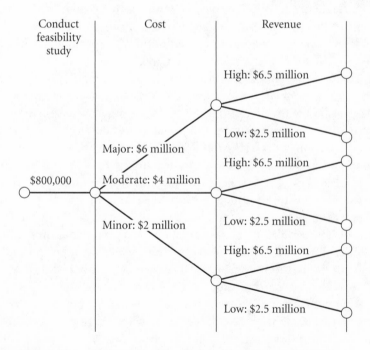

Figure 10.3. Decision Tree for Globus Plant Expansion Project.

Assuming that the high-revenue and low-revenue scenarios are equally probable (the probability of each event is 0.5), expected revenue is:

e(Revenue) = 0.5 × ($6.5 million) + 0.5 × ($2.5 million)
= $4.5 million.

Assuming that major, moderate, and minor expansion costs are equally probable (the probability of each event is 0.33), expected cost is:

e(Cost) = 0.33 × ($6 million) + 0.33 × ($4 million) +
0.33 × ($2 million)
= $4 million.

Consequently, expected profit is:

e(Profit) = e(Revenue) − e(Cost) = $4.5 million − $4.0 million
= $0.5 million.

Note that the expected profit of $0.5 million is less than the $800,000 cost for the feasibility study. This means that we will not be able to cover the expense of the feasibility study if we carry out the project. The decision should be not to spend money on the feasibility study and not to carry out the project.

REAL OPTION APPROACH. With the real option approach, we take a multistep approach to decision making, where during each step, we incorporate newly gained information into the decision analysis. In this example, we begin by estimating the profitability associated with each of the three investment scenarios. The results for scenario A, a major expansion, are:

e(Profit|Major expansion) = e(Revenue) − e(Cost|Major expansion)
= $4.5 million − 6.0 million = −$1.5 million.

These computations tell us that if we proceed with an attempt to engage in a major expansion of production capacity after we carry out the feasibility study, we will lose money. However, if we know that we will lose money, we will never carry out a major expansion because it does not make sense to go forward with a money losing proposition. Consequently, our expected profit is zero.

This is an important point and lies at the heart of the real option approach. What we have done is to use new information—in this case, knowledge that we will lose money by investing in a major expansion— to adjust our thinking about the future prospects of an investment.

The numbers for scenario B, a moderate expansion, are:

e(Profit|Moderate expansion) = e(Revenue) −e(Cost|Moderate expansion)
= \$4.5 million − \$4.0 million = \$0.5 million.

In this case, the numbers tell us that with moderate expansion of capacity, we expect to make a modest profit of \$500,000.

For scenario C, a minor expansion, the numbers are:

e(Profit|Minor expansion) = e(Revenue) −e(Cost|Minor expansion)
= \$4.5 million − \$2.0 million = \$2.5 million.

The highest level of profit, \$2.5 million, will be gained by undertaking a minor expansion of capacity.

Assuming the probability of encountering each of the three scenarios described above is equal (the probability being 0.33 in each case), the expected overall profitability is:

e(Profitability) = 0.33 × (\$0.0) + 0.33 × (\$0.5 million) +
0.33 × (\$2.5 million)
= \$1.0 million.

The expected profitability of \$1.0 million would more than cover the \$800,000 cost of the feasibility study.

The decision is to spend the \$800,000 on the feasibility study, and if the study shows that scenario A needs to be followed, don't pursue further investment; if scenario B emerges as the expansion prospect, invest in moderate expansion of capacity; and if scenario C plays out, invest in minor expansion of capacity.

Use of the real option approach need not stop here. Let's assume that Globus goes ahead with the feasibility study whose results lead its management to conclude that engineering and production requirements demand that they build the "moderate expansion" production facility. Meanwhile, the marketing department is carrying out a careful market research study to determine which of the two revenue scenarios is more likely to arise. A question that Globus managers must address is: Should the company immediately begin building the new facilities, or should it wait until it has better marketing information?

Using a conventional approach to computing profit:

e(Profit|Moderate expansion) = e(Revenue) – e(Cost|Moderate expansion)
= $4.5 million – $4.0 million = $0.5 million.

Using a real option approach, Globus takes into account the revenue prospects. They are, for scenario 1, high revenue:

e(Profit|Moderate expansion and high revenue)
= e(Revenue|High revenue) – e(Cost|Moderate expansion)
= $6.5 million – $4.0 million = $2.5 million.

In this case, Globus will realize a substantial profit, and it should certainly proceed with the investment.

For scenario 2, low revenue, the prospects are:

e(Profit|Moderate expansion and low revenue)
= e(Revenue|Low revenue) – e(Cost|Moderate expansion)
= $2.5 million – $4.0 million = –$1.5 million

In this case, Globus will lose money, and it should abandon the investment. Note that if Globus abandons the project, its expected profit is zero, *not* –$1.5 million.

Assuming the probability of realizing the high revenue and low revenue scenarios is equal (the probability is 0.5 in each instant), the expected overall profitability is:

e(Profit) = 0.5 × ($2.5 million) + 0.5 × ($0.0) = $1.25 million.

This computation of $1.25 million in expected profit is greater than the $0.5 million computed using the traditional approach to computing profitability. These results suggest that before proceeding to build the new production facilities, it is worthwhile to wait until the marketing study is complete in order to determine whether anticipated revenue will be substantial enough to justify building the plant.

OTHER CONSIDERATIONS. The example provided here clearly oversimplifies what happens in the real world. For instance, you should recognize that every number used when employing the real option approach is a guess. In our example, the costs associated with the three cost scenarios are guesses. The expected revenues generated in the marketplace are guesses. The probabilities of the different outcomes are guesses. Clearly, when applying the real option approach to an actual problem, you need to use the best estimates you can come up with so that you are working with good guesses.

Also, in our simplified example, there are two identical payoff scenarios for each investment situation. In the real world, you will encounter diverse payoff scenarios. In addition, in the example, probabilities are assumed to be the same across the three investment scenarios and across the two revenue scenarios. In the real world, the probabilities will differ.

Finally, in this example we have not dealt with an issue that is supremely important in the arena of financial options: timing. When investing in stocks, you have a clearly defined period of time in which to exercise an option. American options allow you to exercise it up to the close-out date, while European options allow you to exercise it on the close-out date. Your decision is governed by your knowledge of the value of the option, which is easy to obtain because stocks are continuously traded and have publicly listed purchase prices. If the stock price is high enough, you exercise the option; if not, you do not.

In contrast, real options are not traded in the marketplace, so their value is not easily determined. This has implications for timing decisions. In our example, we conclude that before investing in physically building a moderate-cost production line, we should wait until we have more information on market conditions (How many chassis do we think we can sell?). But it is not clear how long we should wait. Two months? Six months? A year? There is no definitive answer to this question given all the uncertainties.

It is unlikely that you can use the real option approach mechanically, where you plug various numbers into a formula and come up with clear guidance on what to do. The important thing to bear in mind is the rationale underlying the real option approach. That is, it promotes the making of phased decisions, where you embed new information you gain into your assessment of the costs and benefits of future courses of action. It provides a guide for decision making rather than definitive results.

CONCLUSION

Running a business is risky business. To appreciate this, you need only look at who the big business players were twenty years ago and then look at how they are faring today. Everyone knows that starting a new enterprise is risky and that only a small fraction of start-ups are still in business five years after they begin operations. But corporate behemoths also live risky lives. Not long ago, companies such as U.S. Steel and AT&T ranked at the top of the list of the biggest, most stable business players in the world. Now many of the giants no longer exist (U.S. Steel) or their impact has been reduced considerably (AT&T). The fact is that the business world is constantly changing. One year's sure thing is next year's joke.

All business management is risk management. Whenever business managers make decisions, they are operating in a world of uncertainty. Their decisions may be on target, making them look like business geniuses—or they may be wrong.

At no other time in the history of modern business was the gap between perceptions of brilliant decision making and reality more apparent than at the outset of the new millennium. In the last years of the twentieth century, the leaders of dot-com companies made pronouncements as if they were visionaries. They spoke with certainty about the dramatic changes in the terms of business that define the New Economy. They preached that stock prices of unprofitable companies were justifiably high because business reality had changed, and stocks were being valued according to their potential worth. But just a few months into the new millennium, it became clear that the pronouncements were a sham. The stock market lost more than $1 trillion of value over the next two years, indicating that the old values still predominated and that if you cannot make a profit, your business is not worth much.

The principal lesson of the dot-com experience is that the business fundamentals are always there. A company that does not understand its market, or that regularly spends more than it makes, or that has sloppy business processes in place, or that cannot plan and implement its projects effectively, or that is unprepared for regulatory surprises is a company foredoomed to fail. In this chapter, we have seen that business risk can be decomposed into market risk, financial risk, operational risk, project risk, and regulatory risk. For businesses to survive in a world of uncertainty, the risks associated with these five areas must be monitored and handled effectively. Otherwise, the businesses will face an abundance of grief.

CHAPTER ELEVEN

Operational Risks

Operational risk is the risk an organization experiences as it carries out its basic operations. Consider the following examples of operations-related problems organizations encounter:

- A compressor failure on a refrigerator leads to the spoilage of $1,300 worth of food at Michael's Delicatessen.

- A sales clerk at Rachel's Clothiers incorrectly tallies the price of blouses purchased by a customer, undercharging the customer $13.00.

- An airline pilot ignores an alarm that indicates the plane is dangerously close to ground, with the result that the aircraft slams into a mountainside, killing everyone on board.

- A loose belt on a grinding machine results in 827 defective widgets being produced before the problem is detected and corrected.

- When writing down the telephone number of a client, an account executive inadvertently transposes two digits in the number and is unable to reach the client for a follow-up call.

A review of the items in this list suggests that operational risk is different from other types of risk because it is not concerned with managing the unknown but is dealing with established processes. Consider the nature of the problems described above. A piece of equipment that has functioned reliably for years suddenly breaks down. An employee who routinely engages in sales transactions makes a computational error. An airplane pilot does not follow prescribed procedures when a warning alarm sounds.

Contrast these problems with problems that arise on projects. For example, you encounter a cost overrun on your project because the technical team underestimated the difficulty of doing a job when they made their original estimates of cost. Or a customer rejects the deliverable you provide her because she says that it does not meet her needs. Or you find that the requirements your project has been addressing change radically when a new customer arrives on the scene.

Project-related problems arise because projects are filled with uncertainty. The standard definition of project holds that it is a unique undertaking that is carried out in a fixed block of time, with a defined beginning and end (Project Management Institute, 2000). The fact that it is unique tells you that the past is an imperfect guide to the future. No matter how many times you have carried out a particular type of project, things may play out differently the next time. (More is said about project risk in Chapter Twelve.)

Or compare operational risk with market risk. The chief element of risk you encounter when releasing a new product is whether it will gain market acceptance. Through market research, you can reduce the risks associated with new product introductions by understanding the marketplace thoroughly, but even here, there is a chance that the market will reject your product, as experienced in the cases of Corfam and New Coke detailed in Chapter Ten.

Of all the types of risk you encounter in life, operational risk is the most manageable because it is not dealing with great unknowns. You are not speculating about future states of affairs as you are with most other types of risk. With operational risk, the principal risk you face is taking a misstep while implementing well-defined work efforts.

A little reflection reveals that one of the great areas of management success of the past hundred years, quality management, is about managing operational risk. At the end of this chapter, we examine the risk-quality link in detail and will see that well-established quality management tools, such as control charts, fishbone diagrams, and Pareto diagrams, are really tools designed to deal with operational risk.

SOURCES OF OPERATIONAL RISK

There are many ways that the processes you carry out when conducting your business operations can go wrong. Following are some of the more common sources of operational risk.

Lack of Well-Established Procedures

Consider the case of a newly established mail order company. At the outset, it has only one employee, its owner. She personally takes all orders for goods over the telephone. She writes them down on scrap paper, and during her free moments, she fulfills the orders. As business volume increases, she hires a number of people to register incoming orders and additional staff to fulfill them. She formalizes the order-taking process by creating a standard form for capturing customer requests and develops a process where the customer order is handled efficiently by a newly created order fulfillment department. As volume increases further, she develops formal procedures for monitoring inventory and restocking products when supplies get low. Two years later, when her company is processing $12 million in orders annually, she installs an e-commerce system that allows customers to order products over the Internet and to pay for them on-line with credit cards.

This case illustrates how businesses need to develop increasingly formal procedures as they grow and mature. In the beginning, it is okay to run operations in an ad hoc fashion because the number of transactions is too small to warrant complex procedures. However, as business volume increases and the business grows more complex, the establishment of formal procedures becomes increasingly important.

Businesses whose procedures lag behind their increasingly complex operations continually drop the ball when dealing with customers and suppliers. Orders written on a piece of scrap paper get misplaced. Inventory of hot products is quickly depleted, leading to stock-outs, while the inventory of white elephants mounts. Customers are shipped the wrong products. Some are overbilled, which makes them angry, while others are underbilled, which means the company loses money. At a certain point, the organization begins choking on its inefficiency and ineptness. Customers cannot tolerate its poor service, so they abandon it. Delays in collecting accounts receivable create cash flow problems. Corresponding delays in paying vendors causes some of them to stop working with the company. Ultimately, the company may go out of business simply because it did not develop adequate procedures to carry out its work.

Today, organizational competence is defined largely in terms of the effectiveness of the organization's procedures (Frame, 1999). For example, ISO 9000 certification is granted to organizations that demonstrate that they have processes in place that enable them to offer high-quality goods and services. Note that ISO 9000–quality audits do not examine goods and services per se, only the processes for developing them. The same holds true for CMM certification (Caputo, 1998). (CMM stands for the capability maturity model. It focuses on assessing the maturity level of information technology shops.) CMM audits attempt to determine whether IT shops have processes in place that reflect a growing maturity in producing and maintaining software.

Clearly, organizations wary of encountering problems in their operations need to tighten their procedures for doing business. This entails adding new procedures when needed, updating existing procedures, and discarding obsolete ones.

Poorly Trained Workforce

If you have employees who are not adequately trained, you will face operational snafus with predictable regularity. I recently had an experience at the supermarket that demonstrates this reality. The checkout clerk on the sole open line clearly did not know much about her job. When charging for romaine lettuce, she keyed in the code for Boston lettuce. When charging for avocados, she keyed in the code for Rome apples. She charged me for two six-packs of beer when there was only one. I purchased fifteen items; she made eight mistakes. As bad as these mischarges were, things became horrific when she tried to correct the errors. She began pushing buttons indiscriminately. The cash register locked up. Ultimately, the store manager needed to reset the cash register in order to straighten out all the mistakes. Meanwhile, the line of customers waiting to purchase groceries grew long and unhappy (as did I).

Poorly trained workers can make fatal mistakes. A review of the nuclear disaster at Chernobyl shows that employees at the site did all the wrong things in their attempts to handle the emerging crisis because they had not been trained adequately to deal with emergency situations

(Condon, 1998). Their missteps turned a bad situation into a nightmare. An examination of the Three Mile Island nuclear accident similarly finds that poorly trained personnel at the plant exacerbated a bad situation (Cole, 2002).

Everyone acknowledges the importance of training. Images of poorly trained computer operators running $10 million computers, poorly trained sergeants flying Black Hawk helicopters into battle, and poorly trained bookkeepers maintaining a company's accounting records are frightening. However, although people recognize the importance of having a well-trained staff, they balk at paying the price for competent training for their employees. There are a number of reasons for this:

- Training is viewed as an expensive overhead item: it does not often lead to immediate results that contribute to profitability.

- While employees are being trained, they are not working. Training usually disrupts ongoing operations.

- There is often a lag between the time when an individual undergoes training and then applies the new skills.

- The efficacy of training is not always obvious. Certainly, training employees on the proper use of equipment has evident payoffs; however, the benefits of soft skills training (for example, management training, effective communications training) is often not clear.

- With the high turnover of employees, it hardly seems worthwhile spending money to train them if they are likely to leave the organization in a matter of months.

When it comes time to determine whether to train their employees, managers must carry out a benefit-cost assessment. They should ask: What are the consequences of having an ill-trained workforce? Will their incompetence cost us customers? Will it lead to financial losses? Is it dangerous in a physical sense? The price of training employees should then be balanced against the cost of ineptness.

Incompetence

The incompetent person is one who is regularly unable to achieve reasonable goals that are part of his or her work. Examples include parking lot attendants who routinely damage cars they are parking; financial analysts who consistently proffer bad advice that causes their clients to lose their savings; the ship captain who misreads his compass when navigating his vessel; and the night watchman who sleeps on the job.

There are many sources of incompetence (Frame, 1999). Certainly, lack of proper training is one. If you are trying to drive a truck for the first time and have never had truck-driving lessons, you will do a bad job. The consequence of lack of training was discussed above. But there are plenty of cases where even well-trained people behave incompetently despite their training. So we must look for other sources of incompetence as well.

One obvious source is tied to natural ability. Not every school child is cut out to be an Albert Einstein, just as not everyone who aspires to play basketball is a Michael Jordan. I know that you could put me through ten years of piano lessons, and I still would not be able to play a piano competently.

In the world of work, the Peter Principle prevails: people tend to be promoted beyond their level of competence (Peter and Hull, 1969). Thus, they are put into positions where they behave incompetently. Peter preached that in time, every post tends to be occupied by an employee who is incompetent to carry out its duties. If this is so, then how does any work get done? Peter maintained that productive work is achieved by workers who have not yet reached their level of incompetence. Given enough time, even these workers will become incompetent.

Another source of incompetence is tied to attitude. For example, don't expect people who lack a good work ethic to work hard. Do expect people who do not believe in accountability to blame others for shortcomings when things go wrong. Watch out for impatient people who are always looking for shortcuts: their attempts to circumvent established processes often lead to disaster. I experienced this fact firsthand when I was a boy. One summer, I had a chance to tour a factory owned by my great uncle Tom. In this factory, workers cut, bent, and stamped sheet metal for the purpose of making metal lockers. I was most impressed by what I saw at the metal stamping workstations. They were powerful and noisy and instantly transformed sheet metal into such items as door handles and ventilation fittings. Uncle Tom pointed out that two of the men in this work area had lost several fingers. I asked "How?" He answered: "We have safety devices built into the stamping machines because these machines are dangerous. Some of the workers find it a nuisance to work with the safety devices, so they disable them. Those are the fellows who are missing fingers."

There are various steps managers can take to lessen risks associated with incompetence. For example, they can attempt to make sure their employees are well trained and educated in appropriate areas. Or they can carefully screen job applicants to identify and weed out incompetents.

Increasingly, businesses are dealing with the problem of incompetence by designing work processes that reduce the opportunity for employees to function incompetently. A major thrust of the business process reengineering (BPR) movement of the early 1990s was designing work processes that had fewer people physically handling fewer things (Hammer and Champy, 1993). For example, until recently, when customers placed orders in most companies, the customer identification number might be entered on the initial order form and then reentered into a number of additional forms. The BPR perspective holds that not only is it a waste of effort to enter the customer number separately onto different forms, but each time the identification number is keyed into the computer, there is a chance that it will be entered incorrectly. The BPR principle for addressing this situation is to design a process where the customer number needs to be entered only once.

The negative side of developing smart processes that reduce the possibility of employee error is that they contribute to the dumbing down of work. To the extent that most significant decisions are handled by systems, this leaves little challenging work for employees to carry out. During the heyday of the dot-com companies, articles appeared about the discontent of workers in places like Amazon.com, where only the best applicants were hired and then were given mindless work (Leibovich, 1999). Clearly, a major challenge associated with introducing smart processes is to figure out how to employ them productively to reduce operational risk, while at the same time to develop an environment that encourages innovation and boosts employee morale.

Inattention

A major contributor to operational risk is what I here call *inattention:* the loss of focus that arises when someone is carrying out a task. Because of the loss of focus, mistakes are made. Three sources of inattention are identified here: fatigue, distraction, and tedium.

FATIGUE. Many experiments have shown that people who are asked to carry out tasks when they are tired often make mistakes because they have difficulty concentrating on their chores. Recent studies suggest that on-the-job fatigue is growing in the United States and other industrialized countries. They attribute it to the downsizing of organizations, which commonly results in workers' having more work to do than previously. As they work longer hours on the job, there will be an increase in operational errors induced by fatigue. The best way to treat this risk factor is to cut back on overtime assignments and have employees work a regular work week.

DISTRACTION. On April 6, 2001, Reuters reported that a Vietnamese truck driver veered his truck into a bicycle and motorbike, killing three people, because he noticed a snake slithering around inside the cab of his truck. Vietnam is home to some deadly snakes, so the truck driver's concern is understandable. Nonetheless, the distraction caused by the snake led him to ignore the job he was carrying out—that is, driving a truck—and as a consequence, three people died needlessly ("Killer Crash," 2001).

In the United States, cellular phones have proved to be more deadly sources of driver distraction than snakes. So many accidents have been tied to the use of cellular phones by drivers that a number of states have made it illegal for drivers to use them while operating their vehicles.

There are plenty of opportunities for distraction in today's world. Many office workers, for example, have a radio playing quietly in the background as they work. The degree to which this helps calm them and contributes to their productivity or distracts them from the job is a matter of dispute. Clearly, if the radio is playing too loudly, it distracts surrounding employees who are trying to do their jobs.

TEDIUM. Uninteresting, repetitive work is tedious. When work becomes tedious, people's minds drift and they make mistakes. In today's world of airport security, one of the greatest challenges facing security managers is to keep security personnel alert in an environment where the work is terribly tedious. A characteristic of most operational activities is that they are repetitive. The men and women who work in call centers handle scores of calls each day. Those who work on an assembly line carry out the same steps over and over when they produce their widgets. Traders on stock exchanges, who spend whole days making buy and sell orders, must guard against becoming numbed by their efforts.

There is no easy fix for the problem of handling tedium. Employers should do their best to keep jobs interesting, a daunting task when work is inherently repetitive. Frequent job rotation works in some environments. For example, on assembly lines, workers can work a few days at one workstation, then switch to another for several more days, then switch again, and so forth. Another way of handling tedium on the job is to hire people who can deal with it. Some people take comfort in stable, repetitive processes, and these folks are likely to do better with tedious work than people who demand frequent new challenges.

Poorly Maintained or Obsolete Equipment and Software

The equipment and software you employ in your operations can make you or break you. Two sources of problems stand out: (1) your equipment and software are poorly maintained, and (2) they are out of date.

The term *maintenance* refers to a series of activities that are carried out on equipment and software to keep them functioning properly. One type of maintenance is *preventive maintenance.* For example, when you replace the oil in your automobile's engine every three thousand miles, you are engaging in preventive maintenance. Studies show that the using clean oil in car engines extends their lives indefinitely. Fouled oil, in contrast, creates wear and tear that causes engines to break down prematurely. Consequently, a little investment in fresh motor oil saves the hassle and expense of breakdowns. What holds true for cars applies to other equipment and software as well. To quote the old adage, an ounce of prevention is worth a pound of cure.

Another type of maintenance is *repairs,* called *debugging* in the software arena. Even well-maintained equipment can malfunction from time to time. Similarly, complex software code inevitably has bugs that need to be fixed. When equipment or software fails, you need to be able to repair it. If you organize your efforts to fix problems quickly, you can reduce the pain of breakdowns dramatically.

A third type of maintenance is *improvements,* called *enhancements* in the software arena. Rapid technological change forces both hardware and software products to undergo continual evolutionary modification. It is not unusual to find that one month after you have a piece of equipment installed in your facility, a maintenance technician arrives with a new component to upgrade it. With software, upgrades are commonplace; you may find that the version 2.1 software package you bought in January has been upgraded twice to stand as version 2.3 by October.

Expense and inertia are two enemies of effective maintenance. First, effective maintenance can be expensive. Studies of both hardware and software systems suggest that maintenance costs can far exceed purchase price. In the software arena, for example, maintenance can easily constitute 60 to 80 percent of the life cycle cost of a system. When you have just bought a piece of equipment or software for $60,000, you don't want to hear that it will cost you $200,000 to maintain it over the next three years.

Today, when buyers price equipment and software, it is smart policy to ask for a quotation of life cycle costs. Life cycle costs include maintenance costs beyond the initial purchase price of the product. Be prepared to suffer sticker shock when you hear the cost quotation. Maintenance is not cheap. However, by learning what maintenance costs are, no matter how painful the revelation may be, you develop a realistic sense of what it will cost you to employ the product effectively.

A second enemy of effective maintenance is inertia. A few years ago, I learned that the son of a friend of mine had just bought an expensive car. "Your son's going to have a lot of fun with that car," I told my friend. He looked at me glumly and replied, "Sad to say, my son is not a maintenance guy. That car will be on the scrap heap by the end of the year."

Many of us, perhaps the majority, are not "maintenance guys." Effective maintenance requires substantial discipline. You need to be willing and able to dedicate time, money, and energy to prevent things from breaking, and when they finally do break, you spend additional time, money, and energy to repair them.

The key point is that your equipment and software need to be maintained properly if you want your operations to proceed smoothly.

REDUCING OPERATIONAL RISK

Unlike insurable risk, project risk, or most forms of business risk, operational risk is not focused on great uncertainties. You are not speculating on the likelihood that your house will be inundated by a flood, or that you underestimated the cost of doing a job, or that your new product will be rejected by consumers. Rather, you are dealing with glitches that arise when implementing established processes. The types of problems that transpire and their consequences are well known: tired workers make mistakes, old equipment breaks down, and uninformed staff make bad decisions.

As we have seen, anticipating and handling some of these problems can be accomplished readily, while dealing with others cannot. In managing operational risk, you should focus on those things you can control (Lebell, 1995).

Case Study: Murphy's Law at Travel-Rite

This case study, taken from an actual incident, nicely illustrates the basic nature of operational risk. It shows that operational risk is fundamentally tied to how procedures are carried out. As you read the case, ask yourself: What are the root causes of the problems being illustrated? Also, think about lessons that can be learned from the incident and what steps need to be taken to capture them.

> Mike Jones had worked at Travel-Rite as a bus driver for five years. He enjoyed the job. In turn, Travel-Rite was pleased with Mike, because he was courteous with clients and had a flawless safety record.
>
> Mike was driving twenty-five tourists from Washington, D.C., to New York City on Interstate 95. He noticed that his fuel gauge showed that his twenty-nine-passenger minibus was getting low on fuel, so he pulled into a gas station along the highway. At the fuel pump, he told the station attendant to fill up the fuel tank. Ten minutes later, the tank was filled, and Mike pulled out of the gas station. The bus traveled about twenty-five meters, and then the engine died. Mike tried in vain to restart the engine.
>
> It turned out that the gas station attendant had accidentally filled the fuel tank with gasoline instead of diesel fuel, which was what the bus required. The only way to deal with this would be to drain the gasoline out of the fuel tank and remove all traces of gasoline in the engine. The gas station lacked this capability, so the gas station manager arranged to have the minibus towed to a nearby garage. Meanwhile, Mike telephoned Travel-Rite's headquarters to tell them of his predicament. The headquarters staff arranged to have the tourists picked up by a bus service operating out of New York City. Two hours after the bus breakdown, the tourists resumed their journey.

The minibus was towed to the garage, where mechanics attempted to determine whether the engine had been damaged by the gasoline. The chief mechanic telephoned Travel-Rite headquarters to deliver his report and was put in touch with Jennifer Chen, Travel-Rite's president.

"There's no problem cleaning up the engine," he reported. "In fact, we've already got it working. However, you appear to have a problem with your transmission, because the bus won't go into second gear. We looked at the transmission and saw that it's damaged."

Jennifer was shocked to hear this and immediately telephoned the automobile dealer from whom she bought the buses. When he heard the story, he understood the nature of the problem.

"The transmission was damaged when the bus was being towed," he said. "The drive trains of buses are a bit complicated. You can't just hook them up to a tow truck and start towing them. Several steps have to be taken to prepare them for towing, and obviously the tow truck driver didn't do this."

Jennifer felt sick. What began as a routine refueling had turned into a disaster. Clients had been inconvenienced. Her new bus had been damaged. All this was happening far from headquarters, so resolution of the dispute with the gas station, tow truck company, and garage would have to be carried out remotely.

A nice thing about operations from a management perspective is that they are process driven and largely repetitive. Consequently, they lend themselves agreeably to lessons learned. If you learn that a step in the process works improperly, you can fix it, and this leads to marked improvement in the overall process.

So it is with Travel-Rite. Although the switch of gasoline for diesel fuel set off a chain of unfortunate events, in the final analysis, the problems highlighted weaknesses in the company's travel procedures that needed fixing. By reflecting on the causes of the problems and identifying solutions, Travel-Rite reworked its procedures and became a stronger organization.

A week after the incident, Jennifer held a lessons-learned brainstorming session with some of Travel-Rite's key employees: three drivers (including Mike Jones, driver of the ill-fated minibus), James Cohen (head of tour bus operations), and Ron Caspelli (head of vehicle maintenance). They discussed why problems arose and how processes should be changed to avoid such problems in the future. Following are some new procedures Travel-Rite adopted as a consequence of the meeting:

- All drivers will be offered a half-day training session on mechanical principles they should be aware of for the effective operation of Travel-Rite's vehicles. Among various topics included in the course, one addresses key issues associated with towing disabled buses.

- All buses will begin their trips with a full tank of fuel.

- Qualified mechanics on key routes employed by Travel-Rite buses were identified at roughly seventy-five-mile intervals along the routes. Drivers should contact the nearest approved mechanic in the event of a bus breakdown.

- Locks were placed on fuel caps. When fuel tanks needed refueling, the bus driver would have to open the fuel caps personally with a key.

The lessons-learned exercise showed that Travel-Rite's procedures were strong in one area: when the bus broke down, Travel-Rite's headquarters staff immediately contacted a New York–based bus company that was able to get a bus and driver to the site of the breakdown in two hours. Although it was regrettable that passengers had a two-hour wait, their wait would have been much longer in the absence of backup procedures.

Case Study: The Unthinkable Happens

This case shows that there are lessons to be learned from the experiences of others as well:

Jennifer Chen, president of Travel-Rite Tourist Company, was watching the local late-night news on television. She was feeling tired after a long day at the office. Suddenly, a news story jolted her awake. The news crew was at a highway accident scene reporting on a traffic mishap that had occurred earlier in the day. Apparently, a truck had run a fifteen-passenger van off the road. The smashed-up van could be seen in the background, surrounded by rescue personnel. The news team reported that three of the van's passengers had died at the scene, and four others had been rushed to the hospital and were in critical condition.

Jennifer recognized the van. It belonged to her chief competitor, Happy Tours. She immediately telephoned James Cohen, the head of Travel-Rite's tour bus operations, and asked him to find out what happened.

The next day, James reported that a large tractor trailer truck had been tailgating the van for several miles. The frightened van driver traveled faster to put some distance between the van and the truck, but the truck continued to hover one or two meters behind the van. Finally, the driver lost control over the van; the vehicle went off the side of the road and crashed. Five people were flung from the van. The three who had died had been sitting in the last row. Apparently, the van's back door popped open, and they spilled out. Police reported that the truck driver had a bad driving history and just five months earlier had been charged with reckless driving. James also learned that the van driver was not a regular Happy Tours employee, but a contract driver who was using his own van. Furthermore, it appeared that his automobile insurance had lapsed.

Jennifer asked James to review Travel-Rite's policies for running its van service to see whether there was anything her company could do to avoid her competitor's experience.

In his book *To Engineer Is Human* (1992), Henry Petroski reminds us that progress in engineering is often built on a foundation of tragedy. For example, the unexpected collapse of a structure causes investigations into the source of problems. Once the problems are identified and understood, engineering practice is adjusted to accommodate the new knowledge. Building codes are also changed, requiring that the new practices be adopted in future structures.

At Travel-Rite, James Cohen's investigation of the Happy Tours experience, coupled with his review of pertinent Travel-Rite procedures, caused Travel-Rite to adjust some of its procedures:

• Each year, all drivers, including contracted drivers, will go through a one-day safety course on dealing with the perils of driving.

• Contract drivers will regularly supply Travel-Rite with evidence that their vehicles are up to date on their inspections by state inspection centers, that the vehicles are fully insured according to Travel-Rite requirements, and that drivers are appropriately licensed to drive passenger buses.

• Travel-Rite will contact its bus dealer about the possibility that the back doors of its vans will pop open on impact. If this turns out to be a problem for Travel-Rite vans, then it will ask the bus dealer for guidance on remedying the problem.

THE OPERATIONAL RISK-QUALITY LINK

The mid-1980s through the mid-1990s experienced an explosive movement throughout the industrialized world to introduce quality management practices into all aspects of business operations. I think this movement can legitimately be called a revolution. Unfortunately, the word *revolution* is grossly overused and in recent years has described everything from changes in people's eating habits to new skateboard designs. But if you think about the meaning of *revolution,* you see that it is associated with "to revolve," that is, to turn around in a circular fashion. What happened in the 1980s and 1990s really turned businesses and governments around. The concept of quality changed radically from the traditional view that quality was something that gnomes in the manufacturing division's quality assurance department did to the realization that quality must stand at the heart of the enterprise.

The journey to revolution was a slow, pedestrian one. One of the first notable achievements in quality management occurred in the 1930s, when a Bell Laboratory engineer named Walter Shewhart invented statistical quality control. Shewhart noted that in manufacturing enterprises where thousands of articles are produced in a day, it does not make sense to inspect each item as it comes off the assembly line (Shewhart and Deming, 1990). The cost of individual inspection would be prohibitive, and defects would still slip through the screening. Rather, by taking small samples of manufactured articles at different points in the day and testing them for quality, you can determine statistically the state of all articles being produced.

Starting in the 1950s and stretching over three decades, the quality management effort began looking like a real discipline. A number of practitioners moved the quality discipline forward and dramatically contributed to reducing defects in manufacturing: W. Edward Deming's refinement of statistical quality control, his promotion of the Plan-Do-Check-Act cycle, and the statement of his Fourteen Points (Deming, 2000); Joseph M. Juran's quality trilogy, plus his recognition of the role of internal customers in defining quality (Juran and Gryna, 1991); Philip B. Crosby's promotion of the zero-defects concept, plus his belief that quality must focus on prevention of defects, not inspection (Crosby, 1979); Kaouru Ishikawa's invention of fishbone diagrams, his fostering of quality circles, and the articulation of his ideas on companywide quality control, a precursor to the Total

Quality Management (TQM) movement) (Ishikawa, 1990); and Yoshio Kondo's focus (1991) on improving quality by developing strong employees.

The efficacy of applying the new quality management concepts was demonstrated most noticeably in Japanese manufacturing companies. In the 1950s, the label "Made in Japan" was synonymous with shoddy workmanship. By the 1980s, it was the mark of quality. In retrospect, we can see that Japanese enterprises did many things right in the post–World War II era, but the single smartest thing they did was to place continuous quality improvement at the heart of their operations. Their products were so much better than those of their Western counterparts that major Western companies began wondering whether they would be able to survive the Japanese quality onslaught. If they were to survive, they had only one option to pursue: produce goods that were as good as, if not better than, Japanese goods. By the 1980s, almost everybody had been converted to the quality management religion.

I will end this brief history of the quality management movement by identifying two important developments of the 1980s. One was the emergence of TQM as an irresistible force. The other was the adoption of worldwide quality management standards under the auspices of ISO 9000.

TQM was an inevitable consequence of the great successes of the quality management effort in manufacturing. Consider that the Six Sigma standard that companies today aspire to achieve means that there is an average of 3.4 defects per 1 million items. Contrast this with defect rates a thousand times higher just a few decades ago. In a remarkably short period of time, we have experienced miraculous improvements in the production of goods on the assembly line.

It was not long before managers began asking: Why can't we achieve the same levels of quality success in our nonmanufacturing operations that we have achieved in our manufacturing operations? The *total* of Total Quality Management means that all aspects of an enterprise's operations should achieve high-quality standards. This includes the operations of the marketing and sales department, finance department, information technology department, and even legal department. TQM fever crested by the mid-1990s, when all major organizations implemented TQM programs to raise their level of quality performance corporatewide.

ISO 9000 has emerged as the world's de facto quality standard for assessing the quality achievements of business units in enterprises. Its focus is on determining whether the processes that organizations carry out promote conditions that lead to the production of high-quality goods and services.

The ISO 9000 definition of quality is important to understand. ISO 9000 maintains that quality is what customers perceive quality to be. This is a remarkable perspective. It means that quality is fundamentally subjective. This perspective stands in marked contrast to Philip Crosby's well-known position that quality is conformance to specifications (Crosby, 1979). Although Crosby's definition makes sense at first reading, a little reflection shows that it contains a fundamental flaw: Why do we want to conform to specifications if the specifications do not truly reflect customer needs and wants? Today, there is strong consensus in business and government enterprises that the ISO 9000 viewpoint is on target. That is, quality is primarily about satisfying customers.

The dramatic transformation of our views on quality management has been largely a revolution at the conceptual level. At this level, quality management has moved from a behind-the-scenes activity to center stage. By the 1990s, everyone was sold on the value of quality. Interestingly, the revolution at the operational level has been more subtle. What quality managers do at the operational level today is not much different from what they did in the postwar years. At that time, practitioners of quality control spent much of their energy looking for nonconformances to the specifications, or to phrase this same sentiment from a different perspective, they were looking for consistency of output. This continues to constitute a major portion of their jobs today.

In today's customer-focused world, we recognize that consistency is usually, though not always, a virtue. Customers strongly support the drive toward consistency. When they seek out quality products, they are willing to pay a premium to buy goods and services that perform exactly as advertised. At the supermarket, they will spend more to buy Excelsior brand cheese than the house brand because they know that it will have a good taste. How do they know this? Because they have been purchasing different brands of cheese for years and are convinced that Excelsior consistently delivers the finest cheeses.

What links operational risk and quality is their mutual concern about nonconformance. The central worry of practitioners in both areas is to avoid surprises. On an assembly line, bells sound (figuratively or literally) when products are produced that vary unacceptably from the specifications. Similarly, in the operational risk arena, alarms are raised when employees deviate from established procedures.

A little reflection shows that quality management is a subset of risk management. Risk management is concerned with reducing the likelihood of experiencing untoward events and, when they arise, lessening their deleterious consequences. In the subarea of operational risk, concern focuses on anticipating and dealing with breakdowns of the processes that keep things going. These are exactly the same issues that quality assurance addresses. Through quality control, problems are identified and then handled.

Recognition of the risk-quality link is good news for managers who are charged to cope with operational risks. What this means is that they have access to a wide array of tools, techniques, and perspectives that have evolved in the quality arena over the years. While all quality management techniques can be employed in managing operational risk, we look at only three here: quality control charts, flowcharts, and fishbone diagrams.

Quality Control Charts

Quality control (QC) charts are the principal tool that quality managers employ to identify nonconformance to specifications. They require regular monitoring of a production process, where samples of goods being produced are examined from time to time to see whether they conform to the specifications. For example, each day, a sample of items may be taken and examined in midmorning and then a second sample reviewed in midafternoon. The average performance of the samples is noted on the QC chart, and special notice is taken as to whether the reported deviation from the specifications lies within an acceptable range. If it does, the process is viewed to be okay. If it does not, the process must be examined to see whether there is a problem that needs fixing.

Figure 11.1 pictures a QC chart for the production of small bars used in micromotors. The specifications require that each bar be 9.4 mm long, ±.1 mm. Consequently, an upper control limit (UCL) of 9.5 mm and a lower control limit (LCL) of 9.3 mm establish the range of tolerable deviations in the lengths of bars that are produced. So long as the sampled bars lie within the LCL and UCL, the process is deemed to be in control. A sample that lies outside the LCL and UCL range is considered an outlier and possibly an indicator of a process that is not working properly. In this case, an examination of the process is triggered to see what the source of problems is, if any.

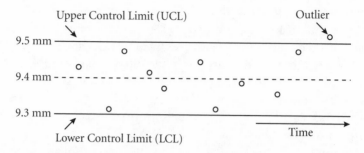

Figure 11.1. Quality Control Chart with a Random Pattern of Variance.

Figure 11.2 shows the power of QC charts to detect patterns of production that might reflect a problem in the process that would not normally be detected. It is inevitable that even processes under control experience some variation from the specifications. However, these variances should be distributed randomly. The variances in Figure 11.1 are more or less random. However, those in Figure 11.2 demonstrate a clear pattern. Although the variances lie within the LCL and UCL, there are nonrandom forces at work here, and they may indicate a problem in the process. Thus, when nonrandom variances are detected, they are treated as outliers. The process is then examined with a view to explaining the source of the observed pattern and fixing whatever is causing it.

The QC chart approach has many applications in risk management. For example, if you track the amount of time operators spend talking to clients at call centers, large variations from the average may indicate problems. One company found that one of its operators spent far less time on the line with customers than the average operator. They were pleased with her performance until they discovered that whenever she had clients on the telephone with foreign accents, she would hang up on them.

As another example, a motor pool examines the miles per gallon achieved for its automobiles after they have been gassed up to see if there is a sudden drop in performance. If a car has been regularly getting twenty-three miles per gallon and then suddenly experiences mileage rates of fifteen miles per gallon, this is a warning that things are not right. A major deviation from average performance may indicate that the car is in the early stages of malfunctioning, enabling technicians to make repairs before it breaks down outright.

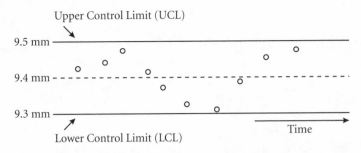

Figure 11.2. Quality Control Chart with
a Nonrandom Pattern of Variance.

The QC principle is routinely employed in project risk management in the form of budget variance charts. These charts, which look just like regular QC charts, track variances in budget expenditure month by month. The measure of variance is planned budget minus actual cost. If the gap between the two becomes too big, it will stand out in the variance chart and may indicate a problem with project performance.

Flowcharts

Quality managers routinely use flowcharts to identify potential quality problems in a process. They step through the flowchart, item by item, and ask themselves if a given item can create problems, for example, whether it can break or serve as a choke point, resulting in a bottleneck. Operational risk managers can employ flowcharts in exactly the same way. Figure 11.3 pictures an order fulfillment process for a small company. As the flowchart makes clear, when an item is ordered, a check is carried out to see whether it is in inventory. If it is, the order can be fulfilled immediately. If it is not, the order must wait for restocking before it can be fulfilled. If restocking has not occurred within two weeks, the order is cancelled. A review of the chart shows that the restocking process can serve as a potential problem area. If for whatever reason, the company consistently is unable to restock items within two weeks, it will lose a good deal of business. It may want to implement procedures preemptively to avoid restocking delays.

Fishbone Diagrams

Fishbone diagrams, also called cause-and-effect diagrams, were originally developed and promoted by Kaouru Ishikawa. Their function

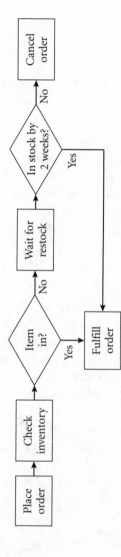

Figure 11.3. Flowchart for an Order Fulfillment Process.

is to identify some state of affairs (perhaps widget production delays) and then to examine the conditions that contribute to it. In manufacturing, fishbone diagram construction often revolves around the four M's: manpower, machines, materials, and methods. Figure 11.4 provides a segment of a fishbone diagram that addresses widget production delays. One source of delays is rooted in manpower problems. As the diagram indicates, workers have inadequate skills for the job. The low skills level, in turn, is caused by the fact that the workers have not been given the training they need. Another source of delays is rooted in problems with methods. For example, poor inventory management leads to production delays. The state of inventory management in turn is caused by obsolete processes.

The employment of fishbone diagrams is relevant for analyzing sources of problems in all operational areas. When used as a tool for understanding why problems exist in a process, it can provide insights needed to determine how the problems and their associated risks can be handled.

CONCLUSION

As we go about our business, all of us face operational risk. Whether we are running a production line or administering an educational program or managing a travel agency, we face the risk that something will go awry as we try to do our jobs. Operational risk, then, is concerned

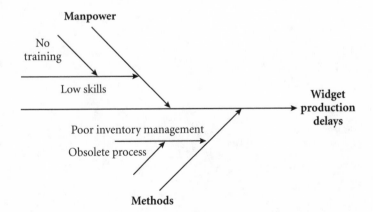

Figure 11.4. Fishbone Diagram Addressing Production Delays.

with mishaps we can encounter during the normal course of our basic business operations.

What distinguishes operational risk from other types of risk is that it is rooted in ongoing processes, whereas business risk and project risk are primarily concerned with future states of affairs. Operational risk addresses questions like: "How can the processes we are employing break down?" In contrast, business risk is more concerned with the future: "If we introduce a new product into the market, will anyone buy it?" The same holds true for project risk: "What is the likelihood that we can deliver our project solution to the client by the March 22 deadline date?"

What this means is that operational risk is more controllable than other forms of risk because it is not focused on predicting future states that have not yet arisen. Handling operational risk generally boils down to following good business practices, such as: "Stick to your defined processes" and "When you have trouble with a process, fix it and implement updated procedures" and "To prevent problems, regularly carry out preventive maintenance efforts."

CHAPTER TWELVE

Project Risk

A nyone who has worked extensively on projects develops a sense that projects are governed by Murphy's Law: if something can go wrong, it will. The prevalence of mishaps on projects is so pronounced that it has generated a spate of pithy variations on the original Murphy's Law—for example:

> *Klipstein's First Law:* A wire cut to length will always be too short.
>
> *Klipstein's Second Law:* A circuit guarded by a fast-acting fuse will protect the fuse by blowing first.
>
> *Jones's Law:* A person who smiles when things go wrong has thought of someone to blame it on.

Projects are filled with risk. To appreciate that risk is hardwired into projects, consider that the definition of *project* appearing in *A Guide to the Project Management Body of Knowledge 2000* suggests that every project is unique (Project Management Institute, 2000). The implication of this statement is clear: if a project is unique, this means that the past is an imperfect guide to the future. No matter how many times you have carried out a particular project-based effort, things will be different the next time.

To see this, consider the challenges that construction engineers face when building a fifty-home housing development. To keep things simple, let's say that each house in the development is built to the same blueprints and that the materials that go into the houses are identical. Obviously, there is not a lot of uniqueness distinguishing house number twelve from house number thirty-three. However, there are a number of unique challenges facing the builders of each house, and these can be important sources of risk.

For example, each house is built on a different lot. Some lots may have a rock substrate, others clay, and still others sandy loam. What lurks beneath the topsoil has important implications for how the house is excavated. Beyond this, some houses may be built on the bottom of a hill, and others may be perched on a hilltop, so the landscaping must be contoured differently for each house to avoid water problems. Or consider that some houses are near utilities (water lines, electric power lines, gas lines), while others are far away. Access to the utilities will vary from house to house, depending on where the house is situated, and this fact will have an impact on how the structure is built.

Many additional sources of uniqueness distinguish the construction of one house from another. The houses may be built in different seasons, so activities such as pouring concrete will be carried out differently in winter than in summer. Governments may change building codes in the middle of the project, requiring work on the second half of the project to adhere to a new set of regulations. And work crews will differ from house to house, probably the greatest source of uniqueness, since each work crew will bring its unique set of skills, competence, and work ethic to the job.

Note that the unique aspect of each project is what distinguishes project management from process management. Processes are based on repetitive actions where you follow a set of well-defined steps to achieve desired results. The principal idea behind process management is to drive out uniqueness by producing things in cookie-cutter fashion. For example, quality control processes are directed at identifying nonconforming outputs in a production environment and eliminating them.

This fundamental difference between projects and processes has important risk management implications. On projects, risks are rooted in ignorance of what is in store for us. We are always facing unknowns. In scheduling a project, we make a best guess of what tasks need to be carried out, how they are linked to each other, and what their durations are. In budgeting the project, we tie our cost estimates to our guess of what work will be carried out and make a number of assumptions about the costs of human and material resources. When assigning people and materials to the project, we establish guesses about what kinds of resources we need, their availability, and how many are needed. Everything we do is based on guesswork.

On processes, in contrast, we have detailed information about what steps will be carried out and how many resources are needed. The cost of resources may fluctuate somewhat, but this is usually not a great source of risk. The real risk lies in the process's breaking down. For example, in a manufacturing process, preventive maintenance activities must be carried out to reduce the likelihood of equipment malfunctioning. In an order fulfillment process, customer orders cannot be handled adequately if inventory stores are not well maintained. Thus, with processes, the risk management effort focuses on handling potential sources of breakdowns.

This chapter examines the types of risk commonly encountered on projects and the different ways that they can be dealt with. It shows how many of the risk events that project teams encounter are hardwired into their projects, owing to the special characteristics of project management.

THE PREVALENCE OF PROBLEMS ON PROJECTS

Historically, project success has been defined as bringing a project to conclusion on time, within budget, and according to specifications. This mantra is so commonly heard on projects that these success criteria have been given a name: the *triple constraints*. Traditionally, project failure has been viewed as the inability to achieve one or more of the three constraints.

With the advent of Total Quality Management (TQM) in the 1980s, the inadequacy of this approach to defining project success and failure became evident. The TQM perspective holds that the ultimate arbiter of quality is customer satisfaction. What this means to project management is that you can get the job done on time, within budget, and according to specs *and still have a failed project* if customers don't use the deliverable or underuse it or misuse it. The root of the problem lies in how the specifications are defined. If the specifications do not address true customer needs and wants, it is no great matter to achieve them on time and within budget.

In 1995, the Standish Group reported on a study it had conducted that offered astonishingly bad news about the state of projects in the information technology industry (Standish Group International, 1995). The Standish Group examined some eighty-four hundred IT projects whose total dollar value was greater than $25 billion. The study demonstrated that most projects experience notable problems. For example, only 16 percent of the target projects were completed as planned; 34 percent failed outright, and 50 percent found themselves trying to recover from problems. These results are astounding. If the Standish Group study reflects what is happening in the IT world at large, it suggests that only one of six projects experiences smooth sailing. Updates to the original study show only marginal improvement to project performance (Standish Group International, 1999).

In early 1998, I had an opportunity to carry out a quick, nonscientific survey of 438 participants in a project management class I was teaching. My students came from a variety of industries, including IT, telecommunications, construction, retailing, and pharmaceuticals. The goal of the survey was simply to validate the Standish Group findings, because I had difficulty believing that things were as bad as they reported. I asked my students three questions about their experiences on their last projects:

1. On your last project, what kind of cost performance did you experience (under budget, on budget, over budget)?

2. On your last project, what kind of schedule performance did you experience (ahead of schedule, on schedule, behind schedule)?

3. On your last project, did you achieve the project specifications (better than specs, met the specs, short of specs)?

The results of my little study confirmed the Standish Group findings:

Budget performance: Over half (55 percent) of the participants reported experiencing cost overruns, 27 percent reported delivering their projects on budget, and 18 percent under budget.

Schedule performance: More than two-thirds (69 percent) experienced schedule slippage (half of this group indicated they experienced serious slippage). Twenty-two percent indicated they were on schedule, while 9 percent indicated their projects were delivered ahead of schedule.

Performance on specifications: Twenty-nine percent reported not meeting the specifications, while 51 percent said their projects met the specifications, and 20 percent indicated their projects performed better than required on the specifications.

Overall, some 80 percent of the respondents stated that they experienced some notable struggles on their projects, results that align closely with the Standish Group findings.

Two facts emerging from the survey impressed me substantially. One was that problems seem to be endemic on projects: four-fifths of the respondents indicated that they encountered notable struggles. Murphy's Law does indeed appear to be the governing law of project management. The second was that relatively few problems were encountered in achieving the specifications, at least in comparison to budgeting and scheduling problems. A little reflection explains what is happening here: given enough resources and time, ultimately we are able to achieve the specifications. Seen from a different perspective, we often need to spend more than is budgeted and take more time than planned in order to achieve project specifications.

It is not only knowledge-based projects that experience problems. They are also common on traditional projects in the defense and construction sectors. In the United States, these two sectors come together in nuclear energy projects funded by the Department of Energy. These projects are largely construction undertakings associated with developing and producing nuclear weapons. In more recent years, they have been geared toward cleaning up nuclear waste. A number of studies have shown that these projects experience terrible problems. For example, one study suggested that a third of these projects were cancelled before completion (after $10 billion had been spent on them), half took three times longer to carry out than expected, and half cost twice as much as expected (U.S. General Accounting Office, 1997). More recent studies suggest that serious problems still persist (U.S. General Accounting Office, 1999).

Why are projects filled with problems? I began investigating this question in the mid-1980s and have reported my findings elsewhere (Frame, 2003). My conclusions are that there are three universal sources of problems on projects, tied to organizational factors, poor management of needs and requirements, and poor planning and control.

Organizational Sources of Project Problems

Projects are carried out in organizations, which are collectives of individuals and groups sometimes working together, sometimes at cross-purposes, with individuals and coalitions pursuing their own interests. Even in the best circumstances, managing people in organizations is a challenging undertaking. On projects, the challenge is particularly daunting because most projects are staffed with borrowed resources over whom project managers have little or no control. This approach is called *matrix management.*

In matrix management, there are three principal categories of players: the borrowed resources who carry out project work, project managers who direct the project efforts, and functional managers who are the bosses of the borrowed resources. Each set of players has predictable complaints about the matrix.

The *borrowed resources* complain that as they are farmed out to different projects, they find themselves reporting to multiple managers who may offer them conflicting guidance. They also complain that these assignments interfere with their regular duties, thereby jeopardizing their ratings on performance appraisal reviews. Additional complaints include: "Each time I am assigned to a project, I spend about a quarter of my time getting up to speed"; "I seldom see a project through to completion"; "On many of my assignments, I find that I am not qualified to carry out the assigned tasks. There's a mismatch between my skills and what is needed on the project"; "These assignments are usually forced on me. Nobody asks if I want to work on them."

Project managers complain that with matrix management, they have little control over the resources employed on their projects. First, they may not be able to get the right numbers of the right people at the right time. It is a common experience for project managers to find that the people sent to their projects are not qualified to carry out their assigned chores. Or they may get qualified people but in insufficient numbers. They may even get sufficient numbers of qualified people, but they arrive on the project too early or too late. Second, once the team is finally assembled, they find that they have little control over team members since they are not their bosses. This creates serious challenges for team building: How do you develop team spirit in a group of people who are borrowed resources, drifting in and out of the project?

Functional managers also have their share of complaints regarding matrix management. For one thing, to the extent that their employees are working in environments that are outside their control, they are unable to determine what they are doing or how well they are working. Other complaints include: "I am overwhelmed with requests for resources, and they always ask for the best"; "I am unable to provide my employees with the mentoring they need"; "I am losing resources that I need for my own purposes within my department."

Despite these well-known problems, matrix management thrives for a number of reasons. First, when it works properly, it leads to efficiency in resource usage and is cost-effective. Second, it is a flexible way of doing business, allowing project managers to put together cross-functional teams more easily than with traditional functional structures. Finally, it can offer employees job enrichment opportunities, as they gain new skills moving from assignment to assignment. But even when matrix management functions properly, it is filled with risk because there are many ways things can go awry.

Poor Management of Needs and Requirements

A major source of risk on projects is tied to difficulties in managing needs and requirements. If needs have not been identified correctly and if the corresponding requirements do not capture real needs properly, then a project is foredoomed to fail because it will produce deliverables that do not correspond to customers' needs and wants. Proper management of needs and requirements is a necessary condition for project success.

Problems begin with attempts to identify needs. One common difficulty is determining who the customers are. At first blush, the answer may seem obvious: the key customer is the individual who is paying the bill. But reflection shows that this perspective is too narrow. Users are customers; ultimately, they will be working with the deliverable that the project team supplies them, and their satisfaction with its features is important. But identifying user needs can be troublesome because users do not hold a monolithic view on what they need. In fact, their needs often conflict: by satisfying user A's needs, you may be suboptimizing user B's needs.

There are also secondary customers whose needs must be addressed. For example, the sensibilities of players in the purchasing department should be taken into account. If you attempt to purchase products from a vendor that is not on the authorized vendors' list, these players have the power to kill the deal. On highly visible projects, the Big Boss may be viewed as an important customer; this individual may monitor project progress closely, and if he or she is unhappy with the shape the deliverable is taking on, then trouble may follow. Your immediate supervisor should be viewed as a customer as well. To the extent your project is rated excellent by other customers, you make him or her look good. To the extent your project generates customer disaffection, you make him or her look bad.

Another common difficulty in defining needs is bridging the gap between the business and the technical solutions that are required to address business needs. The problem arises because technical team members often have little knowledge of the business, while business players do not comprehend the technology needed to implement their products. For example, in financial services companies, few information technology team members really understand the products their companies develop and sell in the areas of derivatives and options. At the same time, the businesspeople have little or no knowledge about operating systems, software protocols, and other technical realities that must be mastered in order to produce the desired results. As a consequence, you have two sets of players who come from different cultures, who do not speak the same language, and who hold different values struggling to work together. It is no wonder that today's software solutions often do not address real business needs.

Poor Planning and Control

Everyone recognizes that running projects that are poorly planned and have weak control mechanisms is an invitation to trouble. If you have not identified what tasks your project will address, you have not bothered to schedule project activities, are clueless on project costs, and have no idea what resources you need, you will certainly experience a host of predictable problems on your project. Similarly, if project control mechanisms are feeble, then you have no idea of where you stand as your project is moving forward. You don't know whether you are on budget, or whether you are meeting your milestones, or whether your project staff are achieving their targets effectively. You are in trouble.

When compared to the two other broad sources of problems (organizational sources and poor management of needs and requirements), planning and control should be viewed as the most tractable. Organizational sources of problems and management of needs and requirements are inherently messy to deal with because they focus on amorphous things like motivation, competence, and communication. This is less so in the realm of planning and control. Plenty of tools and perspectives exist to help project team members plan and control their work efforts more effectively. Schedules can be developed with tools such as Gantt charts, milestone charts, and PERT/CPM networks. Budgets can be derived from definitive cost estimates and can be tracked using cumulative cost curves. Resources can be allocated and tracked employing such techniques as responsibility matrices, resource Gantt charts, and resource histograms. If proper steps have been taken to plan and control projects effectively, then many project problems are dramatically reduced or avoided entirely.

BAD ESTIMATES AS A LEADING
SOURCE OF PROJECT PROBLEMS

Historically, with projects that encountered serious difficulties, problems were attributed to failures of implementation. That is, the project team was not competent, or management did not provide the team with the tools it needed to do the job, or requirements were not articulated effectively. In the 1990s, it became apparent that project problems could increasingly be attributed to failures of estimation. That is, someone—perhaps a salesperson or a district manager whose bonus is tied to generating revenue—promises to do a ten-month job in six months, or a $10 million job for $6 million, or a ten-person chore using six people. If in fact the job requires ten months, or $10 million, or ten people, then promising to do it faster, cheaper, or with fewer resources locks failure into the project effort before any work has begun.

To see this, consider the case of promising to do a ten-month job in six months. If the job really requires ten months of effort, then schedule slippage is built into the project plan. This optimistic schedule estimate will lead to an optimistic cost estimate, since only six months of expenses will be incurred. The irony is that as it grows obvious that the deliverable will not meet its six-month promise date and as project funds are depleted, project team workers and their bosses will begin to panic, creating an operation plagued with inefficiencies. It is likely that the project will experience serious schedule slippages beyond the realistic ten-month estimate and consequential cost overruns beyond the realistic cost estimate.

There is nothing hypothetical about this scenario today. Project teams are experiencing it routinely around the world. The principal cause of optimistic estimates is fierce competition. To win a contract, you feel compelled to promise to do a job faster and cheaper than your competitors. However, if you win the contract, you may ultimately regret your achievement as you see that you cannot meet your promises and face looming project failure.

MANAGING PROJECT RISK

For the most part, the best way to manage project risk is to follow standard good-practice risk management procedures. That is, you should plan the risk management effort, identify risks, undertake qualitative and quantitative risk impact analyses, establish risk-handling strategies, and carefully monitor and control risks once the project is underway.

What differentiates project risk from other types of risk is that we have a good idea of the types of problems project teams are likely to encounter as they carry out their work. We know that there will be predictable organizational sources of problems, inevitable struggles in managing needs and requirements, and problems associated with poor planning and control. We also know that a major source of difficulty on projects is poor estimation. These problems are universal and are rooted in the very nature of projects and project management.

Understanding the sources of project risk enables you to reduce both the likelihood of untoward events arising and their impacts. Because a large portion of the risks you encounter are linked to organizational issues, you should focus your attention on identifying these issues and developing strategies to handle them. For example, experience shows that when employing borrowed resources, project managers have difficulty getting them to develop a sense of commitment to the project effort. Thus, they face a predictable risk that project team members will not give 100 percent of their attention to the project. If this is an inevitable reality, then they should take steps to build commitment to the project where no natural commitment exists. Some commonly employed techniques of team building on matrixed teams have project managers trying to make the team as tangible as possible, implementing reward systems, and employing a strong personal touch when dealing with team members (Frame, 2002).

To make the team more tangible (and remember that project teams are often virtual teams, "real" only in the head of the project manager), they can take some of the following steps:

- Hold a kickoff meeting to introduce the players, describe roles and responsibilities, present a project charter, and invite the project sponsor to give a pep talk.
- Hold effective status meetings to provide team members a chance to get together and learn more about each other.
- Give the team a name and, if appropriate, a logo. Both can be affixed onto a variety of items, such as team caps, coffee cups, ties, scarves, and stationery.
- Engage in a public relations campaign to ensure that the team's efforts are described from time to time in the enterprise's newsletter.

To establish a reward system to motivate team members, they can:

- Hold milestone parties when important milestones have been achieved. What's attractive about milestone parties is that they reward all the team members.
- Recognize publicly the achievements of team players, for example, at the status meetings.
- Write letters of commendation for deserving team members, and make sure that the letters are placed in their personnel files.
- Give team members time off when they have put in heroic hours to further the project effort.
- Recommend to functional managers that key team players receive training to strengthen their job skills.
- Strive to make sure the team players have good tools to do their jobs. This is especially appreciated by technical team members.

To develop a strong personal touch, they can:

- Show a personal interest in the team members by learning something about their interests.

- Maintain an open door policy, where team members are invited to drop in the office for a chat at any time.

- Get out among the troops; engage in some management by walking around.

- Provide clear feedback on the performance of team members.

- Do everything possible to support the team members physically and psychologically.

The point is, when dealing with borrowed resources, you always face the risk of low levels of commitment to the team effort. To deal with this risk, you need to engage in explicit steps to build team commitment.

The same kind of logic applies to handling the other two areas of predictable project problems: managing needs and requirements and poor planning and control. For example, a needs-requirements challenge that affects all projects is the problem of scope creep, that condition where requirements begin to change little by little in order to accommodate change requests from customers, managers, and project team members. The cumulative effect of these little changes can be devastating. The project team that sets out to design a horse ultimately delivers a camel. Meanwhile, cost overruns and schedule slippages arise as the project abandons its original cost and schedule baselines. The predilection for scope creep is universal. The best way to handle this risk is to establish strong change control processes and implement them throughout the life of the project.

The risk of encountering problems arising from poor planning and control can be handled by making sure that your projects follow good planning and control principles and employ appropriate tools. Beyond this, steps must be taken to make sure that project team members are well versed on these principles and tools and that they actually use them. If good planning and control principles are followed, appropriate tools are employed, and staff are competent to carry out effective planning and control exercises, then problems rooted in poor planning and control diminish dramatically.

HANDLING PROJECT RISK WITH EFFECTIVE ESTIMATION

Poor estimates are an important source of problems on projects. If you promise to do more than you can deliver, your optimistic promises will catch up with you. Clearly, to handle this major source of project risk requires enterprises and project teams to implement good estimation practices. Whole books have been written about estimation. My intention here is not to engage in a detailed examination of this topic, but to highlight some key elements that have project risk management implications.

The Estimation-Planning Connection

It is widely acknowledged that good planning is an important determinant of project success. Consequently, project managers and other project staff are expected to have expertise in the planning of schedules, budgets, and resource allocations. A substantial portion of project management textbooks is devoted to understanding and mastering the planning tools.

Planning requires forecasting, because in developing a plan, you are making guesses about what you expect to happen at some time in the future. This means that all the facts and figures that go into a plan are estimates. The estimates can be accurate when you are dealing with a class of projects that you have carried out many times. However, when dealing with first-of-a-kind projects, they may be very crude.

The adequacy of a plan, then, is closely tied to the quality of estimates that feed into it. Good estimates support good plans. Poorly conceived estimates lead to off-target plans, which contribute to project failure. A precondition of effective planning is good estimation.

Estimation and the Project Life Cycle

Project team members develop and depend on cost, schedule, and resource estimates throughout the life of projects. At the earliest stages, before a project has been selected, estimates are developed to determine what it will take to carry out a project. Based on information emerging from these estimates, decisions are made on whether projects warrant support. Later, once a project is underway, estimates are made as part of evaluation exercises to determine what it will take to bring a project to completion. They may show that a project is no longer cost-effective and should be terminated.

Long ago, the construction industry differentiated three levels of estimates that projects encounter: conceptual, preliminary, and definitive. This three-tier system is still useful today and appropriate in all industries.

Conceptual estimates are the crudest. They are made in the earliest stages of the project life cycle, when it is not clear whether a project idea is worth pursuing. For example, a technical marketer may come across a request for proposal that describes an interesting potential project. Before bidding on the project, a conceptual estimate of costs, time frame, resource requirements, and benefits should be carried out to see whether it is worthwhile writing a proposal. Invariably, this estimate is produced in a top-down fashion. That is, rough data are employed in a crude fashion to develop a big-picture perspective on costs and benefits. For example, on a construction project to build a warehouse, the estimating team may derive a cost estimate by multiplying the square meters of building space by X dollars per square meter associated with constructing this type of structure.

Once it is agreed that it is worthwhile to bid on a project, an estimating team may put together a *preliminary estimate.* The data emerging from this exercise are incorporated into the proposal and constitute the promises the bidder is willing to make to the buyer. If the bidder's offer wins, then the bidder must be prepared to deliver its projects according to the promised price and schedule. If the bidder underestimates cost and schedule commitments, it will encounter problems of cost overruns and schedule slippages.

Preliminary estimates may be developed by means of rigorous top-down estimates or may employ crude bottom-up procedures. To carry out a bottom-up estimate, estimators first develop a work breakdown structure (WBS) for the project. The WBS describes the different components of a project in some detail (Project Management Institute, 2001). For example, if you are building a house, the top element is "house." Then this is decomposed into sub-elements, for example, "foundation," "framework," "plumbing," "electrical work," "roofing." Each subelement in turn is further decomposed into sub-sub-elements; for example, "foundation" may be decomposed into "excavate the site" and "pour concrete." This decomposing process is continued until the desired level of detail is achieved.

At this point, the WBS can be used to carry out a bottom-up estimate. Estimators estimate the costs of the work described at the most detailed level of the WBS (called the work package level). When all work package elements have been costed, their costs can be totaled for a total cost estimate. At this early stage in a project's life, however, the WBS will be bare bones, because there is insufficient information to create a detailed WBS. Consequently, the resulting bottom-up cost estimate will be crude.

Definitive estimates are the most accurate estimates. They are developed in a bottom-up fashion from a detailed WBS and used to create a project's detailed budget. Constructing a definitive estimate is time-consuming and costly. Furthermore, it may be that the absence of data will not allow this estimate to be made until the project is well underway. For example, on large Department of Energy projects, definitive estimates cannot be submitted until the project is at least 30 percent into the conceptual design phase, which may be one or two years into the project's life. Definitive estimates made before that time are likely to be substantially off-target.

The Estimation-Risk Link

A review of how estimates are made on projects demonstrates that estimation is an inherently risky undertaking. As we saw in earlier chapters, the level of risk you face in decision making is tied to the amount of good information you have available. One problem when estimating costs, schedules, and resource requirements for projects is insufficient accurate information to make reliable estimates. This is particularly true at the conceptual estimate stage. When making a conceptual estimate, you may surmise that the true value can lie 60 percent above your estimate or 20 percent below. To reflect the level of accuracy in your estimate, you should establish a range of accuracy. For example, if you estimate that it will cost $50,000 to carry out the design phase of a project, you can indicate the accuracy of your estimate by stating that cost will fall in the range of $50,000 + $30,000/– $10,000. That is, it will lie somewhere between $40,000 and $80,000.

From a risk management perspective, the most important estimate you make on a project is the preliminary estimate, because this forms the basis of your commitments to your customers. If you overpromise at this point, you will certainly encounter serious problems on your project. If you underpromise, you may find that you never win any business. The best policy is to be as realistic as possible.

Unfortunately, at the time you make your preliminary estimates of cost, schedule, and resource requirements, you still lack sufficient information to be confident that they are on target. While the accuracy of preliminary estimates varies from project to project, it is common that the true value lies in a range that is 20 to 30 percent greater than what you state or 10 to 20 percent less. These figures show that there is a good chance that you will lose money or encounter schedule slippages on your project.

Common Estimation Problems

People who execute projects have faced estimation problems since the building of the pyramids. Experts have studied the causes of bad estimates over a long period of time and have a good idea of why they arise. What they do not know is how to deal with them.

At the outset of the 1990s, I had an opportunity over a six-year period to work closely with hundreds of AT&T project managers. At that time, before its mid-1990s breakup, AT&T had the greatest commitment to pursuing project management excellence of any major company in the world. Senior managers at the company supported any actions that could improve project management performance. During the course of project management classes that I taught at AT&T, I carried out an exercise where I asked my students to identify typical sources of cost overruns that they encountered on their projects. After the end of a year of assigning this exercise, I had more than a dozen pages of detailed causes of cost overruns. I went through this list and attempted to see whether any patterns emerged. I found some clear patterns and report them here. Although this listing was initially developed as a result of my work with AT&T, I have tested it out on project professionals working in a wide range of companies in different countries and found that the listing highlights universal problems:

• *Bad technical estimates.* When estimating how much it will cost to do a job, or how much time it will take, or how many resources are needed, technical people consistently tend to underestimate the technical difficulty associated with carrying out their chores. They are proud of their technical prowess and assume a can-do attitude when speculating on what they can achieve. As a result, they gravitate toward best-case estimates of costs, schedule, and resource requirements. When technical glitches arise, however, work is interrupted and the technical team focuses its energies on fixing unanticipated problems. This results in increased costs and slippages of schedules.

• *Changing business conditions.* Customers are fickle. Competitors are continually developing innovations with a view to driving us out of business. The economy soars for three years, then tanks. A surge of inflation makes many of our estimates appear laughable. The fact is that the business environment in which enterprises operate is ever changing. Yesterday's brilliant move is tomorrow's folly. Estimates that do not accurately reflect changing business conditions can lead to trouble.

• *Changing regulations.* There is a common perception that business leaders oppose regulation. This is not true. Business leaders recognize that without regulations, chaos would reign and the market could not function effectively. To see the wisdom in this view, all you need to do is visit developing countries that lack effective regulations. What business leaders detest is unexpected *changes* in regulations. Their great fear is that a group of politicians can dramatically change business conditions overnight with the stroke of a pen. When this occurs, their operating environment may change radically. This means that the basis on which estimates were made is no longer valid.

• *Amateurism in estimation.* An important source of bad estimates is what I here title *amateurism.* The great majority of people who make cost, schedule, and resource estimates do not have any idea of what they are doing. When forced to put numbers on their estimates, they pull figures out of the air. They are inconsistent in how they compute costs from department to department. Because they do not employ a systematic process to carry out their cost estimates, they constantly leave out important cost elements, resulting in serious underestimates of project costs. The good news is that by establishing solid cost estimating procedures and training key personnel on good cost estimating techniques, problems of amateurism in estimation can be dramatically reduced.

• *Politics of estimation.* It is important for estimators to recognize that there are plenty of people in the organization who have an interest in providing customers optimistic estimates of what the enterprise can deliver on its projects. Salespeople, for example, are often paid royalties based on the revenue they can generate. So if a customer asks, "Can you do this ten-month job in six months?" salespeople have a lot of incentive to say yes, whether or not their promises are realistic. The same situation holds with district managers whose job security and bonuses are tied to generating revenue. It is easy to generate revenue if you promise customers that you can do the impossible at bargain-basement prices.

Problems arise once the project is underway. The project team finds that it has been given impossible targets to achieve. As its costs mount, it misses deadlines and is unable to deliver the features that are promised in the contract. The project team becomes the focal point of criticism by both customers and its own managers.

The fact that this type of situation prevails in so many enterprises despite its obvious drawbacks reflects the reality that organizational politics often triumph over rational decision making. The best way to handle this type of risk was covered in Chapter Five. Groups can be established to review the realism of promises that have been made to customers before the promises are converted into firm, legal agreements.

TOOLS AND TECHNIQUES FOR MANAGING PROJECT RISK

All the tools and techniques described in this book can be employed in managing project risk. I am highlighting four here, because I have found them useful in my own work and have seen them employed regularly at good-practice enterprises: modeling risk with PERT/CPM charts; using the PERT beta distribution to estimate costs, durations, and resource requirements; incorporating the probability of events into computations by using the expected value concept; and modeling risk with Monte Carlo simulation. The applicability of each of these techniques in managing projects will be discussed briefly. (These techniques are described in some detail in Chapters Six and Seven.)

Modeling Risk with PERT/CPM

PERT/CPM networks provide mathematical models of the project. They picture the interdependencies of tasks, enabling us to examine the consequences of different scheduling scenarios. Today's software packages that are used to create PERT/CPM charts also collect data on costs and resource utilization. Thus, a computerized PERT/CPM routine enables project staff to carry out sophisticated "what-if?" analyses, where the cost, schedule, and resource impacts of different scenarios can be examined. For example, if the project team finds that its project is beginning to slip its schedule, it can explore whether doing some work in parallel can get it back on track without having unacceptable cost and resource implications. It can use the PERT/CPM software to answer the questions: What if tasks A, B, and C, which are now scheduled to be carried out sequentially, are instead executed in parallel? Will it lead to substantial cost overruns? Will it put undue pressure on resources to perform their work in too compressed a time frame?

A more detailed description of the use of PERT/CPM networks to model risk is found in Chapter Six.

Using PERT Beta to Estimate Costs, Schedules, and Resource Requirements

In view of the fact that bad estimation of costs, schedules, and resource requirements is a leading cause of project problems, it stands to reason that project workers should strive to develop solid estimation skills. One of the most valuable tools in the project estimator's toolbox is the PERT beta distribution. Its strength is that it does not require archives of historical data on project performance. When dealing with new project experiences, a common occurrence, you do not have such archival information. With the PERT beta distribution, you do not need it. If you have a good sense of best-case, most typical, and worst-case performance when making an estimate, then the PERT beta distribution can serve your needs in estimating average cost, schedule, or resource performance.

A more detailed description of the use of PERT beta is found in Chapter Seven.

Incorporating Probabilities of Events Using Expected Value Computations

If you know the probability of an event, you have valuable information that can improve your decision making. A standard approach to incorporating this information into risk analyses is to use expected value computations. For example, let's say you envision three cost scenarios for your project: under scenario A, cost is $230,000 with a 20 percent probability of occurrence; under scenario B, cost is $280,000 with a 50 percent probability of occurrence; and under scenario C, cost is $370,000 with a 30 percent probability of occurrence. You can estimate the expected value of costs to be $230,000 × 0.2 + $280,000 × 0.5 + $370,000 × 0.3, or $297,000.

Expected value computations are not limited to cost analyses. On projects, they are useful when looking at the likelihood of doing a job on schedule and when estimating how many resources should be employed. They are also routinely used to calculate contingency reserves. A more detailed description of expected value is found in Chapter Seven. Chapter Eight describes how expected value can be employed to compute contingency reserves.

Modeling Risk with Monte Carlo Simulation

The best-known, and perhaps most powerful, risk management tool is Monte Carlo simulation. The power of Monte Carlo simulation is that it allows you to carry out your project, say, one thousand times and to track cost, schedule, and resource performance over these one thousand trials. As a consequence, it enables you to develop a sense of the likelihood of certain results occurring.

For example, let's say you have contracted to carry out a consulting assignment for $50,000 and want to know the likelihood that you will lose money on this effort. A Monte Carlo simulation might suggest that there is a 23 percent likelihood that it will cost you more than $50,000 to do the job, indicating that you will lose money. Or let's say that you will have to pay a $10,000 penalty if you deliver a product to a client after a given date. A Monte Carlo simulation can offer you insights into the likelihood that you will slip your schedule and pay the penalty.

A more detailed description on Monte Carlo simulation is found in Chapter Seven.

CONCLUSIONS

Because projects are filled with risk, effective project management demands that solid risk management perspectives be factored into the overall management effort. For the most part, the best way to handle risks on projects is to carry out the project effort in accordance with good general management practice. Thus, you should plan well, monitor the team's performance carefully, communicate clearly, treat your employees with respect, and so forth. However, in the realm of project management, experience shows that there are some areas that demand special attention—areas that are breeding grounds for trouble. For example, you should recognize that there are predictable organizational sources of problems, many of which result from the practice of matrix management. You should understand that the project team will struggle to define customer needs, and then will struggle some more to convert these needs into meaningful requirements. You should acknowledge that if the enterprise does not employ procedures that promote effective planning and control and if employees are not up to speed on good planning practice, the project will fail. And finally, you should know that there is a good chance that the cost, schedule, and resource estimates on which the project plan rests are wrong and can result in serious cost overruns and schedule slippages.

While all the standard tools and techniques employed in risk management can be used to good effect in managing project risk, four stand out as particularly useful: modeling risk with PERT/CPM networks; estimating costs, task durations, and resource requirements using the PERT beta distribution; incorporating knowledge of the probability of events into project analyses by using the expected value concept; and using Monte Carlo simulation to model the project.

CHAPTER THIRTEEN

Conclusions

~~~

his book has presented perspectives, tools, and techniques that are being employed increasingly by organizations intent on managing the risks they encounter. The tools and techniques are rather eclectic, coming from a variety of disciplines and practices, including finance, statistics, operations research, quality management, and project management. Some of them are simple (for example, check sheets and issues logs), while others are more sophisticated (for example, Monte Carlo simulation and the use of probability distributions).

It is tempting to see effective risk management as tied to mastery of and employment of its tools and techniques. Thus, you may hold that to be good at managing risk, you should be able to develop best-case, most typical, and worst-case scenarios; you should know how to incorporate expected value principles into the risk models you build; you should know how to set up and run Monte Carlo simulations; and so on.

In most endeavors, mastery of tools and techniques is important. An experienced carpenter equipped with a table saw, drill, router, sander, and lathe can do much more with a large block of wood than a carpenter with a pen knife. The same holds true in the arena of management. Modern enterprises cannot be run without employees who have mastered the essential tools of finance, accounting, information management, logistics, and marketing.

But you must be careful not to allow your regard for tools and techniques to trick you into thinking that their mastery automatically puts you on the road to success. It does not. The reason is that effective use of tools and techniques must take into account the context in which they are applied. Use of a jigsaw to slice a melon does not make sense. Neither does use of a cheese grater to smooth the surface of a mahogany cabinet.

Context is everything in risk management. This means that decisions must be made situationally. A city's emergency handling procedure might state, "In the event of an emergency, the mayor, chief of police, fire chief, and public health chief should assemble at the Emergency Management Center." However, if this center is located at the heart of a catastrophic event, following this procedure is not a good idea.

Risk managers must come to grips with a fundamental reality. The risk events they plan for seldom play out the way the plan states they should. Does this mean that it is a waste of time to plan for risk? Of course not. Plans prepare organizations to deal with untoward events. They reduce the element of surprise. In handling risk events, substantial portions of the plan may be implemented as is. Plans get you thinking about what might happen and what needs to be done. However, in most risk situations, they should not be viewed as a detailed map offering exact guidance on where you are headed and what turns you must take to get to your destination.

The overarching objective of risk managers should be to develop a conscious approach to managing risk in their organizations. If they achieve this, then questions about tools and techniques take care of themselves. A good place to begin is to adopt a defined risk management process. In this book, I have presented a five-step process that is a modest modification of PMI's six-step process: plan to manage risk, identify risk events, examine their impacts, develop strategies to handle them, and then monitor and control them. This five-step process works well for me. However, there is nothing magic about it. There are plenty of other processes that risk managers can use. I have looked at several of these. Not surprisingly, at their heart, they are quite similar.

With a good process in place, it becomes difficult to deal with risk haphazardly. The process sensitizes everyone to the existence of risk and the need to manage it consciously. It also alerts them to the tools and techniques that are available to handle risk within the appropriate context.

Once a process has been adopted, you can turn your attention to what it takes to make it robust. One thing you should do is strive to develop good data to guide you in your decisions. Why live with highly imperfect information if you have the power to strengthen it? One way to improve your data is to begin systematically archiving your organization's experiences. This tune was sung loudly by good-practice organizations in the 1990s and continues to be hummed today. Well-managed organizations are intent on creating archival data that can be used to improve decision making. The data can be derived from accounting systems, monthly status reports, comparisons of project plans against what actually transpired, engineering performance data—or whatever else is relevant in the context of the organization's operations.

You should also strive to gain pertinent information from outside the organization. One popular way to do this is to engage in benchmarking: identifying procedures and performance metrics associated with other organizations in the field. Through the benchmarking effort, you can develop a sense of what your colleagues and competitors are doing and how they cope with challenges. Beyond benchmarking, you should be continually tracking what is happening in the world at large in order to identify risk events that may be generated outside normal business channels. Questions that should concern you include: Is the economy strengthening or weakening? What is happening in global markets? What are the latest technological trends? What are prevailing demographic trends? How are our competitors doing?

You should also recognize the value of what I call embedded information. The knowledge that an organization's employees possess is embedded in their heads. The knowledge of how an organization should conduct its work is embedded in business processes. Smart organizations strive mightily to increase embedded information. For example, they promote training and apprenticeship programs to strengthen their employees' skills and experience. They also regularly update their business processes to bring them in line with the enterprise's evolving business requirements.

In the final analysis, the ability to handle risks effectively is a people issue. People come into the equation in two ways. First, they are usually the cause of risk events, as the following examples make clear:

- Our political enemies consciously set out to ruin our reputation.
- A young engineer's failure to convert British measurement units to metric units causes a $125 million space mission to fail.
- Our competitors have just introduced a product that makes our key product line obsolete.
- An unemployed systems analyst sets his alarm clock incorrectly, causing him to wake up late and miss a job interview.
- An inspection team that is slipping its schedule decides to bypass procedures and carry out only cursory inspection of parts. A week later, one of the parts fails, causing $850,000 in damage to a piece of equipment and knocking out production for a week.

Second, they are the source of solutions to problems we encounter with risk events. If they are alert, perceptive, and well trained, they may anticipate risk events before they arise, enabling us to nip problems in the bud. When problems arise, they can employ their knowledge, decision-making abilities, and leadership skills to minimize the damage that risk events can cause.

Given the centrality of people in risk management, it is clear that the best way to prepare to handle risk is to create an environment where people will not cause problems through their actions and inactions and where they are capable of solving problems effectively when they arise. The prevention of people-induced problems can be partially achieved by making sure they are qualified to do what they are assigned to do. This may entail a substantial dose of education and training. It requires periodic testing and inspection to double-check their abilities. It also demands effective screening of personnel. If you hire unqualified people, problems on the job are near certain. Finally, it is important that the organization has developed good work processes so that employees can carry out their efforts in a tested, prescribed fashion. Even the most talented people find it difficult to function effectively if they are expected to follow poorly conceived processes.

Creating an environment that supports competence gets you halfway to your destination. To complete the trip, you must develop a high level of risk sensitivity throughout the organization. In TQM, we are taught the catechism: "Question: Who has responsibility for quality in the organization? Answer: Everybody!" The point being made is that for organizations to produce high-quality goods and services, everyone needs to keep their eyes open for defects, from the forklift operator in the warehouse to the customer service manager to employees of the quality assurance department. The same principle holds in risk management. Everyone should recognize that potential risk events that can affect the organization lurk everywhere, both inside and outside the enterprise. If they encounter such events, they should sound the alarm.

While risk sensitivity should be introduced into the overall organization, key personnel should be identified who will play an active risk management role. These people should certainly be well grounded in all aspects of risk management. They should attain mastery of the important procedures, tools, and techniques. And most important, they should be able to make the right kinds of decisions as risk events play out, even when the events are not proceeding according to the script.

If you have a defined risk management process and focus on the people issues, you are on the way to handling risk effectively. While important, the details will take care of themselves when good processes and good people are in place.

LAST WORD

The oracles foretold that Oedipus would kill his father and marry his mother. Despite the best efforts of King Laius and Oedipus himself, nothing could be done to change this course of events. And so Sophocles and his Greek contemporaries held that our lives are governed by the fates and that what we experience is preordained. The Greeks were not alone in adhering to this view. Psalm 139 asserts, "All the days ordained for me were written in your book before one of them came to be." The Hindu and Buddhist views that life is a wheel and Muslims' adherence to the principle of *inch allah* also convey a belief that humans have little control over their destinies.

Oedipus would not have made a good risk manager. If the course of your life is preordained, there is not much you can do to manage risk, aside from visiting a qualified oracle who can map your future and reconciling yourself to your fate. If you have the power to affect your future through your actions, then it is possible to manage the risks you encounter. Rather than be a victim of fate, you can set out to shape your future.

The rationale of risk management is based on the belief that the future is not preordained. A large portion of risk management effort entails prognostication in order to develop a vision of the future, for example, identifying risk events by monitoring the environment, developing scenarios of possible future states of affairs, and predicting the impacts of risk events. Once a view of the future emerges, attention then turns to determining what steps can be taken to handle potential risk events in order to reduce the likelihood of their occurrence or to tone down their impacts once they arise. This is done by developing strategies for risk avoidance, risk transfer, risk acceptance, and risk mitigation.

Although the future is not preordained, this does not mean that you have absolute power to make things work out way you desire because, in the words of the great Stoic philosopher Epictetus, "Some things are in our control, and some things are not" (Lebell, 1995). However, even when dealing with events out of your control, you can still take actions that work to your advantage. Proactive risk managers recognize that while they may not be able to influence the occurrence of uncontrolled events, they can still prepare to deal with their consequences. For example, you cannot stop a hurricane heading for your home. However, you can board up your windows to keep them from shattering under the onslaught of flying debris.

Proactive risk managers continuously try to determine what they can do to reduce the likelihood of untoward events and lessen their consequences when they arise. They do not give up easily because they recognize that the steps they take can make a difference. They are not, like Oedipus, fatalists.

References

Argyris, Chris. *Overcoming Organizational Defenses*. Needham Heights, Mass.: Allyn & Bacon, 1990.

Bartlett, J. *Bartlett's Familiar Quotations*. (16th ed.) New York: Little, Brown, 1992.

Bernstein, Peter L. *Against the Gods: The Remarkable Story of Risk*. New York: Wiley, 1996.

Block, Thomas, and Frame, J. Davidson. *The Project Office: A Key to Managing Projects Effectively*. San Francisco: Crisp Publications, 1998.

Caputo, Kim. *CMM Implementation Guide: Choreographing Software Process Improvement*. Reading, Mass.: Addison-Wesley, 1998.

Cole, Michael D. *Three Mile Island: Nuclear Disaster*. Berkley Heights, N.J.: Enslow Publishers, 2002.

Condon, Judith. *Chernobyl and Other Nuclear Accidents*. Milwaukee, Wis.: Raintree Publishers, 1998.

Crosby, Philip B. *Quality Is Free: The Art of Making Quality Certain*. New York: McGraw-Hill, 1979.

Deming, W. Edwards. *Out of the Crisis*. Cambridge, Mass.: MIT Press, 2000.

Frame, J. Davidson. *Project Management Competence*. San Francisco: Jossey-Bass, 1999.

Frame, J. Davidson. *The New Project Management*. (2nd ed.) San Francisco: Jossey-Bass, 2002.

Frame, J. Davidson. *Managing Projects in Organizations*. (3rd ed.) San Francisco: Jossey-Bass, 2003.

Goldratt, Eliyahu. *Critical Chain*. Great Barrington, Mass.: North River Press, 1997.

Hammer, Michael, and Champy, James. *Reengineering the Corporation*. New York: HarperBusiness, 1993.

Herzberg, Frederick, Mauser, Bernard, and Snyderman, Barbara Bloch. *The Motivation to Work*. (2nd ed.) New York: Wiley, 1959.

Ishikawa, Kaouru. *Introduction to Quality Control*. Cambridge, Mass.: Productivity Press, 1990.

255

Juran, Joseph M., and Gryna, Frank M. *Quality Planning and Analysis.* (3rd ed.) New York: McGraw-Hill, 1991.

"Killer Crash After Snake Spotted in Truck." Reuters, Apr. 6, 2001.

Knight, Frank H., *Risk, Uncertainty, and Profit.* Boston: Houghton Mifflin, 1921.

Kondo, Yoshio. *Human Motivation.* Tokyo: Productivity Press, 1991.

Lebell, Sharon. *The Art of Living: The Classic Manual on Virtue, Happiness, and Effectiveness.* San Francisco: HarperSanFrancisco, 1995.

Leibovich, Mark. "At Amazon.com, Service Workers Without a Smile." *Washington Post,* Nov. 22, 1999, p. A01.

Managing Successful Projects with Prince2. London: Stationery Office, 2002.

Maslow, Abraham H. *Motivation and Personality.* New York: HarperCollins, 1954.

National Transportation Safety Board. *NTSB Report Executive Summary.* Public Meeting, Aug. 19, 1997.

Parkinson, C. Northcote. *Parkinson's Law: And Other Studies in Administration.* Cutchogue, N.Y.: Buccaneer Books, 1993.

Paulos, John Allen. *Innumeracy.* New York: Hill and Wang, 1989.

Paulos, John Allen. *A Mathematician Reads the Newspaper.* New York: Basic Books, 1995.

Peter, Laurence J., and Hull, Raymond. *The Peter Principle: Or Why Things Always Go Wrong.* New York: Morrow, 1969.

Petroski, Henry. *To Engineer Is Human: The Role of Failure in Successful Design.* New York: Random House, 1992.

Project Management Institute. *A Guide to the Project Management Body of Knowledge.* Newton Square, Pa.: Project Management Institute, 2000.

Project Management Institute. *Practice Standard for Work Breakdown Structures.* Newtown Square, Pa.: Project Management Institute, 2001.

Rashbaum, William K. "Police Officers Swiftly Show Inventiveness During Crisis." *New York Times on the Web,* Sept. 17, 2001.

Saaty, Thomas L. *Decision Making for Leaders: The Analytical Hierarchy Process for Decision Making in a Complex World.* (3rd rev. ed.) San Francisco: RWS, 1999.

Shewhart, Walter A., and Deming, W. Edwards. *Statistical Methods from the Viewpoint of Quality Control.* New York: Dover, 1990.

Standards Association of Australia. Australia/New Zealand Standard 4360:1999. *Risk Management.* Stratfield, N.S.W.: Standards Association of Australia, 1999.

Standish Group International. *Chaos: Charting the Seas of Information Technology.* West Yarmouth, Mass.: Standish Group International, 1995.

Standish Group International. *Chaos: A Recipe for Success.* West Yarmouth, Mass.: Standish Group International, 1999.

Stevenson, Angus, Bailey, Catherine, and Siefring, Judith (eds.). *A Shorter Oxford Dictionary of the English Language.* Oxford: Oxford University Press, 2002.

U.S. General Accounting Office. *Opportunity to Improve Management of Major Systems Acquisitions.* Washington, D.C.: U.S. Government Printing Office, 1996.

U.S. General Accounting Office. *Major Management Challenges and Program Risks: Department of Energy.* Washington, D.C.: U.S. Government Printing Office, 1999.

White, Josh. "Woman Dies After Bee Sting. " *Washington Post,* Sept. 8, 2001, p. B4.

Index